THE
WHITETAIL
DEER
HUNTER'S
HANDBOOK

THE WHITETAIL DEER HUNTER'S HANDBOOK

JOHN WEISS

Winchester Press

An Imprint of
NEW CENTURY PUBLISHERS, INC.

Printing code
    14 15 16
Library of Congress Catalog Card Number: 82-73791

ISBN 0-8329-3451-8
Printed in the United States

*For Al Wolter, a serious
hunter and dedicated conservationist,
who taught me most of what I know
about whitetails*

Acknowledgments

Portions of several chapters in this book originally appeared in Field & Stream, Outdoor Life, Southern Outdoors, Sports Afield, Petersen's Hunting, and The American Hunter. I am grateful to the editors of those publications for allowing me to revise, update, expand, improve upon, or otherwise reprint those segments of material here.

Contents

THE
WHITETAIL
DEER
HUNTER'S
HANDBOOK

Preface

Every now and then something happens on the conservation scene that sportsmen everywhere and of all persuasions can applaud.

One example was the 1976 proclamation by President Gerald Ford to double the amount of land set aside as national parks as a bicentennial gift to future generations. Another was the passage of the National Environmental Policy Act of 1969, which requires federal agencies to prepare Environmental Impact Statements that must be evaluated prior to launching projects that may have significant effects upon our outdoor heritage. And what about the establishment of National Hunting and Fishing Day, in 1972, to promote a better understanding and fuller appreciation of the valuable roles played by sportsmen in the conservation and wise management of our natural resources?

But all of these landmarks, however noteworthy, are in many minds paled somewhat by another achievement, and that is this country's whitetail deer success story. At least that is the consensus of 4,000,000 people—hunters—who as autumn blends into winter will again this year slip into bright-red jackets in celebration of a ritual that is as old, steeped in tradition, and singularly American as

Thanksgiving dinner. They'll be heralding the opening of the deer season, and by the time the last state season closes about 2,000,000 of them will have collected venison.

In the industrialized, metropolitan, and computer-oriented society we now have, with continual economic and energy demands eating away many natural resources, it seems almost incredible that we should have such an abundance of whitetails. What is even more startling is that not only are deer plentiful almost everywhere but we have nearly *forty times* more deer today than we did a century ago. According to research conducted by the National Shooting Sports Foundation, in 1885 the total whitetail deer population in the lower forty-eight states was an estimated 350,000. Yet in 1978 the herd population was conservatively estimated by the National Wildlife Federation to well exceed 15,000,000!

Sportsmen rejoice over this not merely because with rifles in hand they are the primary beneficiaries of soaring deer populations, but because they, mostly alone and despite heated opposition that continues even to this day, were the ones responsible for bringing it all about.

There is much more to hunting, however, than the technical aspects of wildlife management and the hard-core statistics of the actual dollars and cents contributed annually by hunters to various conservation causes.

As a source of recreation there is nothing exactly to match whitetail deer hunting, and in our space-age world there are few things that are even comparable.

It takes anyone back outdoors for a change, away from the staleness of air-conditioned office buildings, away from the pungency of steam-filled factories, away from the gagging exhaust of congested city streets, and into the fresh air for lungs that need it. It takes the hunter uphill and downhill and offers good exercise for muscles that have become rubbery from too much easy living.

By choice it may take him into deer camps to share the comaraderie of close friends who cherish the same desires to be afield during the crisp golden days of Indian summer and the pure snowy-white days of winter. Or he may prefer to venture into the woodlands entirely alone, as that is one of the best ways to seek and find personal contentment.

The deer hunter who is to see success is required to study and learn about his quarry. And in so doing he cannot help but learn about the land, about other wildlife creatures that share the whitetail's range, about himself, and about the interrelationships and interdependencies of all living things in nature's scheme. And all of these revelations do him good.

But *success* is difficult to define and measure, as it may be afforded in many other ways, too. For one, hunting gives anyone the rare opportunity to be virtually independent, pitting his skills as a rational animal against other animals which have survived by instincts that are as old as time. And this gives the hunter the unexplainable inner satisfaction of once a year being able to step back into the collective history of his species and trying to sharpen his senses enough to survive by them. Suddenly, it becomes easier for him to understand how prehistoric men lived 20,000 years ago, or Pilgrims 400 years ago, or frontier families only 150 years ago, because when men and women submit themselves body and spirit to the effort, they are complete hunters for the time, regardless of their way of life for the remainder of the year. The productive hunt for venison is therefore one of the most inspiring things modern man, searching for a link with those ancestral pioneers who preceded him, is able to experience. The unproductive hunt, venison-wise, lacks only the completeness of the other; it is still a valuable and memorable experience, and it still places things in perspective.

Or perhaps more aptly, as my friend and regular hunting partner Al Wolter believes, "good tracking snow, the challenge of a whitetail's cunning, and thoughts of prime roast venison are things that just may help a man live forever."

John Weiss
Athens, Ohio

Know
Your Deer

A neighbor of mine by the name of Carl Bowman is not exactly an amateur when it comes to hunting whitetail deer, but he may nevertheless be perfectly representative of a lot of this country's deer hunters and the adventures they like to recall. In fact, just last year two encounters with a certain buck made him feel very sheepish indeed.

The location was Georgia, deep in the Chattahoochee National Forest, when only a few minutes after shooting light on opening morning two does emerged from a honeysuckle tangle and very cautiously eased their way down an abandoned logging trail. Short moments later Carl's eyes bulged and his pulse began hammering when an animal with high and wide horns then stepped from the same cover and followed a short distance behind.

"I took one look at his headpiece," Bowman later explained, "and knew at once that buck would make the record book."

The buck stopped about 80 yards away to spar with a small bush, and adrenalin began seeping into Carl's system as he desperately hoped the lady deer, which were now almost directly

A fine examnle of a pure-strain Virginia whitetail. This is the primary "type" species first identified and from which the many subspecies are differentiated. (Photo by John Olson)

beneath his tree stand, would not spot his move to raise his shotgun and spook the gentleman with the rocking-chair rack.

Then Carl looked down for a moment—he isn't sure why, perhaps to check that the plastic caps had been removed from his scope. What he does vividly recall is next looking up again, only seconds later, and not seeing the buck.

"With the exception of the logging trail," Carl related, "the cover was almost impenetrable. Thick clutches of evergreens and high slash piles were everywhere. I finally concluded the buck had simply changed directions, and I felt pretty empty inside."

An hour later Bowman climbed down from his perch to head back to his truck for a late breakfast. He had made his way only 50 yards down the logging trail and was carefully skirting a blowdown which nearly blocked the route when without warning there was a crashing of brush and pounding of hooves as the same buck he had seen earlier jumped from a perfectly hidden bed on the opposite side of the cover and bounded away.

"That deer was moving so fast," Carl lamented, "that he almost cooked the pine cones as he made his escape. He was out of sight before I even had a chance to raise my gun."

Bowman was immeasurably discouraged and convinced his aging years had turned him into a bumbling idiot. But that is not the end of the story, because two days later he had another encounter with the same buck.

He had decided to wait on a different stand not far away and considered it a real stroke of luck when the trophy loped into view along the edge of a small clearing. Then the unexpected happened again. Suddenly the buck froze in position, and when Carl felt the wind shift slightly so that it was now on the back of his neck he knew the whitetail had detected danger in the air.

Well, the buck wasted no time swapping ends and then began quartering away. Bowman took the only shot he had and drove the rifled slug square into the middle of a small sapling, and that was that. A few leaps on nimble legs, white banner astern, and the deer evaporated, not to be seen again that season.

My reason for describing at length what happened to Carl Bowman in Georgia's swamplands is certainly not that it was in any way unusual. On the contrary, it was completely typical of the experiences tens of thousands of hunters have each year while pursuing whitetails.

Were a poll taken, and hunters completely candid in their answers, the results would undoubtedly confirm a suspicion I have long had. My hunch is that when comparing animals downed per shots fired, even in the case of very accomplished hunters, the whitetail buck is missed more than any other big-game animal in the world.

As a matter of illustration, consider another hunter (whom I will not embarrass by naming) who has been fortunate enough to have had the necessary time and money to have enjoyed big-game hunts on just about every continent of the globe. His office walls are literally jammed with head mounts. You name the species— greater kudu, leopard, lion, Cape buffalo, mountain goat, bighorn sheep, caribou, moose, elk, Kodiak bear, wild boar—and he's taken at least one impressive specimen. Which of the many species commands his highest respect? For which species was it impossible for a guide or outfitter to arrange a "guaranteed" trophy hunt, regardless of time or money that might be invested?

Well, singled out on one wall that they have exclusively to themselves are a duo of whitetail bucks, one a six-pointer and the

other an eight, neither of which by minimal record-book requirements is even worth the bother of measuring. Yet my friend
contends that those two whitetails, one of which was taken last
year and the other seven years earlier, were more difficult to bag
than any of the dozens of other species he has tallied during his
lifetime.

If this is so, how do other hunters with far fewer resources and
opportunities manage to collect decent bucks regularly?

Very likely many things, sometimes even pure luck, contribute
to any successful hunt. But most of those who regularly get their
bucks first recognize the importance of concentrating their greatest
efforts on determining where the deer are. In itself, this might be
looked upon by some as an extremely dubious undertaking in
view of the fact that whitetails live in all of the contiguous forty-
eight states (although California, Colorado, Nevada, and Utah
have very few whitetails) and in eight Canadian provinces. And at
the same time, every hunter should learn as much as possible
about the species and its living habits, while similarly striving to
develop a wide variety of hunting skills.

THE VIRGINIA WHITETAIL

Look at the species itself: *Odocoileus virginianus,* or the Virginia
whitetail, of which there are at least thirty known subspecies
(seventeen of which are available to North American hunters).

Although whitetails are native to North America, having developed in the Miocene and Pliocene periods 20,000,000 to
10,000,000 years ago, the *virginianus* moniker very likely derives
from early colonists who saw this deer first upon sailing into the
James River in tidewater Virginia in 1712. Because these settlers of
the New World dined upon the Virginia deer first and foremost, it
became the "type" species or primary strain from which all others
presumably evolved or might be identified, differentiated, and
duly recognized. *Odocoileus,* the genus name, then came about in
1832 when the naturalist Rafinesque discovered the fossilized
remains of deer teeth in a Virginia cave; the name should actually
have been *Odontocoelus* (for "hollow tooth") but apparently
Rafinesque's Greek was poor, and *Odocoileus* it has remained.

It is worth explaining that though relatively few whitetails existed
around the turn of the century compared with their numbers
today, this does not mean that never until now has the whitetail

been numerically abundant. When Indians held leases upon the countryside, *Odocoileus* and his clan were indeed prospering in many select regions, although the dense uncut forests that predominated almost everywhere else presented far from ideal habitat. As an example, during what is generally accepted as the Indian Era (1700–1800), Michigan's Upper Peninsula had what we might describe as "no deer for all practical purposes" until after the timber companies entered the picture and began leveling the expansive pine forests, which subsequently allowed for a profusion of regenerative ground-story growth. Since deer are browsers and grazers, the range steadily improved in quality, to the extent that it has been recorded that in the early 1800s as many as 80,000 deer were being killed annually in Michigan.

As other states and territories were settled, and agricultural and lumbering practices expanded, there as well whitetail populations exploded, and the needs of a growing civilization prompted a spiraling increase in the demand for meat and hides. The whitetail, of course, served as a major source of supply, and decimation of the species was horrendous. One New York State hunter claimed the then enviable reputation of having killed 2,500 whitetails before he died in 1850. Another, in Delaware, brought to a trading post eighteen deerskins per week for forty-seven consecutive weeks. Hundreds upon hundreds of barrels of venison and tall stacks of hides arrived almost daily in growing Eastern cities by freighter canoe, river barge, wagon, and mule train.

By 1900 the majority of deer had been either killed or pushed off their original ranges, and states began rapidly closing their seasons. In some states, as late as 1925, the mere sighting of a whitetail was as rare and exciting as it is today to see a timber wolf in New York, a cougar in Arkansas, or a black bear in Ohio.

It was the hunter-financed conservation movement that can be credited as the key program that saved the whitetail. First, laws brought a halt to the indiscriminate killing of deer for commercial purposes. Sport hunting came into being, and the science of game management was born. Seasons were carefully regulated, and biology studies enacted so that areas of low deer population were permitted to rebuild themselves, while areas with no deer were repopulated with stock transplanted from the very few high-deer-population areas that still remained.

The deer took to the management programs very well and have

been reproducing themselves ever since. Today, there is not a single state that possesses whitetails that does not allow a hunting season for the species. Indeed, over thirty states presently claim their deer populations well exceed 100,000. Twenty of them have more than 250,000, and three states boast more than 1,000,000.

As to the general range of the Virginia whitetail, it is most often thought to be concentrated within an area delineated by the Ohio River to the north, the Mississippi River to the west, the Atlantic Coast on the east (from the Potomac River south), and then down into the southernmost reaches of Mississippi, Alabama, and Georgia. Within this zone the Virginia whitetail's habitat is quite diversified—southern swamps and pine forests, coastal marshlands and canebrakes, the brushy thickets and vegetative perimeters of rolling agricultural lands, mixed-hardwood mountain ranges, and many other terrain variations.

Since the Virginia whitetail deer is the prototype from which the thirty subspecies are compared and differentiated, it is important to take a brief look at its basic physical appearance.

The Virginia deer is by no means our largest whitetail, yet it very frequently stands as high as 42 inches at the shoulder, although the average is closer to 38 inches. This is something for the novice deer hunter to keep in mind, because many embarking upon their first hunts expect to encounter deer much larger than they actually are, while a more realistic expectation would be to see deer that at their shoulders stand no higher than the average man's waistline.

A whitetail's weight may be even more misleading, especially if a hunter has just spent several hours dragging his trophy out of the hinterland. I many times grin with amusement when disbelieving hunters gawk at the scales, shake them a bit to see if they are working properly or jammed, continue to look very puzzled, and never really do accept the fact that the buck they thought easily field-dressed at least 200 pounds really comes in at only 100 or 115. It's true that the species can weigh as much as 300 pounds, but the average Virginia whitetail strain, on the hoof, is closer to 120 to 150 pounds. Further, since all whitetails are extremely nervous and active animals, their overall body outlines are traditionally slender, sleek, and graceful. Even in the coldest climates they almost never build up layers of fat that can begin to compare to those of their more relaxed mule deer cousins.

The heavy coats of whitetails, which are comprised of millions of hollow hairs, enable them to be excellent swimmers and also protects them from bitter cold weather. The only time deer have trouble in winter is when they can't find enough food.

The Virginia whitetail's coloration varies with the region and also the changing seasons, since whitetails shed twice a year. The spring/summer coat, due to predominantly warmer temperatures, is solid, thin hair that is typically reddish brown. As the cold time of year approaches, the lighter coat is exchanged for a much heavier one consisting of grizzled gray-brown hairs containing millions of tiny air pockets to aid in insulation. As a side note, many people worry unnecessarily about whitetails being able to survive prolonged subfreezing temperatures. Many times I have seen deer with a crusted layer of snow covering their backs, the insulating hair being so effective in preventing the escape of body heat that the snow doesn't melt. Because of the air pockets, the hide is also tremendously buoyant, allowing deer to swim very long distances in icy water with no discomfort whatever. When whitetails do find themselves in trouble during the winter months, almost always the difficulty is an inability to find enough food.

The Virginia whitetail possesses a shiny black nose with a pair of white bands directly behind it on the muzzle. The remainder of the face is brown, with the exception of white circles around jet-black eyes. White also appears inside the ears, just beneath the chin on the underside of the lower jaw, on the throat in a patch design that measures about 4 inches in diameter, on the abdomen and lower belly region, along the insides of the legs, and on the underside of the tail. The remainder of the body generally is brownish, darker along the dorsal region and gradually becoming lighter toward the ventral region. All of this aids in a highly effective camouflage effort that allows stationary deer many times to go entirely undetected, as they blend so well with the surrounding terrain. When the animals do go into motion, especially when they are alarmed, it is the waving white "flag" that is usually noticed first. Bucks, it seems, do not erect their tails as often as does. One theory is that the flashing white of a doe's tail serves as a guide enabling fawns to follow their fleeing mothers through the densest and darkest cover.

The antlers of whitetail bucks are single-branched, meaning that numerous tines evolve from a single main beam, which curves around in an inward arc above the head. More detailed information on antler growth and configuration, as it relates to trophy evaluations and the rut, will appear in later chapters.

The hooves of whitetails are remarkably refined in evolutionary terms. Millions of years ago, deer had five toes on each foot, and the animals stood on the soles and pads as humans have always done on their feet. As the evolutionary process began, the first toe (or what would correspond with either our thumb or big toe) completely disappeared. The second and fifth toes gradually became smaller and smaller and moved toward the rear of the foot (we refer to these on deer today as "dewclaws"), and the third and fourth toes became greatly enlarged, forming what we now speak of as hooves. So in reality, deer today don't actually walk on the soles of their feet as did their ancestors but rather upon their toes. But make no mistake—this is no disadvantage to the whitetail, as the cleft-foot arrangement is quite fast, and when the hooves are splayed (that is, the two main toes are spread widely apart) the result is an unfailing capability to navigate hard, soft, or slippery surfaces. The only thing deer have difficulty with is solid glazed ice.

WHITETAIL SUBSPECIES

As civilization continued to expand beyond the first colonial settlements and deer very similar to *Odocoileus virginianus* were discovered, scientists concluded that none was really different enough to warrant its own unique species classifications; they all constituted only slight variations or subspecies of the Virginia deer. It is therefore hardly necessary here to laboriously detail the many individual characteristics of each of the thirty subspecies as other writers have attempted in other texts. In a majority of cases one might even have to get out calipers and biological charts to tell most of them apart. Since their ranges invariably overlap to the extent that at least marginal crossbreeding occurs, even laboratory examinations are many times unable to determine specific subspecies mixtures of individual deer. Most important, the whitetail subspecies all have the typical whitetail personality; variations in behavior patterns that do occur now and then are more results of unique cover and terrain conditions than they are of subtle genetic differences.

For the sake of completeness, however, there are just a few major variances in the lineup of whitetail subspecies any hunter might encounter in one region or another, and they should be noted here. And we should also discuss those regional pockets that predictably see greater concentrations of any of the particular subspecies. Keep in mind, though, that the North American Big Game Awards Program, a joint effort of the Boone and Crockett Club and the National Rifle Association for the purpose of maintaining official trophy records, groups all the related subspecies except one with the "type" species, *Odocoileus virginianus.*

The exception to the above is the Coues deer, *Odocoileus virginianus couesi,* which has been granted separate recognition because of its degree of isolation from the other subspecies and consequently the great unlikelihood of there existing various intergrades. The Coues inhabits the rugged mountain slopes of southern Arizona (and therefore is sometimes referred to as the Arizona whitetail or even fantail because of the abnormally wide appearance of the tail when it is thrown aloft), throughout southern New Mexico, and along the west coast of Mexico.

One thing that especially distinguishes the Coues—which, by the way, is quite diminutive in size, seldom exceeding 100 pounds—is that the racks of bucks typically take on a basket appearance; the beams and tines seem unusually snug and many times almost touch in front. I have no ready explanation for such a characteristic, existing in widely separated areas, but antler configurations of this type are also very common throughout the "low-

The Florida Key deer is our smallest whitetail. This mature adult weighs only 35 pounds. The Key deer is close to extinction, not because of hunters but because of building contractors who bulldoze away their tropical habitat for condominiums and shopping malls. (Photo by U.S. Fish and Wildlife Service)

country" swamp areas of South Carolina. Since the Coues also has rather large ears and a grayish winter coat, it is sometimes mistaken by novice deer hunters for a young mule deer.

Another unique whitetail subspecies is the Florida Key deer, *O.v. clavium,* although this deer may not be hunted because of its continual bouts with near extinction over the years. The Key deer, which stands only about 22 inches tall and weighs only 45 to 65 pounds, is the smallest of the whitetail subspecies. At one time the entire herd population of Key deer was reduced to about thirty animals as a result of man's development of most of the south-Florida islands and the subsequent destruction of the Key deer's habitat. Today, the subspecies has been increased to about 300 in number, and most of these are restricted to a wildlife refuge on Big Pine Key.

The largest deer, the one that is the most widely distributed, and also the one I'm best acquainted with is the Northern Woodland whitetail, *O.v. borealis*. The average weight of a mature Northern Woodland whitetail buck (on the hoof) is probably somewhere between 135 and 165 pounds, but it is becoming increasingly common for huntsmen to show up at checking stations with specimens well over 200 pounds. The 1976 deer season in my home state of Ohio, in fact, saw several deer recorded over 300 pounds, and there were two road-killed bucks that weighed over 400 pounds! The largest Northern Woodland whitetail ever recorded was a 511-pound monster from Minnesota, followed by deer of 491 pounds and 481 pounds from Wisconsin. Eight of the top twenty-five record whitetail heads listed with the Boone and Crockett Club are of the Northern Woodland subspecies, including the world record, taken near Sandstone, Minn.

The winter coat of the Northern Woodland whitetail is generally a grizzled brown, the darkest of any of our deer. And the accepted range of this subspecies is easy to envision. Mentally picture the Mississippi and Red rivers as the western boundary, the Atlantic Ocean as the eastern boundary, and the Ohio and Potomac rivers as the southern boundary. Everything within this area to as far north as the whitetail is found is the range of the Northern Woodland subspecies. In other words, paint a swath that includes all of Maine and New England, down through New York, New Jersey, Delaware, and Maryland, across Pennsylvania, Ohio, Indiana, and Illinois, up through Michigan, Wisconsin, and Minnesota, and then from eastern Manitoba through Ontario, Quebec, and into New Brunswick and Nova Scotia, and wherever one might elect to hunt within this area he is unquestionably in the midst of where the world's largest whitetails live.

Sometimes comparable in body size to the Northern Woodland whitetail is the Dakota whitetail, and even more of late the Kansas whitetail. The primary reason for both subspecies often being so large has to do with their Midwestern habitat, which consists of much of the nation's most fertile agricultural land.

The Dakota whitetail, *O.v. dacotensis,* which has produced eleven of the top twenty-five records, has a range that includes the southern prairie areas of Manitoba, Saskatchewan, and Alberta in Canada, all of North and South Dakota, most of Nebraska, and the eastern portions of Colorado, Wyoming, and Montana. This is a deer of the gullies, draws, valleys, and timbered river bottoms. Physiologically, during the winter hunting season the Dakota whitetail takes on a dark-brown coloration, though not nearly as dark as that of the Northern Woodland subspecies. Antlers are likely to seem heavier and of much greater massiveness, but this is mostly an illusion since the tines sprouting from the main beams are usually somewhat shorter and stubbier than those of other subspecies.

The Kansas whitetail, *O.v. macrourus,* finds itself sort of sandwiched in between several other subspecies, and over countless generations this has precipitated such an extensive amount of cross-breeding that the pure Kansas strain has just about entirely vanished. The northern limits of the Kansas whitetail's range are in fact the southern limits of the Dakota and Northern Woodland whitetail subspecies. The western boundary is the foothills of the Rockies. The easternmost limits of the Kansas whitetail's range sees the predominance of the Virginia whitetail, and to the south are the various "Texas" subspecies. Three of the top twenty-five record heads are of Kansas whitetail lineage, and like the Dakota strain the Kansas deer takes on a somewhat dark appearance with bucks traditionally sporting heavy main antler beams from which emanate rather short, thick tines.

Whitetails residing in Texas deserve laudable mention if only because they constitute an estimated one-third of the entire nation's deer population, or approximately 4,000,000. Texas also records the nation's highest deer kill every year, usually over 350,000, which to some may seem surprising in view of the unfortunate fact that there exists very little land open to public hunting; as much as 90 percent of all of Texas falls under private ownership, and hunting therefore usually requires trespass permission along with a substantial trespass fee.

The vast majority of Texas whitetails are *O.v. texanus,* a subspecies that is also to be found in portions of Kansas, Oklahoma, southeastern Colorado, New Mexico, and south of the border. In addition to being the most abundant, the *texanus* strain is also one that varies widely in physiology. Throughout the northern counties, mature bucks may frequently average no more than 100 to 120 pounds on the hoof, while the same subspecies hunted in the

The Columbian subspecies is another exciting whitetail. There is no hunting this deer, found only in the Northwest. Only a small number of Columbians remain because superhighways and housing developments have consumed its habitat. (Photo by Washington Dept. of Game)

south Texas brush country are just as often real busters. As to antler configuration, the main beams and tines are often very slender but widespread, and brow tines are unusually long in many cases.

Another whitetail subspecies to be found in Texas is the Carmen Mountains whitetail, *O.v. carminis.* The Carmen Mountains whitetail is quite similar to the Coues deer in several respects. Like the Coues deer, it is not very large, bucks carry rather compact racks, and it is somewhat restricted to a rather confined area. Known also sometimes as flagtails, Carmen Mountains whitetails are limited to the Carmen Mountains on both sides of the Rio Grande (separating west Texas from Mexico) and especially inhabit those mountain-range pockets of the higher elevations (over 5,000 feet). The Carmen is a worthy trophy, but not much hunting for the subspecies is actually engaged in for the single reason that most of the Carmen's range falls within the Big Bend National Park, where hunting is prohibited.

The Northwest whitetail, *O.v. ochrourus,* is another subspecies that may attain very large size. This deer is an interesting one, because while it is very plentiful and frequently carries an impressive widespread rack, it is one of the least publicized and least hunted. The reason should be obvious. With a general range that

There are thirty whitetail subspecies. Some number in the millions and have vast ranges, while others are restricted to very small pockets. This fantastic Florida whitetail trophy lives only in the Everglades. It should not be confused with the Florida Coastal whitetail, which ranges along the Gulf Coast and into Alabama and Mississippi. (Photo by Florida Game and Freshwater Fish Commission)

includes the west slope of the Rockies from British Columbia to Wyoming, and then westward just touching northern California and into Washington, Oregon, and Idaho, this is also prime mule deer country. And as mulies are always more easily collected than any strain of whitetail, they predictably draw much more hunting emphasis. Often, the Northwest whitetail is unusually light-colored (typically a cinnamon brown) as compared to the other whitetail subspecies. None of the top twenty-five record heads is a Northwest whitetail.

As we noted earlier, numerous other whitetail subspecies pockmark specific areas of the North American continent. Along the Atlantic Coast, for example, where many offshore islands are home to transplanted subspecies that have evolved with their own distinct, albeit subtle, differences are the Bulls Island whitetail, the Hunting Island whitetail, the Hilton Head Island whitetail, the Blackbeard Island whitetail, and several others. In Florida we find, in addition to the Key deer, the Florida whitetail, which is mostly concentrated in the Everglades region. Also in Florida, and found too in southern Alabama and Mississippi, is the Florida Coastal whitetail. Along the Gulf Coast of Louisiana and Texas is the Avery Island whitetail. And there are approximately thirteen other whitetail subspecies to be found south of the border in Mexico, Latin America, and throughout South America.

To repeat, however, it is generally not necessary to know which particular subspecies you may be hunting at any given time unless you have the lifetime ambition to collect all of the different varieties or perhaps want to select a specific race to concentrate upon in the hopes of eventually having your name in some record book.

2

The Whitetail's World

One thing that has always fascinated me about whitetail behavior and how deer relate to their habitat is that the brushy hollows, cedar swamps, juniper flats, hardwood ridges, riverbottom thickets, pine plantations, and other places where deer live are seldom very serene places. But this should come as no great surprise to those who have spent long hours quietly and unobtrusively sitting somewhere as the outdoor world gradually became oblivious to their presence and resumed its normal course of activity.

Songbirds render a continual cacophony of sounds ranging from musical chirpings to harsh, scolding renditions as they flit from bush to branch and play tag through an overhead umbrella of green and brown. Incessantly chattering squirrels rustle in the fallen wardrobe of autumn and when high in the limbs vigorously shake the outermost extremities of leafy branches as they search for and pluck acorns and hickories; in good squirrel country there may seem an almost continual rain of cuttings from above.

There are nonanimal noises that customarily permeate the places where bucks and does live, too. The wind whistles and

This is the whitetail's world, with its own special chemistry of sounds, sights, and smells that are unique to that specific region. Through the use of super-keen senses, the deer monitor these features continually and may exhibit a variety of reactions depending upon their interpretation. (Photo by Jack Swedberg)

clacks together the limbs of close-standing trees. Hollow sounds punctuate the stillness as black walnuts or the pebbly-textured fruits of the osage orange now and then fall to the soft earth with distinct thuds. There are the clinking noises of rolling gravel on ever-shifting talus slopes, and the disturbances of tumbling rocks and boulders loosened by time and eroding weather. Brooks and streams bubble and there are many other noises.

The places where whitetails live also have their characteristic smells, such as the earthy aroma of spring as green shoots push up through damp, black loam and of cattle droppings in the bottom-lands. In autumn, wild fruits fall to the ground to rot and eventually saturate the surrounding air with an alcoholic vinegary odor that is unmistakable, and on freezing winter days a crisp freshness seems to prevail. In arid country there is the overwhelming pungency of sage, and in high country the cleanness of pine and wintergreen.

A wealth of visual activity, in addition to the movement patterns of the forest's creatures, is sure to be in evidence. I'm mostly thinking of the movement of the earth itself as it allows the sun to bathe the landscape from various angles and in so doing brighten

and then shade the countryside in differing and continually changing proportions with an aliveness that sees fingers of golden light
reach and touch and then retreat. Limber stalks of ground-story
greenery dance as eddies of wind push them one way and then
change their grip to pull them another. And leaves in their late-fall
kaleidoscope of colors flicker erratically with every shifting breeze
until eventually they sift downward from their parent branches and
are swept laterally away by some vagabond air current.

This is the whitetail's world. It's a home range, usually an
ellipse-shaped chunk of real estate of less than 1½ square miles
where he is born and lives out his entire life, but also within which is
a much smaller "core area" of usually less than 50 acres or so
where he can predictably be found most of the time. Further, he
recognizes this home range for its familiar sounds, smells, and
sights. As a spotted fawn he has grown to adulthood among this
particular profusion of individualistic activity, and in monitoring it
continually through the use of highly refined and specialized
senses he is easily able to recognize as well any deviations in
sensory stimuli that may occur from time to time. These variances
are the signals that alert him of the intrusion of someone or
something that does not belong on his home turf and may not
have his best interests in mind.

This is certainly not to say that if man or other potentially
threatening interlopers were absent the whitetail would be a placid
creature. On the contrary, "hypertensive" might be a good word
to describe the whitetail's anxious personality, which entails a keen
alertness, distinct fear of anything of an unknown origin, and yet
the ever-present ability to separate and catalogue component
parts of his environment.

THE SENSES OF DEER

Observing whitetails at close range—which I have been privileged to do many times—is undeniably one of the most
exhaustive, anxiety-provoking, and mentally taxing activities anyone could experience. The animals, as we have seen, are almost
never still, except when they are scrutinizing something very
closely for long periods and have yet been unable to evaluate it
thoroughly. In these instances I have seen them remain absolutely

motionless for five minutes at a time without as much as the twitch of an eyelid. Usually, however, a whitetail's radar does not require nearly this long and the animal hurriedly makes up its mind and either returns to its previous state of nervous alert, sneaks away through the cover, or bolts, all depending upon the interpreted immediacy of the evaluation.

The introduction of totally alien sounds, smells, or sights is most alarming to deer, such as the coarse rasp of canvas or nylon coming in contact with thorn-riddled brush, the crunch of a flat foot upon a brittle branch or newly crusted snow, the odor of an approaching man, or perhaps a moving man-form silhouetted against the skyline.

Alarming sensory stimuli need not always be of human origin, however, to have the same effect of alerting or spooking deer. Anything sudden, unexpected, or atypical of the home range the whitetail has come to know intimately will spook him.

One cold dawn while waiting in a tree stand in Michigan's Upper Peninsula I observed a ruffed grouse drop down from its nighttime roost in a nearby spruce. As it was pecking around on the ground, about 25 yards away, a whitetail doe trotted into view. Neither was aware of the other's presence or of mine, but when the deer approached just a bit too close the grouse whirred from the cover, sending leaves flying in all directions amidst a frenzy of beating wings, and this had the effect of sending the deer over the next ridge like she'd just been turpentined. Squirrels, armadillos, foxes, and other creatures, when they are unnoticed by deer and then make sudden moves, often trigger similar reactions.

But it is the whitetail's sense of smell that is its greatest asset. Deer can scent the approach of enemies or mankind long before they can see or hear them. Experiments have shown that deer, in controlled situations, are fully able to scent man for as much as half a mile away. While a deer's sense of smell is far more developed than most hunters realize, however, there are certain times or conditions, as we will see later in this book, when it is totally inadequate for protection.

Deer also possess excellent hearing. They constantly flick their ears back and forth to strain for the slightest sounds much in the same way as a human squints to see better. A windy or stormy day makes deer extremely nervous and jumpy, because the back-

Whitetails are "edge" animals that use every rootwad, canebreak, or brushy thicket to their advantage in hiding and moving. This suspicious buck has momentarily stopped feeding to play the "stand still" game. Next, he may go back to feeding, run, or drop to his belly to hide behind the fallen log. (Photo by Bill Byrne)

ground sounds of rustling leaves, clacking tree branches, and howling air movements make it impossible to classify sounds, and the wind also homogenizes the various air currents to make locating intruders by smell almost impossible. The deer begin to feel almost as though these senses they need have become useless, or at best highly inaccurate, and this makes them as uneasy as a cat in a room full of rocking chairs. For the same reasons, deer do not frequently hang around loudly rushing streams or riverbanks. They'll come to drink and then leave, or they may cross, but staying too long increases their vulnerability, as the sound of the rushing water makes the accurate detection of other sounds highly uncertain. Yet we have to qualify this. First, not only is the sound of water unsettling to deer, but there is an ingrained suspicion, passed down through hundreds of generations of those species of animal life customarily preyed upon, of waterholes or drinking locations along watercourses, because these are places where they are most likely to be ambushed. Now it is true that various areas of the country where there are timbered river bottoms are often prime places to find large numbers of whitetails, because of the heavy brush, willows, saplings, and succulent vegetation. And if the water is only serenely gliding along, any deer in the vicinity may just as well be bedded close to the edge of the bank as anywhere else. But time and again, from my experience, if the water is loudly bubbling and churning, the deer will sometimes be quite far back from the edge of the bank, such as in a hillside thicket or on a bench adjacent to the flow. I think they choose these spots so that they can distinguish between the sounds of the water and other noises.

This ability to catalog sounds sometimes borders on the incredible. I am not exactly sure how a whitetail's sensory classification process operates, but the hunter can bet that in most cases it is unfailingly accurate. As an example, since I hunt the fringe areas of farm country very frequently, it's not at all unusual for there to be in the immediate vicinity grassy bottomlands, small meadows, gradually sloping hillsides, and similar places where cattle or other stock is grazing. Separating these places are small woodlots, brushy hollows, stands of saplings, clumps of dense vegetation, and the like. The steers, because of the patchwork design of the interspersed cover, are frequently hidden from view when emitting noises associated with feeding, bickering among themselves, constantly moving about, and so on, yet deer in the area seldom pay them any mind. Perhaps it is the unique way in which cattle or other stock moves, with a certain rhythm or cadence to the footfalls. But just let the farmer or rancher quietly walk into the area to check his stock or count heads, and the deer are immediately aware of his presence and soon thereafter are usually gone.

With regards to vision, deer are remarkably equipped and yet also very limited. From laboratory studies we know that the eyes of all creatures possess varying numbers of minuscule nerve endings known as rods and cones. Rods are light-intensity receptors, and cones are the color receptors.

We as humans have a great number of cones, which allows us to enjoy precise color discrimination under ample light conditions. But since we are few on rods, as light levels diminish so does our depth perception and our ability to distinguish among the hues. Whitetails, on the other hand, as well as other lower mammals, have virtually nothing in the way of cones; their color perception is almost nonexistent. In other words, for the most part whitetails are colorblind, seeing everything in varying shades of white, gray, or black or in the same way we see black-and-white television. Nature is always careful in its allocation of sensory or any other mental or physiological equipment, giving any creature what it needs to survive but no more to confuse the issue. And since whitetails are not animals of prey, they simply have no great need for color discernment. With regards to being preyed upon themselves on occasion, however, they are extremely adept at detecting the slightest of movements around them through the use of an over-endowment of rods, which also allows better than average visibility under very low light conditions and even after full dark. Consequently, and because of their desire to evade man, deer have become very nocturnal animals, and after dark is when they do the bulk of their feeding, moving, and mating.

It is a generally accepted rule, then, that the most productive times for encountering deer are toward dusk in the evening and then again very early in the morning, as these are the times when deer are just coming out from their daytime seclusions or gradually drifting back to their bedding sites.

Further, many hunters believe that full-of-the-moon periods make hunting very difficult, because with an increased amount of nighttime light the deer are so active in their feeding and traveling that they delay coming out until quite late and similarly the following morning head back to their daytime resting places earlier than usual, making morning and evening stand-watching for the hunter a sometimes dubious proposition.

Conversely, on no-moon or pitch-black nights, even though deer may still be quite active during the late hours, they are not continuously so, meaning that they are likely to come out earlier in the evening and linger around just a little longer in the morning.

Any sportsman can use this knowledge to his hunting advantage, but for the moment consider what the wearing of various types of clothing entails. As I said, deer are colorblind, and this would seem to indicate that a hunter could wear any color without fear of being easily detected by deer. Unfortunately, this is not the case. Certain colors or color combinations are much better and more effective than others.

To a whitetail a yellow jacket or coat, or one of fluorescent orange, or perhaps light green or light blue, appears as either white or very light-colored. Medium red appears as light gray, as do medium blue and medium green. Dark colors such as crimson red, forest green, or navy blue may appear very close to a very dark gray or black. But since any color is really only a combination of different wavelengths of light, what a hunter should be most concerned with is not some specific color he may elect to wear but rather the tonal quality of the color, or in other words the light and dark renditions those colors exhibit as compared with the light values of the surrounding cover he plans to hunt in.

Because of this I always recommend that any hunter *not* wear solid-hue garments of any color but instead ones of different color proportions, such as the long-popular red/black or green/black checked lumberjack coats. Remember that the outdoors is a latticework of different shades and light values, and the best way to blend is to wear garments that duplicate or simulate the same light-intensity mixtures as are around you.

In some states, for safety reasons, hunters are restricted in this by laws that now require the wearing of varying amounts of hunter's orange or some other fluorescent color which has a highly reflective sheen to it, making the hunter readily identifiable to other hunters in heavy cover or during the low-light hours of dawn and dusk. But the disadvantage of the fluorescent colors is the extremely bright renditions they present to deer. It is not the red or yellow or orange color the deer are likely to be alerted to but the fluorescing quality of something very bright or shiny in tonal value that vividly contrasts with the surroundings.

The hunter wearing a solid-orange jacket and standing on a brushy hillside, for instance, appears to a deer as a big white placard that quite obviously stands out as unusual, different from surrounding environmental components, and worth much closer scrutiny and evaluation. If the "white placard" moves, of course, the deer requires no more sensory input and immediately takes some type of evasive action. But if it remains perfectly stationary for long minutes, the deer then, if he hasn't already, brings into play his other senses to aid in the classification of what he's looking at. Maybe he will be successful in picking up some scent or sound, and maybe he won't, but that doesn't really make much difference, because the bottom line is still a pale vertical rectangle that just doesn't belong, and that alone suggests it's time to sneak away.

So good advice is to avoid the use of solid colors but especially those that exhibit very bright or highly reflective tonal qualities such as fluorescent orange. Yet a hunter will want to comply with all regulations that exist in his region, and he'll also want to be visible to any other hunters who may wander through the area. One tack that accomplishes this is the use of camo-orange clothing. This is of the same fluorescent color, and thereby satisfies laws in most states for safety considerations, but instead of being solid it is a mottled design of many different orange tonal values that better blend with the light/dark tonal values of the cover. Camo red and camo yellow are also available, but in any case the hunter should be sure to check what his state's laws allow.

Remember at all times, too, that regardless of any color combination you may elect to wear, a deer sees in monochromatic shades of gray, and that of far greater importance to the whitetail is the rapid detection of the slightest movements. Light colors, by the way, even tend to magnify movements and make them more noticeable. Since movement (or, rather, the critical aspect of *not* moving) is so important, we'll touch upon facets of the subject many times in later sections.

A couple of other things about the senses of deer and the way they perceive things are also worth noting here. Regarding auditory stimuli, it's interesting to mention that deer seem oblivious to the sounds of gunshots. Sometimes on opening day, near heavily populated areas, the repeated noises of rifles going off in the distance give one the impression there is a war going on. Yet I regularly take aim on complacently feeding bucks amid such background noises and the deer seem totally unaware or unconcerned about them.

Whitetails also seem not afraid of the sounds of farm machinery or vehicular traffic on nearby gravel roads or highways. Many times I've pulled over onto the berm of a county road to photograph deer feeding in adjacent cover and they've offered themselves as willing models for long periods. They just don't seem to give a hoot. But open your car door and begin to climb out and then just watch them scat!

In many cases, deer are not afraid even of man himself, as they seem to sense that man, in those unique circumstances, means them no harm. Trout anglers often look up from their midstream preoccupations to see deer placidly feeding on lush vegetation at bankside not a far distance away. In climax forest areas, where prime deer food is scarce, loggers and pulpwood cutters move in with raucous chainsaws and axes, fell huge trees, and meanwhile as they are working at the bases of the trunks of the tall trees, deer often move in and begin nibbling away at the tender leaves and twigs at the other end. All this proves the unpredictable nature of the quarry, usually timid and shy, aloof, super-sensitive, wary, evasive, and yet still at other times curious or downright dumb, subscribing to patterns of behavior only another deer could understand or explain.

So what I've been trying to drive home here is that there is a wide difference between what a deer sees, smells, or hears and what a deer sees or smells or hears that frightens it. The hunter may not have a ready answer for why whitetails sometimes act as they do, but if he employs all necessary measures to reduce the possibility of alerting or scaring his quarry he's ahead of the game, ahead of the other hunters in the field, and over the years he will have many deer to his credit.

WHAT THEY EAT

Wildlife biologists claim it is far easier to make a list of what deer will not eat than what they have been known to forage upon. One study several years ago revealed approximately 614 different types of plant life in North America that whitetails consumed at one time or another.

As a result, too many hunters commit the error of discounting the importance of food location and type; they assume that since whitetails are so easily appeased with regards to dietary requirements, it is virtually impossible to use food as a clue to location.

Now, I'll agree that I would never base my entire hunting strategy solely on a whitetail's food preferences, and you shouldn't either. But food does indeed play a crucially important role in the lives of whitetails and to a substantial degree influences their movement activities, so every hunter should have at least a minimal working knowledge of the foraging habits of deer. Look at it this way. Understanding what deer eat and the ramifications of other patterns of feeding behavior is just another small part of the picture puzzle of their lives, and when all of the many different pieces are assembled and viewed in their proper perspective the hunter is the beneficiary of insight that is certain to help him make more accurate judgments and decisions in the field. Amateur hunters, of course, will blindly stumble onto good bucks occasionally because the law of averages says they must. But for the dedicated whitetail scout who looks upon his sport as a craft and ongoing learning process, far greater satisfaction is derived from repeated successes that are direct results of putting into use building blocks of knowledge and experience.

Let's begin, then, by mentioning that whitetails anywhere don't generally spend a tremendous amount of time feeding, as the act requires the use of sensory and thought-process energies that otherwise might better be invested in keeping tabs on whatever is likely going on around them. In another manner of speaking, when deer are actively and enthusiastically feeding you might say they have one-track minds, and this makes them vulnerable.

Therefore, nature has made ruminants of the members of the deer family, which means that they possess stomachs containing four compartments, enabling feeding to take place rapidly and with only minimal amounts of chewing and swallowing. The food ingested goes first into an upper stomach known as the rumen, where it is temporarily stored. Later, after the deer has retired to a safe resting place, from which it can resume more intensely monitoring its environment, it regurgitates the partially chewed food to complete the job. When the "cud" is well masticated and then swallowed a second time it enters the next compartment of the stomach, known as the reticulum, and from there travels to the omasum, through the abomasum, and then into the intestines for the remainder of the digestive process.

Adult whitetails require about 10 pounds of food intake per day. In the spring and summer months when vegetation, grasses, and young shoots are in bountiful supply much of a whitetail's foraging may be of a grazing nature. But into the fall and then especially through the winter months, when ground-level greenery may for the most part be depleted or perhaps even covered with snow, above-ground browsing becomes the predominant method of food intake.

The most favored foods of the 614 varieties mentioned earlier include red maple, white cedar, aspen, oak, white acorn, piñon nuts, juniper, poplar, dogwood, witch hazel, staghorn sumac, mountain maple, wintergreen, fir, arborvitae, greenbriar, pine, serviceberry, and yew. When these species are in short supply, second choices may include hemlock, arbutus, ash, honeysuckle, and willow.

Of the purposely planted or cultivated crops, corn, alfalfa, clover, cabbage, soybeans, rye, lespedeza, winter oats, and trefoil are all eagerly sought and eaten.

Of the orchard or fruit crops (either wild or domesticated) the most popular choices are apple and blackberry. Blueberry, elderberry, and cranberry are the next favored.

Those are the basics. But from here on any discussion of whitetail feeding habits becomes somewhat complicated and may require a good deal of individual interpretation. We can list here some preliminary thoughts on the subject, just skimming the surface, but then any hunter will have to pick up the ball and make his own inquiries and evaluations (we'll tell how) in order to pin down the feeding activities of deer living in his particular region or in the locale he plans to hunt. There are regional differences which may see the presence of certain types of forage existing in one area but not in another, annual fluctuations that may see boom mast crops or plentiful supplies of certain other foods one year but then perhaps scant supplies of the same foods the following year, and latitudinal influences that may allow relatively easy year-around feeding by deer residing in warm climes while their cousins farther north during the same months may be "yarded" in confined quarters and forced by high snows that restrict their movements to exist on starvation rations.

For all the variety of foods they eat, whitetails often exhibit very selective dining habits. It is true there may exist a wide variety of acceptable food types in their respective home ranges, and deer will of course eat less nutritional and less palatable foods if that is all that is available some year or the next. But in most cases there will be one or two or three specific types of food they especially favor in a given area, and when those foods are either plentiful or concentrated, they will indeed influence the movements of the local deer population.

But remember as well what we said about regional differences. Perhaps in Maine or New Hampshire the main attraction may be apples. In the brush country of south Texas it may be a shrub known as huajilla that possesses feathery multiple leaf fronds. In Kentucky, or anywhere else for that matter, the perimeter rows of soybean fields adjacent to good deer habitat are almost certain to be regularly visited by whitetails. Anywhere, a lush field of alfalfa will attract deer from surprisingly far distances.

The important thing is *your* evaluation and interpretation of the area *you* will be hunting. If you'll be hunting in Sumter County, South Carolina, forget that your pal living in Vermont consistently takes big bucks near apple orchards; in Sumter County, which is mostly swamp country, 99 percent of all the apples to be found are neatly wrapped in plastic and sitting on the shelves of your local neighborhood grocery stores.

It is not at all difficult for a hunter to appraise whitetail food conditions in his area. One of the best ways to begin is by consulting someone who is well acquainted with the study of trees, vegetation, plant life, or crop species. This might be a local game protector, a wildlife biologist, or someone affiliated with the U.S. Forest Service, Bureau of Land Management, or an agricultural extension agency.

Whoever you make contact with, however, show him the list of highly preferred deer foods presented earlier and ask which are fairly abundant in your region and under what kinds of soil or terrain conditions they usually grow so that you can locate them when you're later in the field scouting for a place to hunt. You might even want to obtain a pocket-size paperback book of trees and plants, with color identification pictures, for ready reference in the field. Bear in mind, though, that while it may be interesting, it won't help you to know what deer commonly forage upon during the spring and summer period. As we noted earlier, these are likely to be depleted, brown and dead, or covered with snow later on, and the deer will almost certainly have shifted their attention to other foods. What the hunter needs to know is what the fall/

When scouting for a place to hunt, it's often possible to find a "browse line" where twigs and buds are all nipped off to a uniform height above the ground. (Photo by Bluford Muir)

winter foods are, and which specific ones are abundant that year, scanty, or entirely absent.

With these thoughts in mind while scouting, the hunter is more likely to take notice and then more thoroughly evaluate any particular area if he chances upon a certain hillside that is layered with acorns, or a hollow dense with red maple saplings, or a stand of rather isolated white cedar or some other favored species.

There is another thing worth doing, but this is an after-the-fact approach, so to speak. Whenever a sportsman bags a deer and is field-dressing it, he should examine the stomach contents to see what that deer had been feeding upon. If he traditionally hunts a certain county year after year and keeps a record, it is easy, in time, to become an expert on the food preferences of the area's deer population. Speed up the learning process if you wish by asking your hunting friends to do the same with deer they kill and to relay the information to you.

One thing worth saying with regards to the browsing nature of deer during the fall and winter months is that the food absolutely must be within their reach. Many times it's even possible to see a "browse line" along a stand of young maples, aspens, or poplar saplings where deer have nipped off all leaves or small twigs to a uniform height off the ground. Such signs of where deer have been feeding are easily recognized, because deer have no teeth on the top jaw at the front of the mouth, only a rough-textured "grinding pad," and so every sign of browsing has a ragged and torn appearance.

If it appears that browsing deer have fairly well depleted the prime food source in any given area, up to a certain height, they may have since altered their feeding patterns so that these particular areas are no longer being visited. Obviously, even if there is still a plentiful supply of twigs and so on but they are all 7 feet or more off the ground, the food is inaccessible to the deer, and depending upon other food or sign about the area the whitetail scout might want to discount the place from any further consideration. This very thing is even why a great majority (some studies say 90 percent) of winter-killed deer are fawns and yearlings. As food supplies grow short during January, February, and March, the younger, smaller deer are simply unable to reach as high as the larger deer and are therefore the first to starve.

Another thing we should consider is water. I have never been too concerned about the location or abundance of water sources, even though many other hunters diligently strive to find places along streams or brooks where deer have come to drink. The reason I downplay the importance of water is that I am of the opinion that deer are able to find ample quantities of what they need almost anywhere. Even though there may not be ready evidence of a lake, river, or stream in the immediate area, there are certain to be countless other water sources, some of which are more or less permanent, such as seepages, springs, and trickles. Then there are the temporary water sources that are usually plentiful; deer can easily find them, but they only exist day to day or week to week, such as rainwater puddles and the like. Along the

Except in arid or desert regions, don't worry about deer having enough to drink. That does not influence their behavior to a substantial degree, because they are able to find what they need almost anywhere. If there are no lakes, streams, or rivers, they'll drink from springs, seepages, and rainwater collection puddles. (Photo by Kesteloo)

edges of fields planted to domesticated crops and grains, I very commonly come upon deer drinking from tractor ruts.

One exception to all of this might be in the case of arid country where there is far less likelihood of puddles, seepages, and such. In these areas it's worth the effort to determine the locations of farm ponds, ranch tanks, "resatas," spring-fed streams (natural streams during these times may be in the form of dry washes), and other water sources. I am not saying that hunting the area around a pond or spring is necessarily a top tactic to employ (though it may well be, because of the likelihood of lush greenery the water source encourages there), but knowledge of such water locations may help in piecing together the puzzle parts as to how deer travel to and from such places.

Lastly, another thing deer take a fancy to is salt, and if a hunter lucks upon a natural salt lick he is almost certain to find the surrounding area entirely marked with hoofprints. A stand overlooking a natural lick might easily result in quickly filling your license, but artificially baiting an area with a salt block of the kind set out for livestock is illegal in most states. Even where it may be entirely permissible, any kind of baiting (some hunters have been known to use apples and corn as well) indicates a hunter too lazy or inept to want to work at his sport or earn his venison.

3

How Whitetails Live and Move

While it is undoubtedly the whitetail's refined senses which enable him to outmaneuver hunters rather than his speed and agility, this is definitely not to sell these latter abilities short. But in most cases, it has been estimated, for every buck a hunter sees, five additional bucks see or smell or hear him first and escape entirely undetected.

Several years ago I had a ringside seat for this very type of occurrence, allowing me to observe something few hunters see during a lifetime dedicated to the outdoors.

I was hunting in Tennessee's Cherokee National Forest and had built a stand near where two deer trails converged to cross a saddle connecting two very steep ridges. It was a natural deer runway, numerous sign littering the area was scorching hot, and early on the second evening of my watch six whitetails suddenly materialized in the distance. When I first saw them they were about 200 yards away and threading themselves slowly through dense cover adjacent to one of the steep hillsides. Through 9×36 Bushnell binoculars I identified five of them as does and the sixth, trailing slightly behind the others, as a very large buck. Even though I was only able to see fleeting glimpses of polished horns through the dense screen of cover I gave him eight points and 180 pounds, and my heart was pounding like a triphammer because if they continued along their present course of travel they would eventually pass directly in front of my stand.

Then things started to go haywire. Out of the corner of my eye there was suddenly a flash of orange in the distance—another hunter!

He was cautiously walking through the cover, but by the way he was moving I could tell he had no idea whatever the deer were around. Then I saw another hunter, moving parallel with the first but about 100 yards to his right, and then still another hunter to his left. They were working a deer drive!

"Dammit," I muttered under my breath. "I don't know where they came from, but they are going to ruin everything."

The trio of hunters was still about 300 yards away from the deer when six heads suddenly jerked up, and it should not be difficult to guess what happened after that.

Continuing to watch the entire episode through my field glasses, I saw the deer first freeze in position for long minutes, training all of their senses in the direction of the approaching danger. Then two of the deer, both does, became restless, swung around hard to the right, and very quietly skulked out a side door. Moments later the other three does began sneaking perpendicular to the hunters, eventually skirted the one on the end, and then disappeared into the darkness of thick evergreens. The buck was even more crafty. Simply sidestepping a few short yards, he hunkered down and with front legs extended far ahead then belly-crawled into the very middle of the tangled leafy branches of a blown-down tree. Next he lowered his head until his chin was touching the ground, and remained still.

The hunters eventually walked right past the buck, one of them coming within 20 yards of the bedded animal, and continued on. When they had proceeded still another 100 yards or so, the buck scrabbled backward from his hideout, like a crawfish, and then slunk away toward the pines in search of his lady friends.

The whitetail's habitat adds greatly to the difficulty of centering sights on him. First of all, it is tremendously varied in terrain types, food, vegetation, altitudes, and especially climate or weather conditions during the hunting season.

Deer adapt, and pattern their behavior to their surroundings. Seldom do they like to travel across wide open spaces, yet when you least expect it that's exactly what they'll do. (Photo by U.S. Fish and Wildlife Service)

This makes it difficult for the deer-hunting writer to reach all segments of his audience. Hunters in Minnesota, Wisconsin, Michigan, and throughout the New England states are north-woodsmen, and many firmly believe the pursuit of whitetails is either impossible or impractical without good tracking snow. Hunters in Iowa, Kansas, Oklahoma, and the other Plains states, on the other hand, will scoff if too much time is devoted to any talk of "ridge-running," which is the favored hunting method throughout southern Ohio, Kentucky, West Virginia, and down into the Ozarks. Yet Mississippi, Alabama, Louisiana, Georgia, Florida, and Carolina hunters almost never see snow hunting, have not much to speak of in the way of "high country," and are not confronted with dry, plains-type terrain interrupted by swales and coulees. The deer they know is swamp-bred and most often encountered sneaking through tropical forests of gum, tupelo, and cypress, bounding ahead of packs of redbones and blueticks, or splashing withers-deep in black water to ward off swarms of biting insects. Their neighbors to the west are still another breed of hunters who face still different environments; whitetails, they say, are animals of dry, dusty, rattlesnake-infested country punctuated by expanses of cactus, cholla, mesquite, and prickly pear, where the sounds of something flushing out ahead are as likely to be javelinas or coyotes as deer.

Regardless of where the whitetail lives, however, he is still a whitetail, and although he adapts his activities to the types of country he lives in, his habits are nevertheless very much the same. One common thread that is typical of whitetail behavior in all terrain conditions is that the species does not at all care for open spaces, like the pronghorn antelope or mule deer, but almost always will be in, near, or around whatever cover is available, and the more broken-up or irregular the cover the better. The reason for this is that there are many more sides or designs to jumbled or irregular cover formations, allowing the whitetail many more options. In other words, he is an animal of the edges. Yet even this has to be qualified somewhat, because when spooked and attempting to place distance between himself and the hunter a deer may well chart a nonstop course directly through the middle of the heaviest cover imaginable.

BUCKS, DOES, AND FAWNS

Whitetails anywhere live in what is known as a matriarchal society, meaning that with the exception of the breeding season or perhaps during bitter winter periods when they yard in areas of concentrated food and cover, does and their offspring live together and bucks keep pretty much to themselves, running with other bucks upon occasion but more often being loners.

This does not, as some hunters may infer, have anything to do with bucks supposedly being more wary or crafty. It is true that bucks, in most cases, are extremely secretive, but it's not likely that does are any less intelligent. There may be several explanations for their apparently less crafty behavior. One thing is that a doe's fear of man may not be as well entrenched because of fewer potentially harmful encounters. In other words, in most areas does are not legal game. Where they are, as in specially set seasons to facilitate herd reduction, they can become as sneaky and evasive as any mossyhorn ever was. Another influence—but this is only pure speculation—may have to do with the sex roles of does and bucks. It is a doe's basic inclination to lure or attract male suitors and also to care for offspring, and both of these are more easily accomplished by more often stepping into more open places and remaining for longer periods of time. Bucks, in a sense, are couriers, with the major role of carrying and protecting the seed, and one way of keeping their private lives private is by clinging to any and all available cover.

Young fawns are playful and just like inquisitive children. They are wild by instinct, but all of their suspicions, craft, and evasive tendencies are taught to them by their mothers. (Photo by Bill Cross)

As to this matriarchal way in which whitetails live, even when bucks, does, and fawns *are* keeping company, which is not often, the buck is not the lord and master. It is nearly always an old doe who leads the group and is in charge of travel directions and other activity decisions.

The paintings one often sees depicting a buck, doe, and fawn standing in some moon-drenched, pine-studded clearing or other scenic setting are phony, contrived for the single purpose of selling calendars and Christmas cards. Family groups like this simply do not exist in the world of the whitetail, or very, very rarely. The buck is primarily a rapist and adulterer, and when his pleasures have been satisfied with one doe in heat he abandons her and seeks out another and then still another. He assumes no responsibility whatever for rearing any of the offspring or staying around for any other protectionist measures. In fact, it is more common behavior for a buck, if and when he now and then does join a small band of other deer, to violently and forcibly chase away all fawns or yearlings. As a matter of record, does in heat will chase away their former season's offspring, too.

When a whitetail doe first gives birth, either at the age of one or two years, she has a single fawn, but every spring thereafter twins are the rule. Sometimes, in prime habitat, triplets and quadruplets occur, but sex composition, concerning the species as a whole, is very close to 50-50.

A doe fawn weighs an average of 4½ pounds at birth; baby bucks are about a pound heavier. The mother may drop her fawns wherever she happens to be at the time. At the age of only ten minutes, fawns are able to stand and walk on wobbly legs, and the doe hurriedly leads them away to a secluded place as predators may be attracted by smell to the actual birthing location. Fawns, of course, are spotted so they easily blend with the cover. They are also odorless, and they instinctively know to lie flat when anything approaches.

It is a doe's nature, after hiding her fawns in cover, to move away herself to watch for danger and lure potential predators from the area. Predictably, however, she'll return to the offspring six to eight times a day to nurse them.

After about a month the fawns are able to trail after their mother and now begin a weaning process in which they gradually imitate her feeding upon tender young grasses. With each day, the solid food intake increases and the requirement for milk diminishes. At this young age of only four weeks a fawn is easily able to outrun a man; as a general rule, however, young does remain with their mothers throughout the coming winter months, not taking out on their own until the following spring, but young bucks may begin fending for themselves at the age of only six or seven months.

The way in which young deer learn from the doe mothers is fascinating. Ordinarily, very young fawns are like inquisitive children, always searching and smelling, tasting, getting into mischief, and expressing curiosity about the world around them. While on summer photo missions, I have had them walk right up to me as I softly whistled or snapped my fingers. They registered no fear simply because they had not yet been taught to.

But observe a slightly older fawn, especially when it is in the company of its mother, as it will almost continually watch and imitate her. When the doe's head jerks up, so does the fawn's. The doe peers off into the distance for long moments, and so does the fawn. Then the fawn looks at its mother to see if what she is looking at has alarmed her. She stamps her front hooves, and the youngster tries to do the same. Finally the doe lowers her head to feed again, and so does the fawn. Almost immediately up comes a big head again, and so too a little one. I stand up and wave my arms. Now the doe for sure recognizes me for what I am. She bolts, snorting loudly many times and with her tail waving from side to side (which says to the little one, "Follow me away from here"). The fawn, barely successful in its attempts, makes little sneezing noises as it runs. From that time on the fawn is imprinted with a distrust of man and knows how to react in a similar situation.

While whitetails do not adhere to any type of herding tendency or inclination, they are gregarious to the extent of benefiting their own individual welfares. It seems they instinctively know that there is safety in numbers, because of the many more eyes, twitching noses, and keen ears on the alert, yet that too large a group will stand out. Also, in many regions there are only small areas of what we might label "prime" cover and food types, and these tend to serve as natural drawing cards to bring together deer that otherwise would not seek company. As a result, deer are frequently seen consorting in twos, threes, and fours. Sometimes there will be even more in a group, but not very often. In those instances in which deer apparently seem present in large numbers, watch closely and you'll probably note that they did not enter the particular area together and will not leave together.

This is a good time to describe the repertoire of communicative sounds and noises deer make, because such sounds are used mainly to warn others of danger. A fawn often bleats like a lamb

Deer prefer to keep company so there are additional eyes and ears alert to danger, but too many all together and they are more conspicuous. Large numbers of deer therefore consist of several different bands that happened to be lured to the same food source. When deer feed, they always post a "sentry" as shown here. (Photo by Kentucky Dept. of Fish & Wildlife)

when it becomes separated from its mother and is attempting to let her know its location. Adult deer, to warn of danger, produce raspy coughs and whistling noises through both their noses and mouths by gathering air deep from within their torsos and then vigorously exhaling. Some hunters have been known to imitate these blowing, snorting sounds to bring a buck's head up for a clean shot at the neck region when an animal is feeding in dense, shoulder-high cover.

During the mating season bucks and does sometimes also produce low, guttural grunting noises, but I am not sure why. Whitetails make stamping noises with their hooves, too; this is often done to warn other deer that something is amiss, or it may be an effort to elicit some response from something they have just seen, smelled, or heard but have not yet been able to classify.

It is quite possible, of course, to see deer almost any time of day. But if we were to take an "average" whitetail and examine closely an "average" day in its life, here is basically what the agenda would entail.

The deer, either buck or doe, would come out of hiding about four-thirty in the afternoon or approximately an hour and a half before full darkness, and the first activity would likely see it beginning to drink or feed. Deer generally walk along very slowly, nibbling at this shoot or that twig, because they sense that the faster they move the less accurately they are able to monitor the pulse of everything going on around them.

This initial feeding activity in most cases sees the deer gradually moving in the direction of lower elevations, drifting progressively farther away from their bedding locations that were much higher, but this is not a steadfast rule. If the favored food source in the area happens to be acorns, which are frequently found along the ridgelines, the animals may move laterally to other areas of similar elevation, or they may even travel to substantially higher ground. But usually within an hour or two after complete darkness has fallen, the whitetail's appetite has been appeased, and so too any requirement for water, and he lies down again to begin chewing his cud. This secondary bedding attitude is very frequently seen in open places such as grown-over fields, in the middle of crop areas, in brushy bottomlands, in the tall grass swales of open plains regions, and similar places, although at any time during the night hours the deer may again rise to its feet for more feeding or whatever, and then it's back to bedding and chewing again.

About one hour before dawn the deer will characteristically become active again. It begins "topping off" its rumen once more as it gradually drifts back to much heavier cover for daytime bedding.

The daytime bedding behavior of whitetails is fairly well defined. We've noted that the animals typically move to higher ground and into heavier cover, but it's not that cut and dried. In most cases does and fawns, and often yearling bucks, do not travel nearly as high as the older male deer. Look for these does and young bucks to select heavy-cover hiding places in hollows and ravines and other low areas, but just as often halfway up some hillside where there are grassy, open areas. One of their favorite bedding places is on benches or where hillsides have a terraced effect.

Larger bucks, on the other hand, seem seldom content to take beds in such locations unless the area is very remote and there are dense stands of pines or similar cover for concealment. Instead, they invariably prefer the ridges, sometimes smack dab on their crests or just slightly over one side or the other.

Ridgelines and other high elevations offer several distinct advantages to whitetail bucks. First, as the sun comes out and warms the

The daytime bedding tendencies of trophy bucks are fairly well defined. In severe, unsettled weather they retreat for heavy cover, not because of the cold or rain but because it is quieter there than on the open hillsides where the wind and weather make their senses of smell and hearing unreliable.

countryside, thermal air currents begin to rise, carrying with them the sounds and scents of everything going on below to forewarn a buck of the approach of anything that may not have his welfare in mind. In many cases bucks will bed almost directly above does and fawns, using them as sentries. If the does become restless and either sneak away or bound off, the buck knows something is not right with the world and has ample time to slip away himself.

The most highly favored bedding locations of bucks are the ends or points of ridgelines just before they drop off, or promontories or outcroppings, both of which, in addition to offering a bird's-eye view in several directions, also allow two or three different escape options.

When we say that bucks typically prefer to bed on high ground, and that is where they are most likely to be found through the daylight hours, we have to ask just how high is high. This is important because there is a world of difference between terrain elevations commonly found in the various states throughout the whitetail's range. In some areas, prime deer cover may be almost perfectly flat, in other areas gently rolling, in others hilly, and in still others mountainous. I've learned from hunting in South Carolina's swamp counties that bucks and does alike use high-ground bedding areas that may consist of not much more than very slightly raised areas, only a couple of feet higher in elevation than surrounding marshes and bogs. Yet in the Daniel Boone National Forest in central Kentucky, a hunter may have to hike uphill for at least an hour to find himself in the type of areas that bucks thereabouts seek out for daytime bedding.

As in making individual interpretations as to different foods that may exist in certain areas, as described earlier, the hunter will therefore have to evaluate the desirability of various terrain elevations in his area, too. A good general guideline is to seek the highest ground available in the immediate area; that is where most bucks will usually be found most of the time. Also, since I related earlier that any given buck may have a home range of as much as 1½ square miles, the hunter will have to base his judgments not solely on singular terrain features but rather on terrain "areas" as a whole and how they relate to the entire picture of deer activities in that region.

It can be said as well that deer do not always bed in the same terrain area but that bedding behavior may vary somewhat depending upon feeding movements to new areas as previous ones become depleted, and in accordance with changes in wind direction and weather. And even when deer are consistently bedding in certain areas, the same *exact* spots are not always chosen, except perhaps in those cases in which a buck has found a very special site such as a promontory where everything is in his favor.

When the days are quiet and sunny, bedding locations may be spang in the open, or relatively so in the types of areas described above, but as weather turns stormy much heavier cover is sought out. This is not because the deer are seeking protection from the elements. They are virtually immune to rain, snow, and cold temperatures, as evidenced by the fact that in Canada, whitetails live as far north as the 53rd parallel, where winter temperatures often dip to 30, 40, and 50 degrees below zero; if deer were adversely affected by cold or stormy weather they would hardly be native to such latitudes.

The reason the deer retreat for the heavy cover, and I briefly touched on this earlier, is that windy, stormy weather makes whitetails extremely restless and nervous. They are no longer as easily able to detect, classify, and catalog sounds and scents because of the competition from the noisy weather and the erratic air currents it creates. And so rather than allow themselves to remain exposed and therefore vulnerable in more open areas, they retreat to cover, perhaps feeling that hiding from ready view somewhat compensates for their temporarily impaired sensory abilities. Thick pines are especially sought, again not because such areas are warmer or anything like that but because deep within such dense cover it is quieter, and therefore "safer." When the wind stops blowing in a day or two, bedding sites may again be located right back on the exposed hillsides and ridgelines, even in bitter cold weather.

Finding and identifying bedding sites is relatively easy for the alert hunter with sharp eyes. The deer that made them will have long since vacated the premises, but that is of no consequence because the hunter now knows of the types of locations they are seeking in that area and under those weather conditions. This, in turn, may enable him to "pattern" the behavior of deer in his region; if he can duplicate the finding of identical conditions elsewhere, he is likely to find beds in many of those locations, too.

When the ground is dry, a whitetail's bed will simply appear as an elliptical depression measuring about 3½ feet long by 1½ feet wide where grasses, leaves, forest duff, and other ground cover have been matted down by the body weight of the animal. In snow, the ground may be packed down in a similar manner, showing body size in a type of "pocket" in the snow, but just as often the deer's body heat will have melted the snow to reveal damp leaves or semi-dry ground in the bottom of the bed.

A good tip to keep in mind is that if the hunter discovers a cluster of two or three beds or more, say on a bench or hillside, these have likely been made by does, which, as I've said, are not necessarily communal by nature but more so than bucks. The hunter might now want to examine higher elevations or heavier cover areas in the immediate vicinity in the hopes of finding that lone bed indicative of the presence of a buck.

The value in locating bedding sites is not that a whitetail scout is likely to be successful in later sneaking into the area and killing a bedded deer. It does happen upon occasion, but as I have emphasized the sites are usually so strategically located or positioned

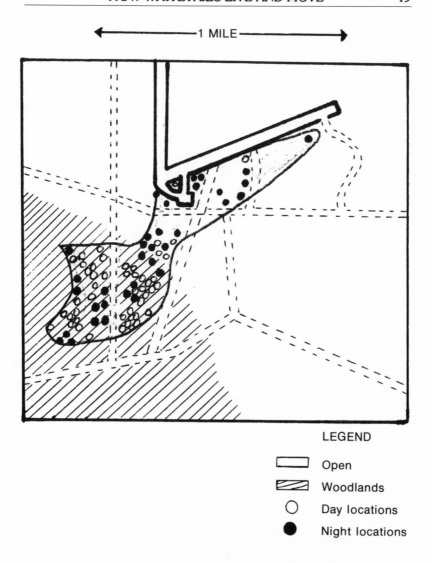

←————1 MILE————→

LEGEND

⬜	Open
▨	Woodlands
○	Day locations
●	Night locations

Whitetails live out their entire lives in a home range that usually averages less than 2 square miles. They use numerous trails for trading back and forth, and also special escape trails. Shown here is the home range of one deer as determined by radio-tracking equipment. Notice how the range overlaps roads. Notice also that the deer spends most daytime hours in cover but at night ventures into open fields, along edges, and along roadsides.

as to make any approach by an intruder an almost entirely futile proposition. Rather, the discovery of bedding sites is beneficial in that it allows a hunter to locate heavily traveled trails leading in and out of the vicinity. Then at some later time he can quietly enter the

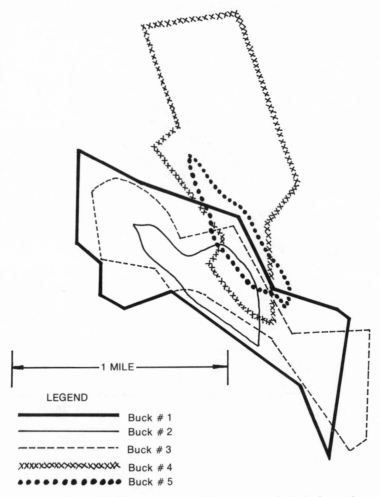

Home ranges of deer almost always overlap, with numerous individuals sharing the same habitat. Here are the home ranges of five different whitetail bucks, as determined by electronic transmitters attached to their collars.

area, assume a waiting station overlooking a trail leading to or from a bedding site, and be in good position to intercept deer coming down from their daytime seclusions or moving back up after full morning light.

Another plus in knowing of regular bedding places of deer, as we'll see in Chapter 8, is that during the midday hours when deer are not actively moving about, hunters can select those terrain locations that have revealed in the past the greatest numbers of beds to organize drives to move the deer out and in specific directions to where their partners are in wait.

THE HOME RANGE

Compared to mule deer, which are migratory, whitetails are homebodies, even though this may not seem at all the case when a spooked buck takes off through the cover apparently with a ticket to the next county. But it is true, and those headlong dashes whitetails execute, unless they are frightened out of their wits, are usually of very short duration. Just as it seems as though a buck is really building up speed (about the time he has vanished from sight) he may commonly come to a quick halt, fade off into a thicket to one side or the other, and resume his lurking and spying. He may even at this time begin executing a wide circle, which serves a twofold purpose. It brings him back to the food or security cover he initially sought out, and also gives him a chance to get a peek at what it was that scared him away.

It is virtually impossible to chase deer entirely out of the range region in which they were born and with which they have become intimately familiar. This can be somewhat of a lucky break for the hunter. He can consider a buck's home range as really nothing more than a big house with many different rooms and interconnecting corridors that allow easy back-and-forth access options among them. There are feeding rooms, watering rooms, rooms where mating takes place, and rooms where resting is done.

You might say the "house" a whitetail lives in is therefore much like a home any human resides in. But in addition to the hallways that lead to and connect with the various activity areas, a whitetail's shy and fearful nature requires that his home also be riddled with many secret passageways that can allow him a quick exit in times of need.

Last year Al Wolter and I hunted an area of the Wayne National Forest in southern Ohio and together located a stand site that was, as Al described it, "so hot it was about to burn up." We flipped a coin and I won the toss, so I got to take the stand while Al assumed another one half a mile away. After a one-hour wait an eight-point buck came along. I aimed for the lungs and squeezed the trigger.

The deer angled away downhill and around a point of land and fell stone dead about 75 yards from the point of impact.

Now, the escape route this deer had attempted to use before it died was one that neither Al nor I had discovered in thoroughly scouting the area previously, and once we doped out the situation it became obvious the exit trail took perfect advantage of the terrain and cover to allow any buck to leave the area without fanfare.

With the buck now on the meatpole, Al decided to take the same exact stand I had been sitting on. Along came a spike buck from the *opposite* direction from that my buck had used in his approach. Al touched off his shot, aiming for the lungs. The deer ran, bellied under a wire fence, turned left and went downhill for a short distance, then turned right onto the same exact escape trail, ran a few more yards, and fell dead not 5 yards from where my buck had previously fallen!

The point is that here was one of those secret passageways in an overlapping home range where two whitetail bucks lived, and it was so special and important to them that it was never used, except in emergency situations, maybe because more regular use would have made it more easily noticed.

Incidents such as this, as the years go by, cause me to be more and more absorbed with the essence of the whitetail—the cunning, chicanery, and elusiveness that make him what he is. It's not simply the sophistication of his senses and how they enable him to outsmart hunters but the way in which he takes the sensory information he is continually soaking up and plugs it in to learn exactly what is going on in each and every room of his house.

Within the home-range area we've seen how food availability at various times, including regional differences in climate, may change. We've noted how deer may alter their feeding habits depending upon the moon phases. And we've explained how winds and storms can determine differences in bedding locations. As they have to do with specific hunting methods, we'll be looking at all of these again very shortly. But to conclude this particular section, let's take a brief look at the phenomenon known as "yarding," which is still another way in which whitetails use different portions of their home ranges during different times of year.

Yarding is common whitetail behavior during the winter

In winter, deer "yard" in areas of concentrated food. Because they are so attached to their home ranges, they often starve when food runs out, rather than search for new sources. (Photo by U.S. Forest Service)

months, but it is seen only where there is considerable snowfall that causes deer to congregate in quite confined quarters and typically in large numbers. In areas of lesser snowfall, the animals also seem to gravitate from the more open cover and edges to heavier stuff—such cover may not be far from roads, or it may be deep in the hinterlands—but in any event the deer form only small bands where plentiful food stores are sheltered from the winter weather.

There is a good deal of speculation that the yarding tendency of whitetails in heavy cover, wind-protected areas such as brushy thickets, mixtures of sheltered hardwoods and evergreens, and like places is for the purpose of seeking protection from the elements. I have serious doubts about this, however, because as I related in the section dealing with bedding sites the species is naturally endowed with ample protection from snow and cold air.

The yarding inclination of deer more likely has to do with the movement- and travel-inhibiting aspects of the deep snow itself, and this is a blade with two edges. The deer, being unable to travel freely, are attracted to regions where concentrated food sources will last them through the hard times. Indeed, as commonly happens, the food may not last and many animals may eventually die of starvation, but that does not alter the fact that they must seek out quantity food sources, and this has the effect of seeing numbers of deer grouped in those few desirable regions. But also—and perhaps this is a genetic trait that has been carried over from hundreds of previous generations in which the whitetail's range was well saturated with natural predators such as wolves and mountain lions—it may be that deer instinctively yard because of some sense of security in numbers they wrongly assume they can rely upon when their ability to flee is impaired.

4

Trophy Hunting

A little of the trophy hunter is hidden somewhere in all of us. No matter how much talk there may be about the best eating deer, I have yet to meet the hunter who could honestly say he would pass up a chance at a sly old monster carrying a trophy rack in the hopes of instead bagging a tender yearling spike. Big bucks, both the ones that were collected and the ones that got away, seem also to monopolize the conversation in any deer camp. I know from experience that they draw excited stares when they are being transported home on the roof racks of cars at the close of the season. And when a sportsman thumbs through the pages of an outdoor magazine or hunting book, it's not the pictures of does or forkhorns or gray squirrels or ringneck pheasants or black bears that draw and hold his interest and awe for the longest periods. It's the pictures of the outsize male deer and their stately and magnificent headpieces.

A trophy whitetail, however, must always be considered in terms relative to the locale, the subspecies being sought, and the expectations of the hunter. What I mean to say is that "one for the

This fantastic full-body mount is the Northern Woodland subspecies—our largest whitetail. The deer was taken almost in the author's backyard in southeastern Ohio.

record book" is always a "trophy." But only a very, very small percentage of trophies ever stand any chance of going into the records.

For example, a Carmen Mountains whitetail taken near the Big Bend country of west Texas, sporting a ten-point rack and weighing in at 120 pounds, would be something even the most expert hunter could be extremely proud of. The same would be true of a Coues whitetail that came in at 110 pounds and carried a basket rack sprouting eight thick points. Yet both deer, while very desirable as compared to most others of their particular subspecies, would appear only like overstuffed greyhounds next to a 225-

pound Dakota whitetail from the grain country of prairie Saskatchewan. And that buck, in turn, wouldn't raise many admiring eyebrows when hung on a meatpole beside a Northern Woodland giant from the unglaciated Allegheny Plateau region of southeastern Ohio. That's why I took the time earlier to list some of the more notable whitetail subspecies—to provide some sort of benchmark you might want to refer to upon occasion when hunting in any particular locale.

In the final analysis, then, a "record" deer is a whitetail buck meeting specific minimum antler dimensions as required by the North American Big Game Awards Program. But a "trophy" whitetail can be almost anything that serves as a reward for your diligent efforts (be it a huge buck that does indeed make the records), meets your expectations (be it your first buck), or in any other way is significant with regards to certain subspecies, fond companions, or memorable places.

THOSE MAGNIFICENT RACKS

About April each year, whatever the region of the country, a whitetail buck enters the first stages of a sexual transformation that will continue to heighten through the many coming months until it finally culminates in mating. Several changes take place in the physiology of whitetails, most of which are described in the next chapter, but let's examine first a buck's crowning glory.

From pedicels on his skull sprout the first bulbous signs of antlers. They appear at first as knobs or buttons but grow very rapidly and are usually fully developed within fourteen weeks. During this growing process these bonelike structures are nourished externally by what is called "velvet." Velvet is actually a dense network of blood vessels that takes on a spongy green color and texture, and during this time the maturing antlers are still very soft and susceptible to injury or disfiguration.

I once knew of a whitetail that had one very high and wide antler on his left side, but the bizarre right antler swooped down in a curve beneath his neck, under his chin. The deer probably ran into a fence or experienced some other mishap when his antlers were still in the soft developmental stage during early spring. Except under highly unusual circumstances, however, antlers damaged during the early growth months seldom adversely affect the health of the animal. This particular deer with the deformed rack was only semi-wild. It had been raised as an orphan fawn by a neighbor of mine and while not entirely tame would nevertheless come to the edge of his backyard every morning for a handout (usually an apple Rick threw from a short distance). Anyway, the buck's regular routine made him easily identifiable, and as time passed the normal and abnormal antlers were gradually shed as they customarily are late each winter, and many weeks later he began growing a new rack of perfect symmetry.

By about mid-August a whitetail buck's antlers have reached full size, the blood vessels nourishing them have dried up, and the velvet is beginning to peel away like dead skin. Underneath are ivory-white main beams from which almost any number of individual tines may protrude, and the buck hastens the removal of the velvet by rubbing his rack on various types of trees and brush.

But as far as telling a buck's age, antler size or configuration may lie to you. The reason is that the massiveness of any rack and the number and length of individual tines is crucially dependent upon soil fertility (mineral type and content) and the local type and abundance of forage available to deer in that area. Any amount or type of food intake, of course, first goes to actual body growth and nourishment and only then are excess nutrients channeled into antler growth and development. As a result, if there is a food shortage, or if the food is of low nutritional value, it's the antlers that get slighted.

Generally, however, given adequate food supplies a buck will begin growing his first antlers at about the age of a year and a half, and in all likelihood they will be either buttons or spikes, although forked horns and even small six-point racks are not unusual. With each subsequent year of growth, each new set of antlers both is heavier and has more points; a buck three and a half years old that has dined well all his life, for example, should carry a heavy beamed rack with eight or ten points.

I'd like to mention here that I think too many deer hunters go to extremes in counting antler points. I have actually seen some stalwartly proclaim that a little peppercorn of a bump on a rack

A typical huge rack from Ohio, with twelve "honest" points. All the little tits, bumps, and sprouts are not legitimate points but only curios. For a typical rack, count only the brow tines and the major tines emanating from the main beam.

was truly a point because they could hang a ring on it. When this happens, we get to the ridiculously absurd stage of heated controversy over whether a rack is an eighteen-pointer, a twenty-seven-pointer, or a forty-pointer!

The truth of the matter (we're talking about typical racks, now) is that most fully mature whitetail bucks will have racks with either six, eight, or ten points, depending upon whether brow tines are present. A very few now and then are legitimate twelve-pointers. And that's how all of them should be viewed, considered, and spoken of, with any other Lilliputian sprouts or other projections off the main beam or the major tines being nothing more than curiosities.

We should also say that antler growth continues only up to a certain point. After about his sixth birthday any buck can be considered a very old animal, and one way in which this is commonly reflected is in racks that with each successive year become progressively smaller or sometimes appear very grotesque and unsymmetrical. A buck that has suffered poor nutrition may have a rack that looks even more haggard; at three to five years old, when he should be in his prime, he may have nothing more than long, gnarled spikes. It should also be noted, though, that bucks over five years old are something of a rarity these days. With steadily mounting hunting pressure, and an increase in the number of hunters seeking only topnotch racks, the average lifespan of the majority of this country's bucks is probably not much longer than two and a half to three and a half years at the very most.

Antler size can also indicate other existing situations in the world of the whitetail. For one, when the great majority of bucks in any given area seem to sport nothing more impressive than spikes, forked horns, or small six-point racks, insufficient forage or forage of low nutritional value may not be the sole problem. The difficulty may be that there are simply too many deer in the immediate area competing for what otherwise might be plenty of high-quality food if there were a balance between the range and the number of deer.

One solution often temporarily adopted by local game departments is reducing the required minimal antler size of bucks that may be taken by hunters, such as allowing spike bucks to be taken where previously deer had to have at least forked horns. Another is opening a doe season. Both measures are designed to reduce the overall herd population to the carrying capacity of the habitat so that the remaining deer may prosper. But too many times sentimentalists—and even hunters themselves, as has been the unfortunate situation in Michigan in recent years—recoil at the thought of harvesting does or young bucks and pressure their state legislatures or game officials to abandon such seasons. The bottom line is that the local deer population steadily falls into even more dire circumstances. The next step, if man refuses to intervene to solve the problem, is that nature intervenes and her remedy is suffering and then a massive die-off of animals from disease and starvation.

Antler growth is also a reflection of previous weather conditions. During mild winters, which in turn often see earlier springs and sometimes even later-than-usual falls, any particular locale will produce larger racks simply because the deer have had highly nutritious food that season and, just as important, plenty of it. When winters are long and severe, and spring gets a late start, there is less food, and what does exist is often not of tremendously high quality. Mast crops as well may not be as dense or plentiful, orchards may not survive unseasonal frosts, and berry crops may be sparse. In other words, liken the entire happening to that of a farmer who as a result of fluctuating weather conditions experiences bumper crops some seasons and other times comes close to being wiped out.

ONE FOR THE RECORDS

It wasn't too long ago that trophy heads were scored by a very simple measurement system based upon the length and spread of any particular rack. That, however, allowed many other characteristics of antler configuration to go unmeasured, probably caused many more knock-down, drag-out arguments than we'll ever know, and suggested the need for a more refined method of scoring.

It was the Boone and Crockett Club (organized in 1887 by Teddy Roosevelt) that set to the task in 1949 of formulating a detailed scoring system that would take into account all the features of a rack rather than just those of length and spread. First was the separation of deer racks into two categories—typical and nontypical. Typical racks are those that are almost perfectly symmetrical in their curvature, number of points, and so on. In another manner of speaking, the features and dimensions of one antler are very nearly mirror images of the other. Nontypical racks average out with a higher score than typical racks because of the greater number of antler tines and points. Many nontypical racks are downright freakish with twisted beams and gnarled points seemingly sprouting in a dozen different directions.

In any regard, every three years the Boone and Crockett Club, in cooperation now with the National Rifle Association, recognizes outstanding trophies that meet dimensional requirements to make the record book, and this is known as the North American Big Game Awards Program.

Using a flexible measuring tape and following a step-by-step scoring sheet, any hunter can come up with a preliminary score of his rack to see if there is any possibility of getting it into the books. The minimum required point count or score for a typical whitetail

Here, using a flexible tape, Al Wolter measures a trophy Ohio rack while son Jeff Wolter looks on, wishing it were his.

rack is 170, and the minimum required score for a nontypical rack is 195. For Coues deer, which are a whitetail subspecies scored separately, typical point count must be 110 and nontypical 120.

Should a hunter discover that a rack he has taken meets the minimum requirements he then goes through the standard procedure of first allowing a period for the rack to undergo normal drying and shrinkage, then contacting an official scorer for the club to verify the measurements, and then submitting an application form to the Big Game Awards Committee. This may be followed by attendance at an awards banquet, display of many of the trophies submitted and accepted during that three-year period, and the presentation of medals and/or certificates.

But let's come back down to earth and look at the more realistic possibilities of actually tagging a record-book buck, how to evaluate a rack, and where a hunter's chances are best for big bucks.

I don't mean to sound a discouraging word, but while we may all collect a few nice whitetail "trophies" during our given years, and while for some hunters there is a good chance of getting into the books with any number of other big-game species, for the vast majority of us there is virtually no chance whatever of collecting a whitetail buck that will make the books.

Look at it this way. If a hunter is in excellent health and physical condition, has at least several weeks to spare at a time, and can afford hunting trips that may *each* cost anywhere from $4,000 on up, there is a decent chance of sometime or another in his life tagging a record sheep, goat, Alaskan moose, caribou, brown bear, or whatever. The reason, obviously, is that such species abide in the continent's wildest and most remote corners, and that means two things. First, that type of country is seen by less than one of a thousand of the nation's average hunters with average means, and second, as a direct consequence of this the various individual game species that live in such inaccessible places are permitted many more years to grow to record proportions.

But with whitetails living as they do in close proximity to man and therefore every year coming under heavy fire by anyone who can buy or borrow a rifle, the herd population is kept very closely cropped. Then there are the influences of winterkill and poaching, which account for a tremendous number of deer every year, at least a few of which might otherwise have lived longer and grown larger.

The best set of antlers a buck is likely to have during his lifetime will probably appear sometime between his fifth and seventh year, but as we noted earlier, very few bucks ever live that long.

Another factor to consider is that a buck that does manage to beat the odds by living longer is a crafty old recluse that has somehow managed to survive numerous hunting seasons by keeping his private life *very* private, and over all those years he's learned plenty from it.

One landowner I know in southern Ohio possesses about 300 acres that he hunts, plants, and runs stock upon. I'll wager he knows every square foot of that acreage better than most know

There are many ways to evaluate racks. Mostly, you compare dimensions of the rack to various body features. From a distance this buck doesn't look all that impressive but it is indeed an extremely good deer. Look at how much wider the rack is beyond the ears. (Photo by Kentucky Dept. of Fish & Wildlife)

their own backyards, so understandably he was shocked when one fall he found the remains of a grizzled buck that had apparently died of old age. The antlers were still intact, though gnawed upon a bit by rodents, and the landowner claimed they were so massive they actually looked phony. The point I'm trying to make is that a whitetail buck generally lives out his entire life within a relatively small home-range area. And the 300-acre tract my friend possesses, because it is uniquely bordered on three sides by natural barriers, was very likely the home of this particular buck. Yet never had the landowner ever once even glimpsed this goliath deer, which was estimated by a biologist to be seven years old.

There may be other reasons, too, why killing a record-book buck is highly unlikely for most of us. But keep these simple statistics in mind if you're still determined to try. During the last several Big Game Awards Program periods, spanning nine years, less than half a dozen whitetails have qualified for the record book, and at that a couple just barely made the minimum required point count. Yet during the same period, North American hunters have harvested literally *millions* of whitetails. You calculate the odds of being one of the lucky few who make the book!

None of this is meant to imply that outstanding trophies cannot or will not be taken every year. But the hunter who is after a very good deer rather than just meat for the pot should know what constitutes a good rack and how to judge a rack accurately when its owner is still in possession of it. This can at times be exceedingly difficult, because when your adrenalin is flowing every rack tends to look much larger than it actually is. The same is true of racks that present themselves unexpectedly, or during low light levels, at very close range, or in heavy cover, while even a record-book set of antlers seen far away on some brushy hillside may not look all that impressive.

Probably the best reason of all for learning to judge deer on the hoof is that it will prevent later disappointments. For example, a hunter may come upon what initially appears to be a "fair" buck on the very first day of a scheduled two-week hunt. Should he try to take it, or should he hold out for something better? More to the point, based upon the subspecies he's hunting and the degree of hunting pressure that locale typically sees, what are his chances of finding something better? This is exactly the question frequently asked in states such as Pennsylvania and Texas, where it is not uncommon to see perhaps two, three, or more bucks per day of hunting. In another hypothetical situation, let's say three bucks bust out of the cover during a drive and the hunter has to make a quick decision. Which should he try for? All may look similar, but one of the bucks may really be much better than the others.

As to the actual size of any rack, the best way to evaluate its merits is by comparing the rack to various body features of the deer itself. I say "various" features because there should be several different criteria by which to make judgments, as the animal may be standing in almost any position.

While the easiest shot to make is at an animal standing broadside, this position also poses the greatest difficulty in accurately judging antlers. Judging the spread is all but impossible, but in most cases you can guesstimate the spread as very good if the tines appear extremely high and the main beams of the antlers are heavy. There is a good chance, since whitetails almost never let their guards down, that the ears will be cocked up and forward. If there is time for a careful examination of the deer through binoculars, check how high above the skull and how high above the ear points the level of the antlers seems to be. Antlers estimated to be 12 inches higher than the bridge of the nose, or 7 or 8 inches above the ear points, are good ones.

You're making a deer drive and three bucks suddenly bust out of the cover and come your way. Think quick. Which do you want to try for? The author picks the one on the far right. It's a heavy rack, wide and high, and look at the length of those brow tines!

If a buck is directly facing you, or more likely running directly away, both width and height of the antlers can be easily and very accurately judged. Regardless of the subspecies, most whitetails possess ears that average 7 to 8 inches in length. If the height of the horns therefore stands at least twice as high as the ears or more, you're looking at an excellent rack. The width of a rack is even easier to judge, because at a glance it is easy to compare its spread to either the animal's body width or the distance between its ears. A whitetail's ears, tip to tip, usually measure 12 to 14 inches, and the body width usually measures 14 or 15 inches. Therefore, if the spread of the antlers exceeds either the body width or the width of the ears, you're looking at an antler spread that is minimally at least 15 inches. And since anything between 15 to 20 inches is a very good deer you'd better begin thinking about shooting; bucks in this category aren't likely to be records, but then again they are by no means found behind every bush.

WHERE YOUR CHANCES ARE BEST

Good deer hunting means different things to different people. If what you're concerned about is continual excitement with lots of deer sighted during any given day, there can be little doubt that

Texas and Pennsylvania are the places to hunt. On the other hand, if you're looking for that one special deer, bigger than any you've ever collected before, your chances will probably be far better if you avoid those states. It's not that trophies aren't occasionally taken in both states—they are indeed—but with such high deer populations competing for the available habitat in each area, and with so many other hunters continually on the prowl, the chances of a rendezvous between you and Mr. Big are not good.

For the hunter who prefers to play the numbers game—wants the best chance at collecting *any* kind of deer and isn't especially concerned about taking home a big rack—I suggest first consulting the *National Rifle Association Hunting Annual,* which costs about four bucks and can be obtained by writing to NRA, 1600 Rhode Island Avenue N.W., Washington, D.C. 20036. The annual gives a state-by-state rundown, listing season dates, hunting regulations, and even recommendations as to the consistently best places in each state for whitetail hunting. The annual also provides a national whitetail forecast. This is a tabular breakdown that gives the estimated whitetail population for each state, number of available resident and nonresident licences (this is important, because some states, such as Kansas, do not allow nonresidents to hunt deer), the estimated deer harvest for that year, and the estimated hunter success percentage. All of this is vital data, because, plain and simple, you'll want to be hunting where the most deer are.

For the best specific deer regions in each of the states, again first review the *NRA Hunting Annual* for suggestions. Then, carry this a step further by writing letters to the department of natural resources or division of fish and game in the state you'd like to hunt, asking for a xerox copy of their county-by-county statistics of deer-harvest numbers in recent years.

As far as where your chances are best for a big buck, we can narrow the field somewhat by first stating that if any particular buck is to be worth measuring it will undoubtedly be a member of the pure-strain Virginia whitetail clan, the Northern Woodland whitetail subspecies, the Dakota whitetail subspecies, the Kansas whitetail subspecies, or the Northwest whitetail race, all of which, as far as their individual ranges, we delineated in Chapter 1. Or perhaps, though not as likely, it could be a member of the Texas whitetail subspecies, or more specifically those Texas deer found

There are many ways to decide where your hunting chances are best. First check the National Rifle Association's Hunting Annual, which every year gives a state-by-state survey. Then contact your game department for county-by-county harvest figures. These figures, along with other data conducted by biologists, such as tagging studies, aerial surveys, and the like, tell you two things: where the trophies are, and where the most deer are. (Photo by South Dakota Dept. of Game)

in the brush country south of San Antonio and fanning out from Laredo and running on to Del Rio.

But there are other ways, too, for determining where one is most likely to encounter the largest bucks. For starters, every dedicated big-buck hunter should periodically obtain copies of the *North American Big Game* record book, which is published about every six years by the Boone and Crockett Club. The current issue of this book came out in August 1977 (the next edition will not come out until about 1983), so this is a prime time for an up-to-date look at trophy-hunting achievements, nationwide, during the past six years. The book costs $25. It is profusely illustrated and therefore a handsome addition to any dedicated hunter's home library, and can be obtained by writing to the National Rifle Association (address given earlier).

North American Big Game gives the specific locations where all ranked trophies have been taken. This is invaluable information, because big-buck regions typically have just the right combination of food, cover, water, soil, mineral content, and the like, and this encourages the growth of big bucks but also serves to draw deer from surrounding areas; when resident bucks either die of old age or are killed off, other large bucks slightly expand their home ranges to take advantage of the ideal conditions. The bottom line is that certain areas of the country that have produced big deer with big racks in the past are likely to continue to produce them in the future—not record racks, necessarily, but much larger ones than generally can be found elsewhere.

Now I'll stick my neck out again with my own suggested regions for those who are strictly trophy hunters. Keep in mind that these are not "quantity" deer places but definitely "quality" ones. Among the top choices would have to be southeastern Saskatchewan and southwest Manitoba in Canada. And in the United States I recommend the western end of Michigan's Upper Peninsula, north-central Minnesota, the northwest and northeast counties in Wisconsin, any of the counties in southeastern Ohio, northwestern Missouri, and finally the west slope of the Rockies (eastern Washington, northwestern Montana, northern Idaho, and western Wyoming). In any of these locations, to be more precise, the up and coming places to tag monster bucks seem to be the fringe agricultural lands surrounding small rural communities.

Also remember, though, that just as it is possible to come across a 400-pound man almost anywhere, or someone who stands 7 feet tall, big bucks are most often where you find them. At this very minute, there could well be a big old snaggle-horned hermit living a life of total secrecy not a stone's throw from your own back door!

5

Season
of the Rut

Whether the whitetail deer is intelligent and possesses powers of reasoning is probably debated in more hunting camps than can be calculated. Yet we can say quite positively that the whitetail's natural instincts, over countless generations, have been honed to keen perfection as a result of the strongest of the species surviving, procreating, and passing on their genes to their progeny.

And were it not for the rutting season, which so often reduces otherwise super-wary, super-clever bucks to blathering idiots, I suspect the annual hunter kill would be much, much lower. Still, numerous misconceptions about the rut continue to be circulated, and this is unfortunate, because accurate knowledge of mating behavior, and how it radically alters the whitetail's habits, can be extremely important for the hunter.

At the onset of the rutting season a buck's neck begins to swell, engorged with blood. His testicles drop considerably, and because of his continually increasing sexual appetite it becomes more and more difficult for him to remain bedded in a safe location during the daylight hours.

In the past, hunters have contended that the rut is triggered, usually during the month of November, as a result of cold-air masses beginning to move in from the north, and that these influence the biological clocks of whitetails in the same way that they precipitate mating behavior on the part of several other animal species, such as domestic sheep. But this has never accounted for deer hunting in the Deep South, where even midwinter days may be consistently warm or even hot. I can remember several instances, that bear this out, of scrape hunting for whitetails when I lived in Florida, with noontime temperatures well into the nineties and the deer nevertheless as rutty as hell.

Not surprisingly, the biologists have learned that air temperature is *not* a factor in spurring mating activity in deer. They say it's a post-autumnal-equinox phenomenon in which, at some specific time, the days suddenly begin growing noticeably shorter, and what changes the deer's behavior is the decreasing amounts of daily sunlight. These lesser daily light averages passing through the eyes of deer have a type of reverse-stimulation effect upon the pituitary gland, causing its normal function of regulating body growth to temporarily cease while simultaneously causing increases in the secretion of testosterone (the sex hormone in male deer) and progesterone (the female sex hormone responsible for instigating "heat").

One of the effects of the sudden flow of sex hormones in buck deer is that it causes them to begin adhering to very strict hierarchies. Naturally, the older bucks with the trophy racks are at the top of the hierarchy, the middle-size bucks with six- and eight-point headpieces have lesser status, and the spikes and forkhorns are at the very bottom of the heap.

Any given buck, however, has three inclinations at this time. First, he wants to avoid encounters with those bucks that have higher hierarchal ranking than he, which he does by "reading" the sign left by other bucks in the woodlands. Secondly, he himself wants to leave sign in the woodlands that will serve to warn or inform other bucks lower on the scale than he of his status. And finally, he leaves yet another manner of sign to lure those particular does into his bailiwick that have come into heat and are receptive to being bred.

The method bucks use to communicate their hierarchal ranking among others of their kind is rubbing trees with their antlers. This is a second, more purposeful rubbing behavior, however, that should not be confused with the random rubbing engaged in

The onset of the rutting season sees whitetails change their behavior. They are now more interested in sex than in feeding, bedding, or their usual precautions. Many times their behavior can only be described as wacky. (Photo by Wisconsin Dept. of Natural Resources)

by bucks during late summer when the animals are simply removing the velvet from their racks, and it is characterized by trees and saplings sometimes being almost totally demolished.

This rubbing behavior that takes place at the beginning of the rutting season is *definitely not,* therefore, as other hunting writers have said, for the purpose of polishing or sharpening antler tines, strengthening the neck muscles, preparing for battles with other bucks, working off sexual energy, or anything like that. Rather, it's what the biologists refer to as "signposting," and it is done for the specific reason of communicating information among members of the local deer population. In other words, a rub on a tree is the identifying signal a buck leaves for other bucks wandering through to see easily, that proclaims both his presence and his hierarchal ranking.

This is a tremendous breakthrough for the hunter, as far as his scouting of the terrain he plans to hunt and his desired attempt to peg the whereabouts of trophy deer rather than the presence of only spikes or forkhorns is concerned, and it is the diameter of the tree that has been rubbed that is the all-important clue.

Pay no attention whatever to thumb-size willows, tag alders, and other small saplings, regardless of how vigorous the nature of the rubs may appear, as these are almost exclusively the markings or sign posts of young bucks.

Rubbed trees that range in diameter up to 2½ inches or so tell of the presence of bucks of intermediate ages and statures in the local population hierarchy. These are generally the six and eight pointers, and sometimes those ten pointers not exceeding 3½ years of age, but in any case deer that possess rather low, tight racks with slender beams and tines.

It's the big buster bucks that most hunters would like to tag— deer that are 3½, 4, or even 5 years of age or more that have eight-, ten-, or twelve-point typical racks, or many-pointed, non-typical antlers, but in any case those headpieces which are wide, high, and very heavy beamed. These are the deer that are responsible for the rubs on the largest diameter trees. Usually they're cedars, pines, or smooth-barked saplings, but they are most often from 3 to 4½ inches in diameter or more.

The hunter can use this know-how to his hunting advantage by spending his scouting hours searching almost exclusively for those particular regions where there is evidence of larger diameter trees having been rubbed. I've put this to use myself and being in an area of big rubs has consistently resulted in big bucks.

In addition to establishing their hierarchies, and engaging in their rubbing of trees, the onset of the rut also causes bucks to be much more active. It is valuable for us to spend some time describing this because the new information adds to the picture puzzle of a whitetail's life. And it was a telephone call to my friends Larry Marchington and W.G. Moore in Athens, Georgia, that was helpful in fitting these new pieces into place.

In addition to being dedicated hunters themselves, Larry and W.G. are animal research biologists at the University of Georgia who have received a good amount of national publicity for their sophisticated radiotelemetry studies of deer. Along with the help of several other biologists, and the assistance of several state game agencies, they catch wild deer, outfit them with collar-type radio transmitters, and then intensely monitor them throughout the year. This has allowed them to plot on maps the precise home ranges of deer, their individual movement patterns, how they interact with other deer sharing the same habitat, and by knowing their exact locations at all times even to sneak in closely to watch the specific types of behavior they engage in during the rut. Many of their findings have been so startling, and contrary to what hunters have believed for many years, that they've appeared in such scientific publications as the *Journal of Wildlife Management* and the *Journal of Animal Behavior*, as well as having been heralded at international mammal and ungulate symposiums.

One thing I learned is that when biologists many years ago first released the information that "bucks travel more during the rut," hunters and outdoor writers began erroneously interpreting this to mean the deer travel farther distances, and the fallacy has subsequently been passed down from one generation to the next. What was meant, instead, was that deer "travel more" in the sense that they exhibit increased activity levels, engage in far less daytime bedding, and are more continually on their feet and restless with mating urges, but during the course of all of this are not necessarily transporting themselves hither and yon.

Yet there is much more to it than that and, as Marchington and Moore explained to me, any deer's travel tendencies, more than anything else, are a direct function of deer population saturation levels in given regions. In another manner of speaking, wherever their numbers are relatively few and they are fairly well dispersed, individual animals inhabiting that range typically wander farther distances during *all* months of the year. But as populations peak, and the available range reaches its saturation level, deer become more and more restricted in their movements and travels.

In substantiation of this, I've reproduced the home-range chart of just one of the Marchington/Moore radio-equipped bucks, to show how a buck may just as well confine his rutting activities as expand them. The chart shows the usual home-range boundary and then the locations of all the scrapes and antler rubs the deer made when the rut began. And it is obvious that the bulk of his activity, at the onset of the rut, became highly concentrated in a core area within his home range.

We should mention, however, that does seem to continue to range throughout the year, though still remaining within a generalized habitat where they live out their lives. They are never territorial during the rut or at any other time and may freely trade back and forth through the woodlands, crossing territories occupied by several different bucks.

SCRAPE SAVVY

Within his established dominion, a buck will also make a number of breeding scrapes or pawed-out places on the ground. The breeding rubs on trees are to tell the other bucks to stay away, and the scrapes on the ground serve to attract does in heat. Scrapes are generally circular or elliptical in shape, where the ground has been repeatedly pawed by a buck to bare soil. When the earth has been cleared of leaves, forest duff, and other debris, the buck hunches up his back and urinates. The urine serves as a "carrier" in that it runs down the animal's hind legs and over the tarsal glands, located at the hock, to transfer a musk scent to the scrape; and it is this glandular secretion which attracts does in heat.

Most hunters are already aware of this, and diligently strive to locate scrapes during their preseason scouting missions.

What most hunters don't know is that as in the case of evaluating rubbed trees, it is possible to examine the dimensions of a scrape and determine what size buck made it.

According to recent research in which the mating activities of literally hundreds of bucks have been closely observed, it has been learned that the finding of small scrapes should not be of great interest to hunters. These are the scrapes that are sometimes as small as only six or eight inches in diameter. In addition to being physically small, they'll also appear to have been made only half-heartedly in that not all of the weeds and ground covering will have been pawed away and they are not as deep or muddied to indicate the aggressive nature of a mature buck. Instead, they are invariably the work of much younger deer such as spikes and forkhorns that have not yet reached full sexual maturity. The conclusion by biologists has been that these young deer don't really know why they are scraping but nevertheless are just beginning to feel the first instinctive compulsion to do so.

Scrapes that average 10 to 15 inches in diameter, on the other hand, represent the work of more sexually mature bucks (but not the trophies) that are generally between 1½ to 3½ years of age and usually carry smaller six-, eight-, or ten-point racks.

Consequently, the scrapes I am always on the lookout for are those with a minimum diameter of 18 inches, but preferably more. And the very hottest sign any hunter can hope to find, to indicate the presence of bucks at the very pinnacle of the local hierarchy, are those which may be as much as 2 or 3 feet in diameter. I refer to these as "Jackpot scrapes," and every time I see one it makes my heart hammer.

Scrapes made by a mature buck will also appear to have been worked very thoroughly. They'll be pawed to absolutely bare ground, without as much as a single blade of grass sticking up anywhere within the perimeter of the scrape. There will probably be one or two very clearly defined hoofprints in the scrape as well. Biologist Tom Townsend, at Ohio State University's School of Natural Resources, believes this characteristic to be still another type of whitetail marking signal, but as yet no one is certain as to its purpose or function. There are also likely to be tine marks in the scrape, where a buck has dragged his rack through the dirt. Carefully examine these and note the distance between the individual tine drags as well as the width of each drag furrow itself; if five inches or more separate the tine drags, with each furrow ¾ inch in width or more, you can be sure you're in the bedroom of a very large deer.

Incidentally, when scouting for a place to hunt, to intercept deer returning to the area, watching scrapes and trails is always the best bet; don't make the mistake of deciding where your stand should be as determined by the location of trees that have been rubbed. Larry Marchington's radio-tracking experiments have shown that bucks do not return to the specific trees they have rubbed, unless it is totally by coincidence. The rubs serve only as visual cues to other bucks that may happen through the area, and once they've been made serve no further usefulness to the animal that created them. Therefore, the hunter scouts first, very quickly, for the readily visible rubs on large diameter trees, only to insure he is in a region

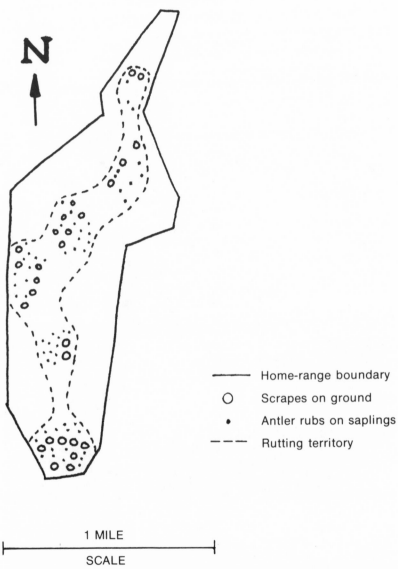

N

Home-range boundary

O   Scrapes on ground

•   Antler rubs on saplings

– – –   Rutting territory

1 MILE

SCALE

The travel tendencies of whitetails depend upon the numbers of deer saturating the range: when there are few animals, the deer travel farther; an abundance of deer has a restricting effect. A radio-telemetry study showed how this buck began confining his movements to a smaller core area within his home range when the rut began. Also shown are the locations of all his scrapes and rubs; doping out sign like this, while scouting, is invaluable to hunting success.

Here the author examines fresh scrape. Biologists say the larger the scrape the larger the deer that made it. The same goes for rubbed trees you find. Small saplings are rubbed mostly by small bucks, so look for large diameter trees that have been almost entirely girdled.

containing big bucks, and then he further refines the search for scrapes and trails to ascertain the best stand location.

Bucks do indeed regularly return to their scrapes, however, but how often is a subject of heated debate around many hunting camps. The scientists say it all depends upon two factors: The population density of deer in the vicinity and therefore how far individual animals customarily travel, and secondly, as a result of this saturation level, how much of a buck's time is preoccupied with does he encounters. If the local deer population numbers relatively few and the animals are fairly well dispersed, a buck may have his mating invitations strung out quite a distance and it may take him as long as three days to "make his rounds." Yet in an area of highly concentrated numbers of deer, with their movements subsequently restricted, a buck may inspect each of his scrapes as often as three times a day.

As a general rule of thumb I like to spend at least several days on my pre-season scouting efforts. But I don't spend all of this continually covering new ground. I like to return every so often to check previous scrapes I've found, to determine which are the ones being tended the most regularly. The whitetail scout will notice that these have been "freshened." More scent will have been added, the ground will again have been pawed to a muddied texture, there may be a fresh hoofprint or two in the scrape, and there may be renewed antler-tine marks or "drags." Those scrapes which are never freshened but in time become weathered—that is, rain-washed, covered with drifting leaves, and the like—are indications of one of two things. Either the rut is drawing to a close and the deer are reverting back to their former patterns of feeding, bedding, and traveling, or the particular buck that made the scrapes has already been taken by another hunter somewhere else.

Look for scrapes to be found almost anywhere, but pay special attention to small clearings, along the edges of woodlots, on game trails, on old logging roads and fire trails, along the edges of power-line right-of-ways, on small knolls and terraced hillside benches, and along the crests of ridges. For every scrape I find in the lower elevations I find ten located higher up, simply because the hillsides and ridges are where trophy bucks spend the greater part of their time.

In bass fishing, to make an analogy, it's common knowledge that the largest of the species favor special haunts. Catch a lunker in a certain location and the chances are excellent that in short time another lunker will move in to take its place. The same holds true regarding habitat sought out by big bucks. Good scrape locations are at a premium. And even though a hunter may kill a trophy whitetail near a series of scrapes the animal has made, another buck will soon move in to occupy the favorable terrain. Many hunters locate a particular ridge dotted with scrapes and there take a fine buck from the same tree stand year after year.

An interesting thing about scrapes is that 86 percent of them (as determined by radio-telemetry studies) are located directly beneath some type of overhanging tree branch. Not even the wildlife biologists are sure why this is so, but there have been countless observations of bucks standing on their hind legs to lick the overhead branches and then exploding with rage, jockeying against the resistance of the branch, and breaking it in several places.

The scouting hunter who has a taste in his mouth for deer tenderloin, however, must do much more than simply locate a couple of scrapes and sit down and wait. The radio-telemetry studies have revealed that a sexually mature trophy buck will make an average of between twenty-five to thirty-five scrapes during his rut. Further, these scrapes are usually made in clusters.

For example, there may be anywhere from three to six scrapes in a rather confined one-acre area. Then further down the winding deer trail, perhaps several hundred yards away, there may be an incidental scrape or two, and then still another hundred yards away yet another three-to-six scrape cluster pockmarking an acre of ground. Each cluster of scrapes is usually also surrounded by numerous rubs on trees to serve as types of "fences" that will warn other male interlopers away from the scrapes. A mature buck, by the way, will make an average of 105 rubs on trees during his rut, so the hunter who claims he isn't finding much sign is typically the one not willing to work very hard at his deer hunting.

In all of this it should stand to reason that one of the most successful tactics any whitetail hunter can employ during the rutting season is waiting quietly on stand within shooting range of a frequently tended series of breeding scrapes or along trails leading to such locations. The key word here is "series." A lone incidental scrape may be discovered in almost any location, even in open fields and other unlikely places. But these are usually chance happenings; perhaps where a buck mated with a doe he had been trailing or where he battled with some other buck. Frenzied and enraged, he may have therefore made a scrape at that location, but unless there is numerous other sign within the immediate vicinity, the scrape is probably not on his regular route. Clusters of scrapes which are relatively close to one another, however, and especially those that are freshened from time to time, give evidence that a buck is regularly visiting the area and checking to see if his mating invitations have been successful. The hunter who positions his stand overlooking this sign, with a good vantage of at least two directions, is almost guaranteed to see action if he is patient enough.

OTHER RUT HABITS

Other whitetail habits during the rutting season should also be taken into consideration by the hunter who hopes to score. Typically, whitetails are most active during the hours of dusk and dawn, and bedding sites are sought during midday and midnight. But during the rut, heightened sexual drives cause amorous bucks to stay on the move continually, and therefore a hunter is as likely to see action during midday as any other time.

Also, the rutting stimulus seems to discount other influences which normally affect whitetail movements, such as wind, weather, and moon phases. During the 1974 whitetail season I killed an eight-point buck over a scrape during the early-afternoon hours while high winds buffeted the woodland cover and torrential rains pelted me with such abandon that at first I had a great deal of difficulty seeing the deer through my rifle scope, which was continually fogged and rain-splattered. Had the rut not been in progress, my prize would almost surely have been tucked snugly away deep in the pines or some protected honeysuckle shelter.

Here is something else I have been learning recently. For years, a common belief among deer hunters has been that during the rut bucks not only curtail their lengthy daytime bedding practices but also cease foraging. Now I will agree that during the rut it is much better to watch scrape areas, especially if they are on game trails, rather than other trails that lead to and from former bedding and feeding areas. But I don't buy the bit about loco bucks not feeding—simply because the last five bucks I've killed, which were so rutty they smelled like courthouse restrooms, had paunches that were absolutely crammed full with browse and other favorite food items.

This rare photo by the author shows a ten-point buck mating a doe. During the rut, hunt all day long because deer are more active and on the move and spend less time bedding.

Another thing pertaining to a whitetail's physical health that is not widely known is that severe weather conditions during or immediately after the rut may cause many bucks to perish. They often wear themselves out so completely just before winter, when they require their greatest strength, that they are unable to regain lost weight in time to sustain them through heavy snows and reduced food supplies. A buck is therefore almost certain to be much heavier at the beginning of the season. If the season is long, this is a good hint as to the best time to ply the bulk of your efforts if you are hoping to load up with deer meat. A three-year-old trophy buck that weighs 225 pounds on the hoof in early October may well be down to 160 pounds by the end of December.

Though bucks and does may inadvertently meet up in the woodlands, more often a wandering doe is attracted to the scent of a buck scrape. She may linger around the area for a while to see if a buck will show, but if she is restless with heat she is more likely to keep on the move. Her behavior at first, however, will be to urinate on or near the buck's scrape, thereby depositing her own glandular secretions.

A buck returning to inspect his scrapes will detect the doe scent and without hesitation begin trailing after her like a hound hot on the heels of a rabbit. In the Moore/Marchington studies, in every case the bucks began making grunting sounds and moved off at a fast walk with their noses tight to the ground. The does were generally within 200 yards of the scrapes and quickly located by the bucks. In a sense, then, it could be argued that it is the doe that actually initiates the mating behavior, not the buck. But this only pertains to does in heat, as a doe in full estrus is readily alerted to fresh buck scrapes and will in most cases oblige a rutting buck who has trailed and eventually caught up with her. Seldom will a buck ever attempt to catch up with and mount a doe not in heat, as she is not emitting the characteristic odor that says, "I am ready." Further, in coincidental encounters a doe not in heat will have no part of a buck's advances and will continually dodge and retreat if he tries to get fresh, foiling his every attempt.

There is some question as to how long a buck will remain with a doe he has just mated. It is my opinion, after researching several biological reports, that this depends upon how successful the buck is at impregnating her. If she stays in heat, the buck may remain to service her repeatedly. If the doe conceives, however, the buck will probably lose interest and retreat once more to tend his scrapes in the hopes of eventually having the pleasures of still other ladies.

According to game biologists, a doe will remain in heat for about thirty hours at a time. If she does not conceive during this time period she will lose heat but "come back in" about twenty-eight days later. This may partially explain occasional sightings of mating behavior after the majority of any given region's deer population has seemingly completed the rut.

Unlike mule deer and elk of the Western states, whitetail bucks do not gather harems—not purposely, anyway—though younger bucks are indeed seen running with numbers of does from time to time. The older, trophy buck, however, is usually a loner, especially during the rutting season. In addition, if he is healthy and the herd population is relatively high in any given locale he may well impregnate as many as twenty does or more during the average three-week rut. It is understandable why the weeks to follow see him gaunt, worn, and exhausted!

If a hunter spots a buck from a distance while scouting for a place to hunt later, it makes good sense to move in quietly and spend some time carefully examining the area. If no "series" of breeding rubs or scrapes can be located, the area should probably be discounted from any further consideration. Likely, the buck was on the move, trailing after a doe in heat, and he may never return to that same location again. Sound strategy at this time would be to move to the nearest highest terrain, search for concentrations of scrapes, breeding rubs, and well-used trails, and then build a suitable stand somewhere in the vincinity. Sooner or later the buck is bound to return.

It was briefly mentioned earlier that bucks in rut possess strong hierarchal motives and will seldom venture into the known domain of another buck if they have already established their own mating grounds. But if a roaming buck who has not yet delineated territorial rights of his own (perhaps because he is just beginning to enter the rut) happens into the bedroom of another buck—and remember, home ranges frequently overlap—a battle is almost certain to follow. The "landlord in residence" will rush to the area and engage in combat, attempting to drive the intruder away.

Hunters living in the arid country of the south-central states (Texas, in particular) have long accepted this tenet of whitetail behavior and use a technique called "rattling" to bring rut-maddened bucks in close for a shot.

Using a pair of antlers, which may have been taken from a buck killed the previous year, the hunter secrets himself in heavy cover and begins clashing the antlers together with violent force. He may also shake the horns in a nearby bush, claw them against the bark of a tree, or bang the backs of them on the ground to simulate the sounds of stamping hooves. The idea is to create the fighting sound of two bucks squaring off against one another.

The resident buck, whose territory this encounter is taking place in, will have no part of this intrusion and in a blind fury rushes to the area, ready for defensive battle. Often he presents himself boldly and in plain view, allowing the hunter precious seconds to evaluate his rack and make the decision to take him or not.

Rattling has never been practiced very much outside of Texas and a handful of neighboring states, but it's logical to assume that it should work as well in other regions *if* such select places have

Contrary to popular belief, bucks rarely engage in serious combat and seldom kill each other. But sometimes they hit antlers with such force they become entangled and impossible to separate. Eventually—unfortunately—the gladiators die of starvation.

relatively high deer populations and therefore the good possibility of numerous bucks using the same range. Obviously rattling isn't a good idea anywhere there may be trigger-happy hunters who might mistake you for a deer.

Bucks rarely fight to the death, although some of our more romantic authors describe such battles. It is true that fighting bucks may occasionally gore one another, and if an antler tine pierces the neck, chest, or abdominal region the end result will eventually prove fatal. But more often than not the fight is just a bluff match to determine who's boss. The bucks may rip the ground apart with their hooves, snort, and ram heads together, and using the power of their flank muscles and broad bodies they continue the pushing match until one of the bucks is backed upon his haunches, thrown off balance, or otherwise convinced that he is the loser. Such sparring and fighting is very beneficial to the species, because it allows the superior buck to retain his territory, breed any does which are around, and subsequently pass on to the next generation of offspring his more desirable characteristics.

In late winter the antlers fall. The rut has long since concluded and bucks are no longer idiotic in their behavior. Now, they are just as crafty as ever.

It is indeed common, though, for bucks engaging in combat to hit each other head-on with such initial force that their antlers spring slightly apart and then close upon each other, leaving the two deer enmeshed and impossible to separate. The end result is usually a slow and unpleasant death for both. It would be unsporting to shoot animals in such a predicament, and many hunters, when coming upon such a scene, hike to a nearby farmhouse to seek the loan of a hacksaw. A few minutes of antler sawing (which does no harm to the deer) and the animals are released from their bondage. But often the hunter's reward for his kindness is a goring from an antler swung in his direction or perhaps a slashing kick from a sharp hoof.

It should also be mentioned that hunters often report coming upon a scene in which two bucks are doing battle, with a doe or perhaps several of them standing nearby. The impression, logically enough, is that the two combatants are fighting to the end and the victor will be rewarded with the favors of the damsels in waiting. This is not entirely true. While the winner of the pushing match may indeed mate with any doe present, the battle is not over her. Once again, it is a battle over hierarchal ranking. One buck has entered the territory of another, and the fight would take place even if does were not present.

Finally, we should note that in any given region there are usually only a relatively small number of trophy veteran bucks which are capable of establishing a territory and defending it against all interlopers. As a result, established territories of rather small size are usually separated from one another by "unclaimed" lands of vast reaches. Here, younger bucks with far less impressive headgear retreat to take up residence. They may occasionally spar with one another, and they may even mate during their first year if they chance upon particularly receptive does in heat.

Because of this unclaimed-land phenomenon, many trophy-only hunters, upon spotting a yearling spike or forkhorn buck during the rut, immediately leave the area. Their reasoning is that no worthy trophies are in the vicinity or they would have long since established territorial rights and driven the younger bucks away.

Of all the altered whitetail behavior patterns that can be seen during the rut, it should be repeated that the one of most importance to the hunter should be the location of "active" scrapes an animal is regularly tending. These locations are where he should invest his hunting efforts.

Sometime between late December and mid-January a buck's antlers will fall. Nearly always only one falls at a time, rendering a queer imbalance which the buck tries to rectify by knocking the remaining horn into tree trunks, or kicking at it with a hind foot, until it too topples to the ground. His mating urge has long since dissipated and there is no longer any compulsion to defend territory. Now he may or may not join with other bucks and does which are yarding in specific locations where deep snows have not accumulated to cover what little there is left to eat.

6

Play the
Waiting
Game

In a well-publicized experiment in progress every hunting season during the years 1954 to 1960, the Michigan Department of Natural Resources admitted hunters to a 1-square-mile enclosure at the Cusino Wildlife Station.

Within the enclosure, which was entirely surrounded by a high deer-proof fence, seven hunters spent an average of five hours afield every day of the test, each trying his best to kill a deer.

Since there were an average of thirty-six deer within the enclosure on any given day, seven of which were bucks (some days only bucks were legal; other days either bucks or does could be harvested), it would seem that due to the degree of hunting pressure the kill would have been high, but that was not the case.

During the hunting period staged in 1954 it took the hunters 124 man-hours in the field to locate and shoot the first buck, and by the end of the season that remained the only buck taken! The results for the other hunters during 1955 to 1960 were very similar.

The researchers conducting these tests concluded, in part, that "deer usually are more plentiful than seems evident to the casual observer." Most skilled hunters would add to this that the term

Whitetails are incredibly sensitive to their surroundings and tuned-in to every feature of their habitat. Therefore, prowling around the woodlands is the least effective way to success. The hunter who plunks himself down and waits is the one most likely to have deer approach this closely.

"casual observer" is most often meant to describe unskilled hunters and nonhunters.

In another Michigan experiment the antlers of several bucks were adorned with ribbons—long, fluorescent orange streamers—before the deer were released into an enclosed area, and yet it required 140.5 hours of hunting for a buck to be killed!

And in a South Dakota study of a similar nature, a buck was outfitted with a small radio transmitter that sent out electronic beeps, enabling biologists to know the buck's exact location at all times, and then it was released into a fenced enclosure. Five alleged expert hunters were sent out to find the buck, and they continually failed during the course of seven consecutive days afield. Eventually, the biologists directed the hunters to the deer's location, but still they failed to sight the animal. Finally, the biologists stated outright to the frustrated hunters that one of them, according to the beeping signals, had at one time come within only scant yards of the deer. Not believing a word of this, the hunters returned to the deer's stated location still again and this time routed the animal out, but only after one hunter almost stepped on it lying flat on its belly in high grass.

It's worth repeating that because of the whitetail's refined sensory capabilities and inherent shyness and distrust it is extremely difficult for even the most accomplished hunter to sneak up on some buck and catch him completely off guard. In other words, hunters must accept the fact that attempting to pit their rather dulled senses (by comparison) against those same but far more acute senses possessed by deer is a very dubious undertaking. Those who are more Indian than Anglo may pull it off upon occasion, and so may those who sometimes win during visits to Las Vegas. Then there are the annual accounts of camp cooks bagging their bucks while chopping firewood or hauling water, and everyone knows some kid or housewife who on his or her very first hunt collected a near-record deer, with a running shot square through the heart, using an unfamiliar gun. Such incidents may offer enjoyable reading but they are definitely rare. Consequently, if simply wandering around in the woodlands during the open season and "being lucky" is what any particular hunter is hoping for, he should know that the whitetail buck will not give him nearly as favorable odds as will the Irish Sweepstakes.

If the reader therefore learns nothing else from this book, the material presented in this section alone is guaranteed to help. And the time-proven axiom to bear in mind is that throughout the whitetail's native range, those hunters who are *consistently* the most successful are those who have elected to outwait whitetails rather than try to outwit them.

Successfully playing the waiting game means finding a place

deer regularly travel through, building or installing a stand over-looking the area, and then staying put. If the stand is situated in the right place and if the hunter can patiently bide his time for long hours, his buck will eventually come to him. This might mean investing three or four days or more of waiting during those prime-time hours when deer are on the move. But sooner or later he'll come slowly walking down the trail to your stand. Yes, he will. And being totally unaware of your presence, because there have been no unnatural sounds, sights, or smells to have alerted him, he should provide a relatively easy, close-in shot.

But waiting on stand, it must be emphasized, is not something that can be done arbitrarily or with no forethought or planning. A hunter with ironclad nerves and the patience of Job might well wait until spring flowers bloom without ever seeing antlers if he has gone about the task in a haphazard manner.

SCOUTING THE TERRAIN

Regardless of the county, most hunters will probably have the choice of pursuing whitetails on either private land or public, and the latter includes state and federal properties. In my opinion, with regards to the tactics you'll be using and the level of success you can probably expect, in most areas it really doesn't make a lot of difference. But there may be other matters to consider. First, hunting private land may require paying a trespass fee, which is becoming more and more common, and it certainly will involve a lot of knocking on doors in an attempt to secure permission to hunt. This can be a real hassle for the hunter who lives in a big city and must make a long drive to good deer country; if he lives year-round in some rural area, however, it may be easy.

But also, in the case of private lands maps may not be readily available. You'll probably have to write to some federal agency or another,* and there is no telling how long you may have to wait.

---

*Topographic maps are the most commonly used by hunters. For maps of areas lying east of the Mississippi, write to the U.S. Geological Survey, Map Distribution Center, 1200 South Eads Street, Arlington, Va. 22202. For maps of areas west of the Mississippi, write to the U.S. Geological Survey, Federal Center, Denver, Colo. 80225. In either case each office will send you, first, an index listing maps available for the area you request. Using this index, you can then select appropriate quadrangles you wish to scout, and send in your order form. The price of each map (in all cases, less than $3 apiece) is listed in the map index. The 7.5-minute series maps, which are the most popular with hunters, show an area of roughly 56 square miles (7 miles wide by 8 miles long).

In the case of public hunting lands, various types of maps are usually immediately available. Simply drop in to the district National Forest Service Office, the district Fish and Game Department Office, a Natural Resources Office, or any other office that may be charged with managing state or federal lands where you plan to hunt. Other sources often include local bookstores and engineering offices.

Let's say you've now got an idea of the general area in which you'd like to hunt. The next step is to focus in upon places to begin scouting for a stand site. This is relatively easy, if you'll remember the two basic rules of whitetail behavior we stated earlier.

Rule 1: *Whitetails especially like broken or irregular-shaped tracts of real estate that possess a variety of different types of favored food, heavy cover, and plenty of "edge."* They do not favor endless climax woodland areas where there are tall, mature trees and little ground cover, and of course they do not prefer expansive, open fields and prairie areas where there is no cover.

Rule 2: *For every buck that may be lingering around in the lower elevation areas you'll find ten bucks running the higher ridges and hillsides, if such terrain features exist.* It is not that bucks are never in the valleys, bottomlands, and other lower elevations; they are indeed, and even in open fields and croplands, but usually not until after full dark.

In scouting the terrain, good advice is to get away from the highways, as there is almost certain to be considerable traffic and hunter activity along major thoroughfares, country lanes, and township and county roads. Further, the great majority of these hunters seldom venture more than a couple hundred yards from where they've parked their cars. As a result, any deer living relatively close to the roads may soon be pushed back farther into less accessible areas in order to escape all the commotion. But on the next ridge back, or the one after that, the deer are far less likely to have had their routines and daily movements disturbed.

Be careful you don't go too far back into the wilderness, though. Remember, you're going to have to walk to your stand every morning in pitch darkness, and then retrace your steps after nightfall, and you don't want to have to stumble blind through miles of dense cover. Further, when you kill your buck, you're going to have to drag him out, and you don't want to have to spend a week doing it.

Many hunters wait until the very day before the season opens to do their scouting, but I like to allow much more time than this. The only exception might have to do with a particular area that you hunt year after year, and then it might be possible to make quick checks of previously known hot spots to see which are again this year revealing the most activity. Otherwise, good advice is to allow at least a couple of days of scouting time and try to schedule these relatively close to opening day; if your scouting is done too far in advance, by the time the season opens major changes in the weather, the nature of the cover, or food availability may have caused an alteration in the deer's habits. Yet at the same time, a hunter does not want to build a stand or blind the very day before the season opens, as deer should be permitted to acclimate themselves to the change you've made in their home. On the average, I spend about three full days of scouting, and both the scouting and stand building are completed about four or five days before the season opens.

I suggest you check your map and eliminate from any consideration whatever all terrain that lies within 300 yards or so of any kind of county road or highway. Concentrate your scouting efforts beyond these boundaries. We should note that it is indeed possible to go much farther in than you normally would (as the bird flies, I usually like to be within a mile of some kind of road) if for a goodly portion of the route you can follow an abandoned fire trail, logging road, the shoreline of a river or lake, or perhaps the edge of an extremely long fenceline or some other feature which allows you to maintain your bearings in the dark.

As you begin hiking the ridges and hillsides, do so methodically. I like to first walk the hillside slope, 40 or 50 yards down from the crest of the ridge, then come back down the crest itself, and next work the other slope back in the opposite direction. Carry out your scouting systematically and you'll not only save time but are more likely to find the hottest prospects any given area has to offer.

It's a good idea to take scouting slow and easy; rushing over a lot of ground is almost never as beneficial as thoroughly knowing somewhat smaller sections. And there are many things you'll want to be on the lookout for. Yet as various clues are revealed, try not to consider them singularly (remember, a whitetail's range may be as much as 1½ square miles) but in terms of their relation to the total picture of deer movements and activities in that area. Many

Scouting the terrain should be approached systematically. Spend most of your time on high ground if you want a buck, and look for sign that indicates presence of deer. Pellets are one indication, but they can fool you. Covered with morning dew, they may look fresh but be months old. Also, deer defacate seven times daily, which means a single doe may be leaving large numbers of pellets, giving the impression there are a lot of deer around.

times, when it seems that deer sign is plentiful but randomly scattered and unrelated, I'll begin penciling in my findings on my topo map. It is surprising, but in time, as more and more parts of the puzzle are jotted down, such as the location of beds, evidence of droppings, and other clues, that suddenly, when the overall picture is viewed, a pattern can be seen. Alone, any feature may be almost meaningless, but as more and more features are added and simultaneously viewed in perspective and relation to the others the solution slowly begins to emerge.

Take the presence of droppings or pellets, which are very commonly found while scouting. It is impossible to distinguish between buck and doe defecation. Both appear as numerous capsules, hard and dark-brownish in color, and about ¾ inch long. And unless it is a cold day and the pellets are actually steaming, it can be difficult to ascertain their age. Old pellets, of course, will be dry, hard, and crumbly, but recent pellets that have been rained upon or are covered with morning dew may look fresh even though they may be weeks or months old. Another thing is that a whitetail defecates an average of seven times a day, so a single animal can give the mistaken impression that the place is overrun with a multitude of deer when it is not.

What I look for in pellets are two things. First I keep an eye peeled for large pellets which indicate one or more large animals in the area. The large animal may be either a buck or doe, it is true, but it is not a fawn or yearling. Second, I feel much more confident when I'm consistently finding fresh pellets, moderately old pellets, and very old ones, as this indicates that the deer that made them were not simply passing through but are regular all-season inhabitants.

We've already described a whitetail's feeding habits and what to be on the lookout for with regards to prime food sources. We've seen how the presence of rubs on trees and scrapes on the ground are the hottest buck locations to be aware of. And as to tracks, those are covered a little later. So for the moment, let's take a close look at the one other type of sign or evidence of whitetail activities that should perhaps consume the bulk of your scouting time in the field. We're talking about the presence of deer trails.

Whitetails are creatures of habit, and they have routines that, when not unduly molested, they follow day after day. These routines are carried out almost like clockwork; over a period of weeks and months they will see very gradual changes in accordance with changes in the weather, food supply and type, and so on, but on a day-to-day basis they are highly consistent.

Trails are the hallways or corridors that connect and give access to the many different rooms in the whitetail's house. Any deer, of course, will have alternate routes for use in special circumstances, such as when he is alarmed and fleeing the area, but under normal circumstances the same trails will frequently be used every time the deer travels back and forth between feeding, watering, and bedding areas.

If you keep your eyes open during your scouting missions, these routes are not difficult to ascertain. Sometimes they become so pronounced over years of use by subsequent generations of deer in the area that they may even be mistaken for hikers' pathways! If there is snow or mud present, tracks often indicate the presence of

The most important "sign" to look for is a deer trail. Deer like to follow routes of least resistance, and therefore take the same routes day after day to circumvent natural terrain barriers or dense cover. (Photo by U.S. Forest Service)

a trail. But otherwise, look for barely discernible routes worn through vegetation or forest duff. Deer don't stay on these trails like slot cars but rather have a tendency to wander through the area. Therefore, each trail will appear to be well worn in some areas and yet almost entirely disappear in others. Those places where it is worn are usually locations where the animals repeatedly take a specific line of travel through very heavy cover, or where they are taking the easiest routes to circumvent natural terrain features. Where the trail grows thin, you'll invariably notice the cover is less dense and terrain features are less difficult to navigate. The reason for all of this is that deer always like to take the easiest routes available. So pay special attention to the overall lay of the land. If there is a gap through a natural cover barrier, there is almost certain to be a deer trail there. Examples of these are openings or natural avenues through dense acres of brush, cactus, honeysuckle, or perhaps a stand of crowded pines. Benches or terraced shelves high on steep hillsides, and fire trails or logging roads now grown over and bordered on both sides by dense cover, are also natural deer runways.

Once you've found a deer trail, stay on it and see where it goes. It may eventually lead to an elevated terrain area, and you'll find beds, or it may wind its way downhill to the edge of a cornfield or river-bottom area thick with cedars.

Any trail that is regularly used by deer, regardless of where it goes, could provide shooting opportunities if the hunter waits long enough. But I and most other expert hunters like to increase the chances of seeing deer as much as possible, and one way to accomplish this is by staying on a trail until a location is found where it intersects with another trail. Being able to watch two trails simultaneously doubles your chances of seeing deer. And now and then a hunter will really strike it lucky and find a smallish clearing or other terrain feature that reveals several trails from different directions crossing there; these are priceless gems that may allow a hunter to kill a good buck in the very same location year after year after year.

Once—and this is the only time it has happened in my hunting career—I found a place, a very narrow gap through absolutely impassably thick cactus and thornbrush on a south Texas ranch, where *five* deer trails intersected. They looked almost like spokes radiating from the hub of a wheel. As to the numbers of deer crossing back and forth—well, one time I began thinking it would be a good idea if someone put up a traffic light. The rancher who now owns the land claims that he and his two sons hunt—one at a time, of course—from a stand overlooking that crossing and that every year all three of them fill their tags at that very location.

Watching several deer trails requires that the trails either cross each other, as we have noted, or that they come from different directions to a place where they funnel-spout themselves through natural terrain routes or obvious passageways through cover. Because of this, it is often possible to carefully examine a topo map of the general area you plan to scout and, by closely looking at the contour lines, predict where various terrain features are likely to reveal the presence of one or more trails. Such locations are the gateways or doors leading from one area of a deer's mansion to some other.

In hilly or mountainous terrain, a fantastic stand location is often one situated at the juncture of where two ridges (each with a trail along its crest) come together to form a single ridgeline; another, equally fantastic area is where a very slight saddle connects two distinctly separate ridgelines.

In flatland areas, the landforms I examine first in the hopes of finding several trails are brush-bordered stream or river bottoms, shallow gullies, narrow necks of land that join two large natural barriers such as two lakes, narrow strips of heavy cover leading to feeding areas (or waterholes in arid regions), any clearing area (or more specifically its edges) surrounded by heavy cover, long alleys (such as power-line right-of-ways) through broad expanses of pines or other dense cover, and where swaths of "thin" cover species seem to cut through expanses of "thick" or dense species.

In any type of terrain, another prime location for a stand overlooking trail crossings is where there is "transition cover." In other words, locate yourself on some edge where heavy cover begins to peter out and there is moderately light cover before distinct openness. Bucks, especially, like to lurk around these safety areas in early evening, not wanting to expose themselves in the more open places until full darkness comes. And in the morning, as the sun is clearing the horizon, they seem to like to hang around such edges just a tad longer before heading for their daytime retreats.

Many hunters have their faith in trails shaken when a light skiff of snow suddenly falls and day after day the route they thought was heavily used shows not a single track. What has happened is that the hunter has failed to keep in mind the nature of deer habits, which sees them make gradual seasonal shifts in their movement and behavior patterns; more thorough scouting and the hunter would have probably been able to dope out the shift.

Let's say, however, that you're having difficulty finding any kind of trails. Here are a few additional tips. First, while whitetails are capable of jumping almost any kind of fence, if it is not too inconvenient for them they seem to prefer to run its length and cross wherever the wires or boards are hanging particularly low, where they are broken down altogether, or where there exists some other type of opening or gap in the fenceline. Check along fencelines and you'll probably find a trail and eventually a place where they are crossing; there may even be a bit of hair clinging to the barbs or strands where the animals have occasionally brushed against the fence. In rolling country there may be places along a fenceline where the lowest boards or wires are well off the ground. Deer will often belly-crawl under the fence at such locations.

Another tactic for locating trails is to follow small streams or brooks. Sooner or later, in the soft mud banks of such waterways, you'll discover a place where deer are crossing—a deer trail—and you can follow it into the higher elevations.

LOCATING AND BUILDING YOUR STAND

It's a good idea to do enough scouting so that you're able to build or install stands in at least two different locations. It is unfortunate, but there are always some slob hunters in the field. Most of them don't know what to look for in the way of deer sign. They suddenly come upon a stand someone else has built, figure it must be a good place to hunt, and make themselves at home. Few things are more frustrating than to work hard scouting an area, hike to a location on opening morning, and see some clod sitting in the stand you built. You can claim it is yours and politely ask him to get his butt out of there, but if he won't budge (which has happened to me two times over the years) you're in trouble unless you have an alternate stand site readied.

Sometimes respectable sportsmen will inadvertently mess up your stand site. Once I had a perfect location picked out and a stand built. But on opening morning two other hunters who backpacked into the area unknowingly set up a tent camp only 100 yards from where my stand was situated! I knew no buck in his right mind would venture near my stand with those other guys rattling pots and pans, chopping firewood, and talking; fortunately, I had readied another stand half a mile away and simply changed locations.

There are several tricks in preparing a stand site that will greatly increase any hunter's chances of scoring. The first thing is to determine the exact location where the stand should be situated. It's *not* wise to have a stand spang in the open and right on top of the trail or scrapes you intend to watch, as a buck coming down the trail may spot you from far away and change his course of travel. I suggest you place your stand at least 30 or 40 yards away from the location you wish to observe. And it should be so situated that you have light cover all around you to break up your outline and a heavy-cover backdrop behind you. Second, the stand should be so situated that prevailing winds through the area will not be blowing your scent in the direction you most expect deer to approach from. Third, at all costs make sure the trail you intend to watch is not on an elevation higher than the elevation of your stand. Instead, try to be higher yourself, such as on a hillside, slope, knob, promontory, ledge, rock outcropping, or in any other position that allows you to be above an approaching animal's level of vision. And fourth, make every effort to ensure that when you are in your stand you will not be looking into the sun. The reason is that you will be more visible against your background cover; also, if your weapon is equipped with a scope, the glare of sunlight through the glass may make it almost impossible to see the animal.

If the stand is to be a ground-level one, good choices are behind large boulders, logs, blowdowns, hedges, or similar cover. And one of the neatest tricks you can employ is to have along a drape of lightweight camouflage cloth which can be thumbtacked to small saplings around you; with a few strategically placed branches or pine boughs then placed here and there, your entire outline, save your head, will be almost totally invisible to approaching deer. Another "functional" consideration is to clear the ground around the stand of dry, crunchy, or brittle twigs, leaves, and other debris that may give away your location if you are momentarily careless in moving your feet. Finally, be sure that you have complete freedom to raise, swing, and aim your gun.

The comfort aspect of a ground-level stand is critical, too, because of the long hours of waiting which are often necessary. Many hunters carry along a boat cushion to sit on. Or you might want to take along a lightweight folding campstool. One hunter I know carries to his stand site an aluminum lawn chair spray-painted with camouflage colors. It looks silly as hell. But with his camouflage-cloth drape in place he is easily able to wait quietly, patiently, and comfortably on stand far longer than any of his regular hunting partners, and this may partially explain why over the course of many years he has taken more bucks than any of them.

The best bet of all, however, is some type of tree stand. Whitetails have long been conditioned to expect danger from ground level and consequently they don't tend to look above their eye level. Also, a tree stand allows what should otherwise be a serious concern about wind direction to be not quite so critical; since warm air rises, the hunter's scent is more likely to rise and quickly dissipate rather than exude down, out, and around his

If it is to be a ground-level stand, sitting in the open like this makes you readily visible; deer may skirt your location.

This is the same exact location, but notice how the hunter has disappeared behind the drape of camouflage cloth thumbtacked between saplings, with dead brush to further break up the outline.

Tree stands are the best bet of all, because deer are not as alert to danger from above, and your scent rises and quickly dissipates. Here the author displays three different sizes of the most popular climbing-type tree stand, called Baker stands. Also shown are hand-climbing bars. The ones in the center have not yet been painted with camouflage to hide their shiny aluminum frames.

location. Another plus in favor of tree stands is that they let a hunter establish a waiting location where no dense ground cover may be available, or where the placing of contrived or artificial cover might alert game. Just as important as any of these, from a high station a hunter can look down and through the cover to see approaching deer much more easily and from farther away than if he were on the ground and there were intervening cover blocking his view.

Having upon countless occasions used the commercially manufactured, portable tree stands, and also having built many permanent stands in trees, I am undecided as to which is best. So I'll list the advantages and disadvantages of both and allow you to make your own choice.

The portable stands such as the popular Baker model range in price from $30 to about $80, and most of them offer a mechanical advantage which allows the hunter to use the stand to climb the tree trunk and then have a platform for standing or sitting upon. Most such stands are constructed around bright aluminum frames, so it's wise to beforehand spray them with drab brown and green

From an elevated vantage point, a hunter can see down and through cover so sneaking deer are not likely to go by unnoticed. This is Al Wolter, patiently watching a deer runway in the Wayne National Forest in southern Ohio. He later killed a nice buck here.

paints in splotches and irregular designs in order to render them less conspicuous.

One thing I especially like about a portable factory-made stand is that you can take it with you to your hunting location and bring it out of the woods when you leave. This means there is no chance of some dolt taking advantage of your scouting efforts, finding a permanently built stand, and plopping himself down.

Another distinct advantage of a portable climbing stand is that other than causing a few superficial slices in the bark it won't damage the tree.

Portable climbing stands pose two disadvantages. If the tree you plan to climb is thoroughly wet, covered with snow or ice particles, or has smooth, slick, or scaly bark, there is a certain danger; the stand may slip slightly during the climbing effort, which could possibly send you to the ground minus some skin on your chest, arms, and legs. So try to select what appears to be the driest tree and also one that has thick, rough bark for the stand's climbing edges to grab.

The second disadvantage of a portable stand is that since such stands are constructed mostly of metal, climbing a tree can be a very noisy proposition if you are not extremely careful, and this could possibly spook a deer that is not too far away and presently moving in your direction.

A wooden stand built permanently into a tree has three things in its favor: you climb to your perch safely, quietly, and in only half the time.

However, before a permanent stand should even be considered, check first with your local game department to determine if any special regulations exist. One or two states disallow any type of tree stand, a couple of others have laws as to how high off the ground the stand may be erected, and a couple allow only the use of the temporary portable models.

If you do go ahead with plans to install a permanent fixture, please don't create an eyesore and destroy the integrity of the cover. Saw limbs and pound nails no more than is absolutely necessary. Whenever it is possible, rather than use trees such as hardwoods I try to select one of the scrub species such as a willow or thornapple, or better yet a dead tree that is still sound.

From the scrap pile at your local lumber company you can probably obtain for free some random pieces of plywood to be used for seats and foot rests. Other scraps can be used for steps, like rungs on a ladder. You may even have these materials around your home, but whatever their source, you can lash them to a backpack frame, along with a lightweight saw and hammer, for ease of carrying to wherever you've chosen to build your stand. Then simply nail the makeshift affair into place, preferably from 10 to 12 feet off the ground.

Here are a few more things I've learned about building a stand in a tree. For maximum stability, I like to use three close-standing trees to support the stand, or a single tree that has well-spread limb formations. If only two trees are available at the best stand loca-

For a stable stand platform, use three tree supports. Note that the upper left platform is lashed with rope; use it whenever possible and a minimum of nails. Also, rather than using good hardwoods, select scrub tree species or those that are dead.

tion, and they are 5 feet or so apart, it's worthwhile cutting a stout sapling and constructing a third "leg" to support the stand platform. If you make the stand platform at least 2 feet square, you'll have more freedom of movement, and this will prevent your legs from getting cramped. But an even better idea is not to sit or stand directly on the platform itself; use this for resting your feet, and between two of the three upright tree trunks, about 2½ feet higher than the platform, construct a seat. In this manner you can sit quietly for long hours and yet be perfectly comfortable, as you are sitting in a type of chair. And when building the ladderlike steps, place them fairly close together, because with heavy clothing you'll be able to take only short steps. Finally, with either a portable stand or a permanent one, once the thing is in place, stand heavily on all portions of the stand platform, perhaps even shifting your weight a bit. The idea is to anchor the stand firmly so that if a breeze comes up the thing won't begin creaking in the wind.

The next item of business, once the stand is built or installed, is to get into it. You'll be spending many hours there when the season opens, and so it should be as comfortable as possible, and now is the time to correct any deficiencies. One of the crucial things to concern yourself with at this time is that you have unobstructed shooting lanes in at least two or three different directions from which deer could possibly approach. You'll probably have to cut away a few vines here, saw off a bushy branch somewhere else, knock down a couple of dead limbs, and so on.

CLOTHING FOR THE STAND HUNTER

There are still a few other things any hunter will have to attend to before opening day arrives. Clothing, for one, has a good deal of influence on stand hunting, because if the hunter is dry, warm, and comfortable, the number of hours he can wait quietly and motionlessly will be increased.

Weather is the primary determinant. Most hunters will want to wait until the day before the season opens to make the choice. The best I can suggest is to dress more warmly than you feel necessary, because you won't be doing any moving around to generate body heat, and this means you'll chill very quickly if not properly attired. By using the layer system of dressing you can actually wear less and stay warmer because the various layers will trap dead insulating air in between each article of clothing, and yet if it becomes too warm it's easy to simply peel off the outermost layer. In my mind, for most types of innerwear, cotton is best because it absorbs perspiration. For outerwear, wool is best because it allows a hunter to remain warm even if his duds become wet.

The three areas to be most concerned with are the hands, feet, and head. Gloves are okay, but they may be a hindrance when fast gun handling is required. Other times there is no choice—it is too cold—and you have to wear them.

Footwear can be bulky and cumbersome now, as you won't be

The main advantage of a permanent tree stand is that it is quiet and more easy to gain access to. It's also best for older deer hunters who may no longer be able to shinny a tree with a portable, climbing model.

making boot tracks across miles of countryside and the additional insulation may be desirable. Several pair of wool socks with insulated leather or all-rubber boots make a fine combination if the temperature is not expected to dip below 30 degrees. But if you expect the mercury may really take a dive, I recommend felt liners inside boot-pacs. You might also want to don insulated longjohns and slip a couple of handwarmers into your pockets. If your state requires it you'll have to consider some type of fluorescent outer garment as well, but bear in mind my earlier comments on this subject.

There is an old saying that if your feet and hands are cold, you should put on your hat. This is true, because body heat most readily escapes through the head and neck region, but while many types of headgear may do the job of keeping your noggin and extremities warm, certain hat styles are far better than others for deer hunting.

A felt Western-style hat is great, if you're a cowboy riding a horse. But for a deer hunter who spends most of his time in heavy cover or climbing up and down trees, it is strictly theater. A watch-cap style of hat does a dandy job of warming the head and ears, but nothing for shading the eyes from bright sun.

The hat that is ideal for me, if the temperature is not expected to go below freezing, is a simple hunter's cap with a baseball-type bill and earflaps that can be pulled down if the wind kicks up. The bill of the cap shades my eyes, and very important in my case keeps my eyeglasses from specking with raindrops and snowflakes. When the temperature goes below freezing I switch to an insulated furry trooper's hat with a bill that can be lowered when needed or raised and buttoned in place. By the way, I find hooded parkas totally inadequate. They severely hamper lateral or side vision, which is critical, because a hunter should move only his eyes rather than his head when waiting on stand; a parka may even obscure the tiptoeing sounds of a buck sneaking in from your backside.

In warmer climes, clothing is not such a serious matter. I like my leather birdshooter boots, jeans, lightweight shirt, and a regular baseball cap.

You'll need some type of knife, either a folding pocket model or one that rides in a belt sheath, with a blade about 4 inches in length that you've honed to razor sharpness for field-dressing your deer. Slip a small plastic bag into one of your pockets for the heart and liver. And you'll need about an 18-foot length of some kind of rope. I recommend nylon parachute cord, which serves two purposes. When you arrive at your stand on opening morning, you can carefully lay your unloaded gun on the ground and tie the rope to the sling swivel mounted on the butt of the weapon. Then tie the other end of the rope to your belt, climb to your stand, and pull your gun up after you with the muzzle pointing safely toward the ground. Reverse the procedure whenever you leave your stand. The rope will also be necessary for dragging your buck out of the woods, and this is discussed in detail in Chapter 14. Ten rounds of ammo in your pocket, secured in appropriate beltloops or rifle clips, should be more than enough.

THE VIGIL

On opening morning get up early enough to allow plenty of time. You should plan on being in your stand absolutely no later than half an hour before legal shooting time, as this will allow the woodlands to return to their normal level of activity after your intrusion. You should probably have a sandwich in your pocket, and maybe a handful of hard candies. Take along a small plastic bottle with a lid for heeding the call of nature, because urinating on the ground will saturate your stand area with scent. A small pocket flashlight will prevent you from tripping over roots as you find your way to your stand in the darkness; this is also a safety measure, even when a sliver moon allows one to see sufficiently, because it identifies you as a hunter walking through the woods and not a deer some ass might try to plunk before the legal shooting hour.

Climb into your stand, pull your gun up after you, and load it. Leave the gun's safety on at all times, until you plan to pull the trigger, and at all times keep one hand around the stock as it lies across your lap.

It's not necessary to remain so still that you're like a stone statue, because that is very tiring. But stay as reasonably motionless as possible. Continually scan the cover with your eyes, moving your head as little as necessary, and pay special attention to the trails and scrapes near your stand.

This actual waiting aspect is perhaps the most difficult chore of all for the stand hunter, regardless of whether he is high off the ground or secreted behind cover on a hillside blind. But there are many things you can do to pass the time and likewise prevent your body and mind from tiring.

If you know something about isometric exercises you can relieve cramped body parts without actually moving them to give away your presence. Start with your finger muscles and flex them without moving them. Then your arm muscles. Contract your stomach and chest muscles, and then do the same with your leg muscles. Deep breathing, especially during cold weather, will eliminate drowsiness. And you can wiggle your toes all you want inside your boots, to keep them warm, without moving your feet an inch.

Smoking is not advised for several reasons. It can bring on coughing spells, and although there is no definitive proof one way or another it would seem that burning tobacco would easily alert a deer's sense of smell. For sure, the act of smoking usually requires a good deal of hand movements. Many hunters find they can do without a smoke for a few hours if they have something else to occupy their time. You can have a pocketful of hard candies.

Generally, I am able to remain perfectly motionless on stand for about an hour and a half before I begin feeling overly restless. Then I may very, very slowly rise to a standing position, but only after I have meticulously surveyed the cover. Once standing, I can remain motionless for another half-hour or so. When this begins to get old I may return to a sitting position or go through my isometric exercises again.

Since I'm a writer, I often use this quiet time to work out story ideas in my mind. But I suppose teachers could think about lectures, others could mentally lay out the spring gardens they intend to plant, and still others could ponder upcoming Christmas shopping lists.

But the thing that enables a hunter to see his greatest success is the confidence that the stand is superbly positioned. This alone will generate enough interest and excitement to allow anyone to stay put for long hours. Otherwise, uncertainty gnaws at you, and as shots occasionally ring out in the far distance it becomes all too easy to give in to the temptation of wandering off in search of some presumably better place to watch.

As my friend George Mattis, of Birchwood, Wis., has said, "Hearing shots all around him in the distance, the hunter begins to believe that in this veritable oasis of deer country, he alone is unfortunate to have selected the desert."

So even if you may have waited on a particular stand every morning and evening for several days, and not seen a thing, don't become discouraged! If you're watching well-worn deer trails you can be sure that deer are actively using the area and that your buck will eventually be along. It's sort of a reverse geometric progression, in that the longer you wait without seeing antlers, the increasingly better your chances become. So tough it out!

The first of two time periods in which a hunter is most likely to see deer action from a stand is that two-hour block beginning with the legal shooting hour in the morning. But stay on stand a little while longer! Most other hunters will have by now become so restless that they can no longer remain on their stands, and they'll have begun moving about, maybe doing some still-hunting through the cover. Then there are the others who say to hell with it and begin heading back to their cars for coffee; often, they are tired, bored, trigger-happy, and along the way pop off shots at stumps and knotholes (these constitute many of the shots you've been hearing in the distance). In any of these cases it is very possible they will push deer out which will circulate in various ways to avoid the hunters, and being creatures of habit the deer will use familiar trails. You are watching two of those trails!

Usually by about ten or eleven o'clock, however, even the roaming hunters begin to tire and head for camp, home, or more likely a meeting place along the road for a confab with the boys. You might as well do the same, because by now the deer have been long since bedded and are not likely to come by your stand. But you'll have to exercise your own judgment here. If there is absolutely no hunter activity whatever in your area, it might be well to give it up as early as eight-thirty or nine o'clock. On the other hand, sometimes other hunters wait on stand for only the first hour of daylight and then begin organizing drives for the remainder of the morning and afternoon hours, which sees them moving back and forth between the roads and the deep woods, and they might push something in your direction. Otherwise I suggest using these midday hours to take a nap back at camp or in your car. No sense further exhausting yourself, because waiting on stand is hard work, and you've got another long wait later in the day.

You should be back on stand sometime late in the afternoon, depending upon how long it is staying light, to watch for deer during that final period before full darkness sets in.

Let's briefly examine what happens when you see deer approaching your stand. You may first see does which are followed shortly thereafter by a buck. If apparently no buck is following, and only does seem to be around, carefully scan the edges of nearby cover; a buck may be slinking along and not fully exposing himself like the others. And be very careful not to alert any of the does in any manner. Many times a buck will trail along at a considerable distance, sort of using the does as advance guards to warn of impending danger; if they spook, it's almost a certainty you'll stand no chance at any buck that may be trailing. If the rut is in progress, any buck that comes along will invariably be alone, or perhaps following a single doe. If the rut is not in progress, however, it's entirely possible to see two or three bucks approach your stand.

Regardless of the number of deer, they'll be moving quietly, making no more noise than perhaps rustling the leaves a bit. In fact, they usually appear and then disappear like ghosts. You'll be watching a trail and see nothing, then look in another direction for a moment, next look back at the trail, and there he is!

Take your time. He doesn't see you. He's thinking about how good that grass tastes, under which leaf he's likely to find the next acorn, or, oh boy, what he's gonna do when he catches up with that doe he's been following. He has no idea *you* are around! So you can play it cool and wait for just the right opportunity.

The paradox of stand-waiting is that it is probably the most frequently used method by the country's most skilled hunters who have reputations for bagging trophy bucks every year. Yet it is also the one, single best tactic that can be successfully used by the amateur who is just beginning a career of deer hunting and who may not be as well acquainted with the ways of the wily whitetail.

7

Walk a Little, Watch a Lot

The hunting methods of still-hunting, tracking, and stalking are seldom the most productive ways to pursue whitetails, at least compared to other strategies. However, since all are vaguely similar in principle we can group them together for discussion in this chapter.

By definition, still-hunting is moving very slowly through good deer cover in the hope of visually sighting the animals and getting close enough to get off a telling shot. Tracking, of course, is following hoofprints in soft soil or trailing after "slots" in the snow in the hope of eventually catching up, farther ahead, with the animal that made them. Stalking, on the other hand, is an attempt to close the distance between your present location and a deer sighted ahead, in the hope of getting a better shot.

Using any of these methods, one crucial rule that applies most of the time and can be said to be a determining element in the success of the undertaking is that *the less you walk, the more you see.* If a prospective still-hunter, tracker, or stalker continually keeps this in mind, he will have absorbed the main thrust of this chapter.

WIND: A FRIEND TO HEED, OR FOE INDEED

The combined effects of wind and weather, if one understands basically how they are used by whitetails to monitor their environment, can prove to be the undoing of big bucks year after year. Yet if they are not considered they can have the opposite effect of forewarning deer so far in advance that the hunter may begin suspecting that every animal has left the county.

Wind and weather affect a whitetail's senses of smell and hearing. The scenting ability being by far the more important, the thing to be most concerned with is wind direction, because traveling air currents are the messengers that inform whitetails of the approach of hunters.

Most who have hunted deer are familiar with the bare-bones basics of using wind direction to advantage. These entail, in their most simple terms, moving into the wind at all times so that the hunter's scent is not carried ahead of his progress and so any minor sounds he may make are not amplified or easily detected in the distance. The same applies to establishing a stand site, which should always be downwind from the anticipated direction from which deer are most likely to approach. If hunting into the wind or establishing a stand downwind is not possible, the next best state of affairs is working with a crosswind.

There is a lot more to understanding wind and weather, though, than these fundamentals alone. Many times it may seem as though not even the slightest wisp of a breeze is in the air, which actually is a rare occurrence. And knowledge of air currents as they are affected by air temperatures can cause one to vary his hunting strategies considerably at different times of day. There is, in fact, a distinction between two types of moving air that we should make here and now. "Wind," as we commonly use the term, is moving air that is a by-product of masses of hot air meeting cold, or vice-versa, as various types of weather patterns move across the country, generally from west to east. Then there are "thermal" air currents, which are more localized in nature, travel up and down rather than horizontally, and are caused by changes in the temperature as any given day wears on.

Under stable or consistent weather conditions, thermal air currents drift downhill beginning in the late evening and lasting

A good hunting rule is "the less you walk, the more you see." Wind especially is the hunter's undoing, as it carries the warning of his approach to the deer who are constantly testing the breezes. (Photo by Maine Dept. of Game)

through the early morning. "Downhill" also means down valleys, down canyons, down creek bottoms, and so on, to lower elevations. Then beginning sometime during the late morning the thermal air currents reverse themselves to head back in the opposite direction, upslope, uphill, to the crests of ridges and to the heads of canyons and draws.

Stormy periods also affect the directional movement of thermal air patterns; rapidly clearing weather after a storm sends the currents wafting to higher elevations, and yet a rapidly approaching storm or one that is already in progress causes them to plummet downhill.

When there is no rolling terrain, hill country, or mountains, but everything is relatively flat, thermal air currents drift out of heavy cover areas such as forests to more open places during the evening hours, and this continues until early morning the following day. Then about midmorning there is a reversal, with the thermal drift from the open places toward heavy cover.

One other thing to keep in mind is that *a prevailing wind will cancel out any thermal air movements.*

Now, it's easy to see how any hunter can use this knowledge to better his chances of catching deer unaware. First, deer continually test the wind for any ravels of scent that may indicate approaching danger. When the air "seems" still, however, deer use the thermals to serve as their sentries.

You may have already noticed the effect of this, but not known exactly how or why it was happening. For example, it's one reason why crafty bucks head for higher ground to spend midday. They do it to have a good view of what's going on below, as we stated earlier, but also because the typical upslope drift of the thermals during the daylight hours will warn them well in advance of anything on the prowl. Conversely, "most" deer spend "most" of the night and dawn hours at the lower elevations; that is usually where food and water are most plentiful, but also the thermal air currents have now shifted and lower ground is simply the place to be if those air currents are to be used as warning signals of anything approaching. In flat country, the same principle applies. The deer move into heavy cover to spend the late morning and afternoon, partly to hide and rest, but also because the thermals will be in their favor; conversely, in the evening and early morning they are able to move into more open areas to feed and water and yet still be on radar alert.

It is common to see large numbers of deer feeding in open areas during midday periods immediately after the passage of heavy storms (either rain or snow). As we discussed in the section dealing with feeding habits, the animals are immune to severe weather but retreat to cover more because their sensory capabilities are impaired during such periods. The apparent oddity, then, of coming upon deer feeding in open places after the weather has cleared is again a result of thermal air currents. The upslope drift of the currents, or in flatlands the movement of thermals from heavy cover to open areas, both of which are generally associated with dusk-to-dawn periods, suddenly takes place during, say, the late morning or early afternoon, allowing whitetails to stock up on groceries while still being fully attuned to anything and everything that is going on around them.

Therefore, those who pay attention to weather forecasts often see great success hunting just before the approach of a storm; the animals seem to sense that bad weather is coming, that they will soon want to enter their heavy-cover seclusions, and that now is a good time to take on supplies. Similarly, rough weather may keep the deer holed up for several consecutive days, preventing much feeding, and when the weather suddenly clears they waste no time heading for food.

I said hunters could benefit from such insight, and here's how. When employing almost any method of in-field reconnoitering, but especially still-hunting, plan your movements in advance to have thermal air patterns working in your favor instead of against you. In other words, deer have tied their movements and behavior to the patterns, and if you tailor your movements to them as well you'll stand a far greater chance of seeing game. This means, in hill country, hunting upslope in the direction of bedding sites until no later than perhaps nine or ten o'clock in the morning. Through the late morning and then the afternoon and sometimes even into the very early evening, you absolutely must be on high ground such as ridges and canyon rims. In the flatlands, stay deep in the forests and heavy-cover regions during midday, and work the edges and clearings only during the evening or very early in the morning.

I'm talking here, of course, about stable weather conditions. If it turns stormy, concentrate upon sheltered terrain where there is heavy cover such as the edges of forest facings, the lee sides of hills and ridges, and deep in the pine plantations and cedar swamps. Yet when there comes a sudden clearing after severe weather that has persisted for several days, head straight for the feeding areas.

The hunter who is willing to bear minor discomfort will also see good success during periods of steady, light rain. Here again the whitetail scout should work the feeding grounds, as the animals seem to consider such periods very safe for moving about. The deer will stare intently in certain directions when something arouses their suspicions, but they are farsighted and the rain greatly impairs their vision. The sodden air as well does not carry scent any distance and allows the hunter to move easily and quickly over a carpet of soft ground cover.

One other point might be of value, and this pertains to sunlight. Almost always, those terrain areas that receive direct light all day long, or are bathed with golden warmth at least part of the day, see far greater activity levels than do those dank, damp, perpetually shaded regions. Sunlight is the spark of life. It's where food grows best and where there is the most cover for concealment, and as a result all creatures spend most of their time in sunny places. This is even more true when it is bitter cold. Don't be bullheaded, though. If you've got an educated hunch, and it involves terrain that is typically dark, go check it out. But know that in the long run the sun-bathed terrain will pay off more consistently.

While deer actually seem to seek out sun-drenched areas for feeding and bedding, this is a trait they exhibit more often in those locales where temperatures range anywhere from well below freezing to 70 degrees or so. When much higher temperatures prevail, as in the Southern states or whenever it is scorching hot, deer will frequently seek shade. They'll still be bedded high, but perhaps now under an overhead ledge, under pine boughs, or on the shady side of dense brush or vegetation. Very likely, in such cases, they'll also have a water source nearby.

THE STILL-HUNTER'S ART

Still-hunting is a skill that can be acquired only one way, and that is by actually doing it. It pits the hunter's knowledge of his quarry, his limited senses, and his abilities to slip quietly through the cover against the radar defenses of the deer. For this reason, even though still-hunting is mastered by only a very small percentage of truly expert woodsmen, it is one of the most rewarding and satisfying ways of collecting venison.

The essence of still-hunting is moving several steps forward, coming to a complete stop, and then quietly panning the terrain for two or three minutes before pushing on a few more steps. The amount of ground one covers in a day's time is of no concern; indeed, the hunter who covers *less* ground is invariably *more* successful. I feel that if a hunter covers more than a mile a day during still-hunting operations he's moving much too fast.

It might even be said that one reason so many hunters today have very little success in still-hunting, stalking, and tracking deer is that they take into the field the same impatience that characterizes their everyday lives. In decades past, hunters were more dedicated to the hunt and were willing to invest whatever time was necessary to get their quarry; for many of them it was not merely a sporting adventure but a serious effort to obtain their winter meat. Today's hunter too often carries with him a schedule book of appointments and rushes his hunting in order to be back at camp in time for the evening cocktail hour, or home on time so his family won't be angry that he was late for dinner. The same thing is very true of many stand hunters. Rather than doggedly and persistently sticking with it, many will hunt perhaps only the first day or two of the season, then it's back to the office to take care of absolutely earth-shaking matters that just won't wait, back to the field again, then back home to see if everything's going okay, then to the field again—here, there, and the other place, like a spooked rabbit jumping from hole to hole. Such hunting, based on the clock or calendar, severely penalizes the hunter. That's why I plan my hunts several months in advance and entirely block off certain segments on my calendar. I give advance notice to family, friends, and work associates that during those periods, twenty-four hours a day, I am simply unavailable.

Clothing is an important element in still-hunting. The whitetail scout usually does not have to dress too warmly, because being on the move will generate a good deal of body heat. But he absolutely must dress so as to be able to move as quietly as possible. The best of all fabrics for this kind of work is 100 percent wool (if it scratches, wear very lightweight cotton underneath). Wool is a "soft" material, as contrasted with "hard" fabrics such as denim, canvas, nylon, and so on, and therefore it is virtually noiseless when it comes in contact with brush, pine boughs, and even thorny branches. If there ever is any sound created when such contact is made, it is an almost inaudible "swish" that does not carry far.

A baseball cap with a short bill is ideal; anything more elaborate will be continually knocked to the ground as you stoop to make your way underneath branches or when there are vines and other cover draped at eye level.

Crepe-soled leather hunting boots are fine for still-hunting; compared to bulkier boot-pacs, they allow for easier and more dexterous foot placement, as when stepping between brittle twigs and crunchy leaves. But even better, if the weather permits, are tennis shoes. These can be murder on the feet if the terrain is rocky or littered with root stubs and small ground-level cacti species, but they are the quietest type of footwear I know of.

Advance movements are best made by taking short steps, putting the toe of the foot down first to test the firmness of the ground, and then slowly transferring more and more weight to the ball and heel of the foot. Learn also to recognize what kinds of terrain conditions offer the most silent footing so you can anticipate the best route. Crusted snow, dry leaves and twigs, gravel, and crumbly shale make the most noise when they are trod upon. Whenever possible, therefore, step instead upon flat rocks, moss-covered ground, dry or slightly moist soil, sand, damp leaves, or pine needles.

I like to hunt with my weapon held at the port-arms position, even though this is much more tiring than other ways. If a deer is sighted ahead, the weapon is already partially raised and only a slight additional movement is necessary to bring the gun to the shoulder. Also, if a deer is jumped and begins bounding away, the gun is more quickly put into use.

I especially like to move along just below the crests of ridges (when the wind and thermals allow me to do so), every now and then just barely peeping over the top to scan clearings, edges, and trails on the other side; when the animals are on their feet, plenty of sightings take place using this technique. But in any still-hunting effort, since deer are keeping on the watch for a "whole" man and otherwise find difficulty identifying only "parts," when it is time to stop, look, and listen, do so with just your eyes cautiously peering around a stout tree trunk, through brush, along the edge of a hedgerow, or in some other manner that allows the rest of your body outline to be either fairly well concealed or broken up. The hunter should never allow his silhouette to be skylighted against the horizon. Staying slightly lower, in or near heavy cover that is navigable, also seems to have a dampening effect upon ravels of scent and sound carried away. Another thing is that you'll be far less noticeable if you avoid clearings, fields, and open well-lighted places. Stay just inside transition-cover edges and lurk about in the shadows, wearing basically dark-colored garments of multi-tonal values, and you'll see more deer.

When he accidentally makes a noise, the experienced hunter comes to an immediate halt for at least several minutes, aware that a buck, if within hearing distance, is at this time awaiting the arrival of more evidence that something is approaching. Studies have shown that whitetails have very short memories, and it can therefore be predicted that if no further alarming noises are caused, the animals will soon forget that anything alerted them in the first place. The atypical and yet continually rhythmic noises that penetrate the habitat are the ones that are the hunter's undoing.

I like to still-hunt on the deer trails themselves whenever they are in evidence. First, they are usually somewhat tamped down and therefore less noisy. Also, any subtle noises you now and then do make, I believe, are less likely to trigger an alarm reaction. Deer use these trails themselves, and since they are mildly gregarious they come to *expect* to see movement and hear noises on such routes. Off-trail noises or movements may scare them, but on-trail activity commonly takes place as soft hides brush against cover, as small twigs are daintily stepped upon, because of other deer periodically threading their way through the cover to their own particular seclusions, so such things are not as likely to alarm other nearby deer already bedded. They are fully aware of the movement or noise—make no mistake about that—but since such activity is customary they seem to wait around far longer until the author of the commotion is very close and fully identifiable. In the very few instances in which I have approached bedded bucks to within scant yards, it has been only by making use of this tactic.

A crucial aspect of still-hunting is knowing what to look for and how to see deer, because seldom is the entire body form of a deer recognizable; rather, it is some small part that more often stands out, and then gradually other body parts are discerned until the general outline of the entire deer can be established.

Distinguishing between bucks and does is not difficult, even when antlers cannot initially be seen. Bucks will often be larger, but not always. A big old doe may carry substantial weight if it has been a good year with plentiful supplies of nutritious food. But aside from actual body weight, does nearly always have a more triangular anatomy; by necessity, for birthing purposes, the "barrel" or rearmost portion of the torso at the hips is often quite large compared to the slimmer forward section. Bucks, on the other hand, are traditionally more blocky and rectangular in shape, as seen from the same broadside view.

Whether buck or doe, however, there are other features of the anatomy that allow the astute observer to see deer in cover. Much of any type of cover but especially that found in forested regions is typically of a vertical nature, so the horizontal lines of deer (their backs and bellies) readily stand out as unnatural. The rounded form of the rump and haunch region, and the angular curvature of the neck, are also outlines not commonly produced by tree trunks, branches, or other cover. If you see a deer standing facing you, does often have a pigeon-toed stance, with the knees buckling inward slightly, while bucks are usually more solid on their feet with legs well spread.

Sometimes it is the glint of sunlight on a single antler tine that will give away a deer's location, a wet shiny nose, the white throat patch, or some other clue that when placed in its proper perspective suddenly completes the picture puzzle. When bedded, deer are often detected by their movements. Insects buzz around, and to ward them off a deer may occasionally swish his tail or flick his ears back and forth. Therefore, as the whitetail uses the detection of movement to alert him to intruders, so can the hunter play the same game to see more deer! Many times, while I've been quietly searching the cover with my eyes, the slightest flit of a songbird in the distance has drawn my notice, or perhaps the flickering of a dry leaf in the wind as it alternately reveals its light and then darker underneath sides. Just as often, after carefully studying the "bird" or "leaf" I've found it was a deer instead!

It is the inexperienced hunter, then, who takes a wide-angle panoramic view and looks for "complete" deer in their habitat, and fails to see them otherwise. And it's the veteran who more often looks for details in small areas; often, he sees a small spot of shiny black that could be an eye, a patch of tawny-brown color in consistently green honeysuckle that could be a piece of deerhide, a twitter of movement that could be a flicking ear, a fingerlike projection of something white that could be an antler tine, or anything else out of the ordinary. It is true that the veteran makes plenty of wrong guesses and eventually discovers what he has been examining for long minutes is really only a stump, odd-shaped rock, or some other unusual cover configuration. But the chap who has trained himself not only to look but to see what he's looking at is the guy who serves up venison tenderloin for his family instead of bean soup.

One still-hunting technique that is consistently successful, for hunters who are able to engineer it properly, deserves to be singled out for special mention here. It is one of those methods that we might call still-hunting but purists will maintain—quite rightly— that it also falls into the category of driving deer.

Call it a "two-man still-hunting drive," if you will. It's lethal when employed in very heavy cover areas, either large or small, but preferably where the terrain surrounding the cover is open on all sides, as deer are reluctant, when not pressured, to venture into or bound across open areas and therefore are encouraged to circle and sneak.

The first hunter enters the cover and slowly and quietly still-hunts in a straightaway direction, staying on a well-worn deer trail if it is possible. He walks five or six steps, stops for a full minute to watch and listen, walks five or six steps more, and so on.

After this first hunter has pushed his way about 75 or 100 yards through the cover, the second hunter enters. His job is to trail the leading hunter, slowly and quietly still-hunting as well.

Whether out of instinct or pure enjoyment, whitetails like to play games, and one of them is to widely circle a supposedly lone hunter in order to get behind him, whereupon the deer often closes the distance to have a good look-see at what has been following its backtrail. Sometimes a buck will come up surprisingly close behind the hunter and then eventually snort and bound away in the opposite direction (this is something that will cause a hunter's neck hairs to bristle). Other times the deer will simply circle and then sneak away. Whatever the case, the trailing hunter very frequently has an extremely easy shot at a deer concentrating on the front man and therefore unaware of the trailing hunter. For

If you have a partner, why not make it a cooperative still-hunt? One way is for each of you to take one side of a densely wooded ridge. Deer you push out will go up and over the crest to give him a shot, and vice-versa.

Grassy bottomlands

Open fields

Wooded ridge

Grassy bottomlands

In flat terrain, where cover is heavy, another cooperative still-hunt sees one hunter following directly behind his partner, to take advantage of a whitetail's fondness for circling and sneaking back.

Open fields

Open fields

safety reasons, using this method, both hunters should wear a quantity of fluorescent orange, and never should the trailing hunter take a shot to his immediate front; shots directly to the left or right are the ones most likely to present themselves, and they're also the safest.

A variation of this two-man still-hunt may be even more effective, but there are two differences. It is best suited for working those long steep ridgelines which are only moderately dense with cover. And rather than one hunter trailing behind the other, they both move along parallel to each other.

The ridge may be saturated with pines, brush, or almost anything else, but seldom will bucks travel the entire length of the cover when they are moved from their beds; they know that when they eventually reach the end of the ridge's length there will be no place to go but downhill into the lower elevations, and this is something they'd rather not do. From my experience, they prefer instead to travel uphill or in some other manner remain in the higher elevations.

One hunter takes one side of the ridge, about two-thirds of the way up the side of the hill, and the second hunter takes the other side. The very crest of the ridge separates the two of them, so shots can be safely taken in any direction.

When one hunter quietly still-hunting along jumps a buck from his bed, the deer will usually line out straightaway for a short distance, cut sharply to the right (or left), and go up and over the crest of the ridge to the other side with the intention of then reversing his line of travel to remain on the higher ground. However he carries out the maneuver, though, as the buck comes over the crest, he has a surprise waiting for him. It is often so unnerving for a buck when he unexpectedly is greeted by the second hunter on the other side that he just stands there and gawks, allowing himself to be put down with little effort.

TRACKER'S TECHNIQUES

Any whitetail hunter may sooner or later decide to track a deer. It's against my recommendations as to the most consistently successful way to pursue the species, but if he comes upon extremely large prints in new-fallen snow or soft earth, temptation may override good sense and he'll be off at a trot, hoping eventually to glimpse the animal and be awarded a shot.

Often a hunter who has discovered oversize hoofprints immediately conjures in his mind thoughts of a new state record, and this prompts him to spare no effort. He'll spend numerous hours on the trail, meticulously inspecting each and every print, then running ahead with his adrenalin spigot turned wide open. More times than not he eventually closes the distance to see only a large doe casting what seems like a smug glance over her shoulder before throwing her flag aloft and high-stepping off into the cover.

Some hunters—there seems to be at least one in every camp—make claim of being able to distinguish accurately between buck and doe tracks. I'll admit that I cannot, and nor can those of the nation's better hunters with whom I've had the privilege of spending countless instructive hours afield. Many times certain clues allow us to make educated guesses, but that is all.

But what of those subtle clues that will sometimes hint as to whether tracks were left by a she-deer mincing carefully along or by some antlered patriarch of the woodlands? First, actual size of the tracks, as we've already mentioned, can fool you. Deer are like people; some have big feet and some have little feet. But pay special notice to the track's indentations. The rear portion of a track made by a doe is more likely to be beveled as a result of the way in which does characteristically place the tips of their hooves down first, which supports the majority of their weight, while the heel does not always squat flat on the ground. Since bucks have a tendency to stand firmly and squarely on their feet, this beveled feature is likely to be absent, dewclaw imprints may show, and tracks are likely to be accompanied by slight drag marks emanating from the toe of the hoof to where the buck begins to put the foot back down (compared to the usually "dragless" prints made by daintily stepping does). Along the same line, bucks often exhibit tracks that appear more rounded, the reason being that bucks are generally heavier in body weight, which causes a bit of swaggering to their gait. Does are usually more free-stepping, and because they are lighter than bucks the hooves are subjected to less abrasion and therefore are more pointed. Another indicator that is considered "fairly" accurate in "many" instances is the way in which the tracks appear when compared with one another. A doe has a tendency to walk slightly pigeon-toed, while a buck tends to walk with his legs turned slightly outward and the toes of the hooves somewhat splayed.

In addition to the physical features of the tracks themselves, the directional movements of the deer many times hint of their sexes. Bucks tend to walk in a rather purposeful, straightaway line of travel as they move along hillsides, the crests of ridges, or through cover, while does seem more often to wander erratically as if they can't quite make up their minds where they want to go. Then too, large tracks that travel alone are very likely to have been made by a big buck. Smaller tracks traveling alone may have been made by a spike, forkhorn, or single doe. And even tracks that may be very large, if there are one or two sets of much smaller prints accompanying them, probably were made by a doe with her latest fawns.

Varying types of terrain may reveal tracks with a wide variety of clarity. Morning dew, for example, will often lie to you, making tracks appear moist and fresh when actually they may be weeks old. Tracks found in soft soil, in protected places where they have not been subjected to wind or weather, such as deep in a cedar swamp, under pine boughs, and under rocky outcroppings, may look fresh much longer than tracks exposed to the elements. Tracks made in early-morning snow will appear much larger later that same afternoon after the sun has had a chance to work on them; the clue here is that the tracks will no longer be crisp and well defined but expanded and distorted. Very fresh tracks are those which are sharp and clean around the edges of their contours and show a very thin ridgelike elevation between the toes of each hoof; after they have been rained or snowed upon, or weathered by the wind, these ridges are obliterated. On the undisturbed surface surrounding the tracks there may be a littering of small particles of snow, leaves, or other matter that was kicked up by the hooves; after a period of weathering these will be solidly frozen to the surface layer rather than loose and free, or they may even be partially covered by new snow. The bottoms or depressions of fresh tracks are usually unfrozen and perhaps even slightly damp as they reveal the presence of wet leaves or pine needles underneath, and the outer rim of each track may take on a slightly glazed appearance. If the depression of a track is frozen solid, the deer that made it is long gone.

During rainy or stormy periods in the warmer climates, when the once-hard ground is soft, mushy, or muddy, tracks that have retained their sharpness are very fresh, as pelting rain makes them indistinguishable in short order. Deer tracks that are almost entirely filled with rainwater, seepage water from the surrounding mushy ground, or a light skiff of snow are usually old, but this depends upon the amount of precipitation currently in evidence.

Often, when any particular area of whitetail habitat is littered with tracks, it is easy to overestimate the number of deer using the region. Remember, every time a deer moves forward a step, *four* new imprints are made.

Just last year I was hunting near my home in southern Ohio and had established a stand within range of a lone oak tree that had yielded an especially large number of acorns that fall. Anyway, snow began falling as I waited through the evening watch. One doe came to the oak and spent perhaps fifteen minutes kicking up the leaves and munching upon the acorns before moving on.

When shooting light was gone I climbed down from my stand and went over to where the deer had been feeding, which was an area about 10 square yards in size and located directly beneath the tree. Scanning my flashlight beam around the area I was astounded at the literally hundreds of tracks that pockmarked the snow. Had I not witnessed for myself the arrival of the single doe, or had I chanced upon the location and not thoroughly examined it and found only a single deer's tracks leading in and then a single deer's tracks leaving the oak, I probably would have decided a whole herd of deer had been around the tree that night.

It should be clearly evident by now that about the only way to take after any deer is when the ground is covered with new snow, as other terrain mediums simply do not register tracks distinctly enough to allow steady and continuous pursuit. But certain types of snow and certain times of day make far more desirable tracking conditions.

The most *undesirable* time of day to take up the trail is late in the afternoon, as the tracks from the previous feeding and moving activities of deer in the region are likely to be as much as ten or twelve hours old. The deer that made them may be far away or may have been flushed out by another hunter, and with nightfall soon approaching there is not likely to be sufficient time for proper trailing. In fact, the hunter may find himself forced to rush, and this in turn will cause him to make mistakes or be careless in his movements.

The very best time of day to pick up a trail is very early in the morning after snowfall during the night hours has ceased. Tracks in the newfall will be readily discernible and fresh, and the animals that made them not far off. Ideally, the weather should be either bitter cold or a little on the warm side. In very cold weather the powdered snow allows quiet walking on your part, and in warm weather the snow is heavy and pillowy, which also permits noiseless movements. If the weather has been erratic, with alternate thawing and then freezing, the surface of the snow is likely to have a crust that will loudly crunch with each footfall. By the way, if tree branches, brush, and vegetation are covered with snow, all the better, as such drapes serve as sound baffles to help muffle hunter noises and also partly obscure a deer's range of vision, which may allow a closer approach.

Unfortunately, too many hunters, when they come upon tracks, take off at a trot, feeling they have to make up for lost time and close the distance to the animal, which they suspect is far ahead. I believe a different approach is in order, because from my experience when there is snow cover the movements of whitetails become somewhat restricted and they are less likely to travel far distances if not spooked. Consequently, the moment fresh tracks worth following have been detected, the hunter should automatically assume his quarry is not far ahead and proceed with caution, as a buck that has not previously been jumped is invariably easier to approach than one already routed out several times.

In this style of hunting, slow and easy is often the most productive method, with persistence the key. Some hunters have described trailing after a deer for six or eight hours at a time, repeatedly jumping the animal until it eventually makes a mistake, such as trying to remain motionless in its bed or simply presenting itself in some clearing for just a tad too long. I have no doubt such hunters are telling the truth, but it's a pretty chancy way to hunt deer, and the physical exertion required may even be too much for many hunters. Better, I think, is to ply one's energies upon unalarmed, unsuspecting deer in the hope of making the first encounter the telling one.

When following tracks, don't keep your eyes on those tracks at your feet. Watch tracks as far ahead as you can see them, in hopes of seeing the deer. Here, Bill Weiss follows tracks the right way, off to the side of the trail, in cover, while scanning farther ahead.

In this situation—tracking unalarmed deer—I stay directly on the tracks, as there is a good likelihood other deer are now and then using the trail as well. It might be well to recall here what I said earlier about on-trail activities. Further, when following tracks the trick is not to keep your head bent over examining the ground at your feet. Rather, your eyes should be focused on those particular tracks as far as you can see them off in the distance. In addition to this, your eyes must continually and carefully scan the cover in the distance in the hope of seeing the animal walking along or feeding.

In both still-hunting and tracking, the hunter should pay meticulous attention to everything high and to both sides of his line of travel, as deer frequently double back to bed down on elevations overlooking their backtrails. Many times I have forgotton this and almost to my direct right or left, not a dozen yards away, triggered an explosion of bobbing flags.

If a buck is jumped from his bed, or a moving deer is alerted to the hunter's presence, a slightly different strategy takes over. Often it will be a whitetail's natural inclination, at this point, to initially move out and then begin making a circle or at least occasionally double back to have a closer look at what it is that's following its trail. In this case it's wise for the hunter to *not* follow directly on top of the tracks but instead walk parallel to them, 40 or 50 yards off if possible, and to remain inside whatever edge or screen of cover may be present. The reason for this is that the deer will want to know what is on its trail, and will scrutinize it closely whenever there is a chance, and anything that is off the trail therefore stands a better chance of going undetected.

Tracking is indeed an art. Tracking, still-hunting, and stalking in my mind constitute the most refined and difficult ways of filling deer tags. I don't do a great deal of any of them but have the highest respect and admiration for those who do and see success.

STALKING A DEER

Stalking a whitetail buck may sometimes be necessary when the deer is initially sighted a far distance away—too far to risk taking a shot and maybe only wounding the animal—or when an unsuspecting deer on the move has inadvertently placed some cover formation or terrain feature between the two of you, meaning that a renewed vantage must be gained if there is to be any chance for a shot of any kind.

First, try to anticipate the direction of the deer in the hopes of intercepting it at some point farther ahead. If it's possible to go around the backside of a steep knob, large rock formation, or several acres of dense pines or cactus, and if such cover will hide any noise or movements you may make, it may pay to take off at a trot. Otherwise, since the animal is unaware of your presence, it's better to take it slow and easy.

It is imperative that the primary landscape features between the deer and the stalker not be disturbed or altered; the bobbing hat of a hunter behind a hedgerow will alert the animal, as will other body movements such as your entire head and shoulders suddenly coming over the top of a grassy knoll like a jack-in-the-box. What is important then is to engage the stalk so that intervening terrain features may be utilized to block the view of the animal while advance movements are being made. This means carefully selecting the route ahead, using cover features piecemeal such as logs, rocks, stumps, or bushes that conceal most of the body most of the time (even if it makes the stalk longer in time or distance).

Whenever you take a peek, make sure your head is held low and to the side of the cover rather than high and above.

Should the animal be in sight and happen to look in your direction, freeze! And don't move again until the deer has given you the once-over and then returned to its previous activity. If the deer is in view but totally unaware of your presence, move forward only a few steps at a time, being careful not to step on noisy ground cover, and only when his head is lowered to feed or looking off in the opposite direction. Of course, you should be taking advantage of the prevailing wind direction or your knowledge of how thermal air currents are traveling.

One of the main difficulties in stalking deer is that decisions must usually be made quickly and accurately. But also a hunter must sometimes be inventive and willing to put out just that extra little bit of effort that some others might not be so inclined to invest. This might mean taking off your boots and walking in stocking feet across noisy ground. It might mean belly-crawling 200 yards through thorns when the only suitable approach cover is low to the ground. Or it could require holding your rifle high over your head while fording a chest-deep stream.

How close a hunter should try to get depends largely upon the type of firearm being used. The hunter, to be sure, should have engaged in sufficient shooting practice (we discuss this in detail later) to know his gun's capabilities and the ranges at which he can shoot accurately. As a general rule, however, approach the deer no closer than is absolutely necessary to kill it quickly and cleanly, because the nearer you draw to your trophy the greater the chance of your being detected or making some mistake.

8

The Deer Drive

Driving deer in the old days was quite a thing. Drivers carried their firearms with them, to be sure. But they also had whistles, horns, and even discarded Halloween noisemakers upon occasion. Stomping through the woodlands, we'd hoot, holler, bang clubs against tree trunks, and otherwise saturate the hills and hollows with a fusillade of approaching sounds. The din was supposed to move whitetails in the direction of our partners stationed farther ahead on logging roads, near clearings, or sometimes simply behind a convenient maple near a suspected deer "run."

Looking back, it's understandable why there is nothing I would trade today for the memories of that experience but it is now clearly evident that our drives—no matter how much fun—were confused and disorganized; they constituted little more than gang hunting of a most rudimentary form.

Almost never did the drivers have shooting opportunities. The noise they made enabled crafty bucks to pinpoint their locations easily and then sneak back through the spread-out drive line or

The loud drives of years ago, with many hunters participating, were not the best way to drive deer. Too many hunters are difficult to effectively organize, and the noise enables deer to pinpoint each of their positions and sneak around them.

circle widely and skirt the line altogether. Sometimes deer merely remained hidden in their beds in heavy cover until the drivers passed and then bounded off in the opposite direction. And other times the approaching din had the effect of stampeding the deer, so that the animals did not follow familiar escape trails but lined out in random directions. Consequently, even those standers who had been positioned on known deer trails (most of the time they were not) seldom had shots, and those who did indeed see deer nearly always missed because the targets were in full flight.

Last, and perhaps most important, there was a safety problem that sometimes caused uneasy feelings. With drivers and standers trying to sandwich deer in between, there could conceivably be times when hunters on stand were firing in the direction of oncoming drivers. We never experienced a mishap, nor have I ever personally known another hunter who was involved in a shooting accident. But however remote the possibility, some misgivings nevertheless lingered, clouding what should have been a relaxed and enjoyable hunting atmosphere.

None of this is to say that our mob-hunting efforts of those halcyon years were entirely dismal failures, however, because as the old saw goes, "Even the blind hog will find an occasional acorn." But compared to the sophisticated drive tactics an increasing number of today's deer-hunting parties are using, those of the past were definitely inefficient, overly time-consuming, and sometimes downright dangerous. Further, there is no doubt in my mind that only a fraction of the bucks living in any given heavy-cover region were ever seen, much less tagged.

Basically, though, the idea of driving deer is a sound one. And when traditional techniques are blended with the new, driving whitetails is the all-time best method for group hunting.

Compare, for a moment, the minimally successful bungles and snafus that characterized drive-party practices during previous decades with the well-oiled techniques that are likely to be seen in use this year.

Certainly, there will still be the same cozy cabins and gatherings of hunters in remote regions. But there are also sure to be many hunting parties that don't have the use of some wilderness hideout. Nor may many of the individual party members have a stretch of consecutive days available for deer hunting each season. Likely, these hunters will invest their efforts, perhaps a day or two at a time, upon the many chunks of state or federal land which in many cases fringe large metropolitan areas. Second in popularity are usually the farmlands, ranches, and vast rural tracts lying just beyond city limits.

As a matter of fact, the most impressive bucks of the season may well be killed in these close-to-civilization locales, because we now know that whitetails do not favor expansive climax woodlands. They are primarily "edge" and heavy-cover animals, and their habitat preferences are often quite compatible with the broken and irregular-shaped acreage near where mankind lives and works.

So the hunting party that elects to stage drives close to home, or has no other choice, may well see better success with trophies than the party that sets up a base of operations in some remote region where endless high-canopy forests and poor ground-level browsing conditions often exist.

Regarding the participants themselves, the new trend is that the most highly skilled drive parties consist of very small groups of hunters. This is sound reasoning, because lesser numbers of hunters are far more easy to organize effectively, and this means efficiency skyrockets. Time delays are minimal because there are fewer hunters to position on stand or keep track of on the drive line. With fewer hunters roaming around, the danger potential is greatly reduced. And it's increasingly becoming all too true that smaller hunting parties, especially in the case of private lands, have access to many more places than do veritable carloads of guys looking for somewhere to enact a massive onslaught.

Inherent in the new attitude toward driving deer is acceptance of the tenet that whitetails are habitual and therefore very predictable creatures. Accordingly, the guesswork of past generations of hunters has largely been replaced with intelligent prehunt planning. And the single person responsible for bringing all of this to fruition, regardless of where the drive is to take place, the specific type of drive to be enacted, or the actual number of hunters taking part, is the *drivemaster*.

THE DRIVEMASTER

The drivemaster is chosen to be the leader of the group primarily because of his responsibility, familiarity with the terrain to be hunted, and ability to organize and maintain control over a number of hunters. Almost surely, he will make use of some form of topographic or other land-contour chart. With such a map he will always have a ready reference as to where he has placed standers and drivers, and he will similarly be able to show those in the party the exact locations they are to occupy or move through. The map may even be riddled with X's where deer have been taken during drives in previous years.

The drivemaster will have thoroughly surveyed several different areas to be hunted, and done so well before opening day. In other words, he will have scouted the terrain much in the same way as if he were planning to hunt on his own, but on a larger scale.

Any changes in the countryside which may have occurred since the previous year will be well noted, because these can appreciably influence the behavior of the deer population. Examples of such changes that more commonly take place are locations where logging operations have been carried out, where state or federal agencies have selectively clear-cut or burned areas to promote regenerative growth, where previously fallow fields have been planted to crops, where previous croplands are being permitted to lie fallow in agricultural rotational schemes, where roads or trails have been cut through tracts of land, or perhaps where livestock ponds have been built or waterways diverted.

Further, the drivemaster's plan will be to drive only those regions which have revealed plenty of deer sign, actual deer sightings, and high kill numbers in past years. And in these regions, which can sometimes be very large, he will have narrowed the odds even more by knowing where heavily used deer trails are located, where unusually heavy mast or fruit crops are in evidence that particular year, where deer using the area have their security cover, and where there are concentrations of breeding sign. He will also be aware of the presence of private property lines, state and federal boundaries, fire trails, access roads, restricted hunting areas, where first-aid can be most quickly obtained, and the locations of rural homes or farms in the vicinity.

Since the drivemaster intimately knows the terrain and is acutely familiar with the habits of deer using the area, it is imperative that all members of the hunting party listen closely to his instructions and follow them to the letter. *He* is in command, and if the drive is executed exactly as he has planned, every hunter's chance of taking home venison will be sharply increased.

Without question, and regardless of the specific type of drive to be enacted, the drivemaster will emphasize timing as an important factor for all hunters to keep in mind. All watches must be synchronized, because a driver whose timepiece is only five minutes fast will begin early and soon find himself far ahead of the other drivers. Aside from this being dangerous, it may easily result in the deer being pushed in an unintended direction. Similarly, all efforts may be futile if the drivers commence moving through the decided-upon cover before the standers have had sufficient time to position themselves.

All hunters must also respond on time to the signal that a drive is ended, such as when the drivemaster gives a series of short blasts on a whistle or horn. Timing, again, is very important if the hunting party is to regroup quickly when finished driving an area so they may move without delay to the next drive site. There is nothing more maddening than to "lose" several members of the drive party and have to spend valuable time searching for them.

Also regarding the timing element of any drive, when a deer is killed the drivemaster will (or should) suspend all further driving activities until the animal can be recovered and removed to the hunting camp or a waiting vehicle. There are obvious advantages to this. For one, dragging a buck out of the woodlands can be a laborious and lengthy chore for a single hunter. But with numerous buddies to aid him in tracking down the deer (if necessary) and then carrying out the trophy the task can be accomplished in almost no time at all and the drive activities quickly resumed. Additionally, a man who abandons his assigned post after killing a deer, if the drive is not immediately called off, may in wandering around cause the remainder of the drive to be a useless and disorganized effort. All that is necessary, when a good hit has apparently been scored, is for the hunter in question to call out "Deer down!" whereupon the others farther down the line pass on the good news with similar shouts until all in the party are aware of the happy event. It's traditional for a man who has killed a buck to then take on the job of driver to help his partners fill their tags.

With regards to the logistics of the modern drive, and if terrain conditions allow for it, stand hunters will probably find the drivemaster positioning them so that they will be looking down upon the area they are to watch for passing deer. If it is to be a ground-level stand the elevated vantage point will invariably be from some knoll or rise, or even more likely high on some hillside or ridge. Whatever the case, the hunter should carry along a folding campstool or boat cushion so he can wait quietly, comfortably, and with a minimum of movement. And rather than sitting blatantly in the open at his assigned location, he should take advantage of tree trunks, logs, stumps, bushes, or other cover to break up his outline.

There is an even greater likelihood, however—and this is very contrary to strategies of previous years—that members of the modern drive party who are placed on stand will find the drivemaster has put them in trees. There should be a wooden platform of sorts for the hunter to sit on and a place for him to rest his feet. Such stands may be built in advance of opening day by the drive-party members, or they may consist of the commercially made portable models which can be installed in only a few minutes just before each drive begins.

Whenever possible it's best to have "standers" perched in trees. Use portable stands like the Baker for this. If tree stands are not practical, at least have hunters stationed on slightly higher elevations and behind cover to block their outlines from view.

From an elevated stand position, either on the ground or in a tree, a hunter will have an excellent view of the surrounding terrain and nearby deer trails. A stealthy buck moving cautiously through the area, even if there is heavy intervening cover, will not have much chance of slipping by undetected. With drivers working toward hunters who are perched in trees or on overlooking hillsides or canyon rims, a much greater safety margin is also afforded. Any opportunities for shots by the drivers will usually be on a horizontal plane, while shots at deer by standers will be on a nearly vertical plane.

Never underestimate the whitetail's canny sneaking abilities. This trophy buck has managed to pinpoint locations of several approaching drivers and is using cover to sneak around them.

The drivers, too, are very likely to use different tactics than they employed in former years. For one, the drivemaster will probably have them moving through the cover at a very slow pace, and if any of them are instructed to sound off at all it will only be intermittently and not loudly. There will be no shouting, whistling, or banging clubs on hollow logs. In effect, then, rather than "driving" as it is most commonly termed, what the "drivers" are really doing in most cases is quietly still-hunting in the direction of the standers.

The benefits of this are many. The drivers themselves frequently get good shooting opportunities, and this is something that was almost unheard-of before. In many cases, while quietly or semi-quietly still-hunting through the cover toward the stand sites the drivers may move bucks from their beds only yards ahead of them. And because there is a marked absence of man-noise permeating the cover, the animals are seldom spooked into panic-stricken flight and are not likely to bolt in random directions. Instead, wary whitetails will often move slowly in the mistaken belief they are evading approaching danger. Not alarmed, and using their regular travel routes and escape exits, they will stop frequently to test the wind, cup their ears to listen for distant sounds, and watch their backtrails. Like so many marionettes on the strings of knowing hunters, they can be purposefully and intentionally moved in specific directions, at a slow pace so that relatively easy shots become the rule. In previous years hunters usually had only precarious chances at jackrabbiting animals.

There is often some debate as to how closely the drivers should be spaced. This depends not upon the size of the area to be driven, or the number of hunters participating in the drive, but the cover density existing in the region. When working through stands of rather open pines, where the first branches are well off the ground and there is little second-growth cover, the drivemaster may instruct his drivers to move along spaced as much as 100 yards apart. When moving through nearly impenetrable palmetto tangles, however, drivers may have to close their ranks to within 20 yards of each other to prevent deer from slipping back through the drive line or remaining hidden in their beds.

ADVANCED DRIVE STRATEGIES

Once the annual hunting party has mastered the basics of driving deer they will probably want to increase their expertise by further refining their drive tactics. Very likely they will have learned that there is no single type of drive which is best for all situations. Rather, certain cover and terrain features dictate the need for specific types of drives. And herein lies still another reason for electing a knowledgeable drivemaster. Having carefully scouted and appraised the terrain before opening day, he will know in advance what type of drive is likely to prove the most productive in each area.

My guess is that he will decide upon one of the following six drive variations, as they guarantee far more shots at worthy trophies than what is even remotely possible with more conventional tactics.

The buttonhook drive. This drive variation is designed for hunting rather smallish patches of very heavy yet isolated cover such as where stands of pines, brush, or other dense ground-story growth is surrounded on all sides by open fields, meadows, or various types of natural or manmade boundaries such as high-

Plowed fields

Plowed fields

Plowed fields

There are many different types of drives, any of which may be best for different cover situations. The Buttonhook Drive shown here is the one to use when deer are sneaking back through the drive line.

ways, lakeshores, etc. Therefore, it is most frequently used in areas where the rural countryside is dotted with ranches or farms, or where other types of expansive agricultural or livestock operations are separated here and there by small swatches of heavy-cover acreage.

It's easy to see why executing one of the old-timey noisy drives in this type of cover/terrain situation would be a highly uncertain venture. Realizing that they are enclosed in rather tight quarters (say, ten acres or less), the deer would become alarmed and could spurt out anywhere along the edges of the cover in an attempt to make a run for it. As a result, if the standers didn't luck out and happen to be in the right place at the right time, they would usually only catch fleeting glimpses of white flags disappearing over some distant rise.

The buttonhook drive, however, enables hunters to control the deer. It's a semi-silent drive, seldom are more than seven hunters required, and for safety reasons all should be wearing bright orange.

Two standers are positioned so they are facing the far side of the cover, back 50 yards or so, and preferably in trees or some other high location.

Five drivers space themselves an equal distance apart along the opposite side of the cover. As they begin very slowly moving through the cover, the two end drivers and the one in the very middle sound off, but only occasionally (normal voice conversation is sufficient), while the others remain entirely silent as though still-hunting.

With this technique, the deer will not randomly spurt out along the sides of the cover because when not unduly alarmed one of their basic instincts is a reluctance to cross wide-open areas (the surrounding fields and meadows). Instead, they will try one of two evasive tactics which allow them to be easily intercepted.

They may gradually drift all the way through the length of the cover to the opposite side and upon eventually finding they have run out of concealing cover will next attempt to break from that far edge to other security cover in the distance. Typically, the standers will see the animals slowly sneaking to the edge of the cover and then hesitating or nervously milling around as they decide upon the best escape direction. Usually the deer present themselves in

The Funnel Drive sees hunters moving deer in such a way they must pass through a narrow neck of cover to gain access to an adjacent area. Standers overlooking the neck see deer sneaking through almost the minute drivers approach the other side.

full view just inside this edge; they are either standing still or moving very slowly, and in most cases there is more than enough time for one of the standers (sometimes both) to pick out the deer of his choice and make a safe and very easy shot.

If the drivers are carrying out their duties as they should in this type of drive, it is just as likely that the deer, not wanting to leave the cover, will attempt to pinpoint each driver's location and then dodge, circle, and sneak back through the drive line to get behind the drivers. And since they are only able to pinpoint the noisy drivers, which sound as though they are very widely spaced (because the two center-line drivers are remaining silent), they are actually encouraged to sneak back through the middle.

What often happens, then, is that one of the quiet drivers has a buck suddenly materialize before him at almost point-blank range!

But since the cleverest of bucks are master engineers when it comes to fancy footwork, it is a frequent occurrence for them to still succeed somehow in getting behind the drive line, and this is where the buttonhook maneuver counters their play.

When the drive line has proceeded about three-quarters of the way through the cover, the two silent drivers reverse their line of travel and begin quietly still-hunting back in the opposite direction. Often, one or the other will soon spot deer slinking away through the cover or standing in some semi-open clearing with their senses tuned in to whichever retreating noisy driver is closest to their immediate locations. Seldom do they ever suspect the presence of a still-closer hunter until the crack of the rifle!

The funnel drive, type 1. We know that few are the times when it is wise to drive expansive, unbroken tracts of land. The deer simply have too much room to roam, and circling the drivers will be very easy for them. Much better is to concentrate upon smaller segments of terrain, as this allows better control of the animals' direction. And funnel drives are another way hunters can take advantage of that whitetail trait which, when they are not spooked, makes them very reluctant to venture into open areas or cross natural or manmade boundaries.

The first type of funnel drive is designed for almost any kind of terrain in which heavy cover gradually necks down into a much smaller cover area through which the deer must pass in order to avoid exposing themselves and yet gain access to some other location during the course of their escape. Perhaps a thick stand of evergreens is surrounded on all sides by open fields with the exception of one corner of the pines where a small aisle of brush or high grass leads to and connects with a woodlot. Or maybe there is a triangular-shaped crop of high field corn. Let's say two sides are bordered by meadows, and the third side lies next to a recently plowed field. The near corners of the triangle are surrounded by openness, but the far corner touches a long hollow filled to the brim with blackberry tangles.

If danger (the drivers) approaches from a distance (in either of the cover situations just described, or similar other ones), any deer bedded in the evergreens will attempt to slip very quietly out the back door (the narrow neck). Stand hunters placed in trees overlooking the neck may expect to see action the minute their partners begin nearing the far side of the cover. Seldom are more than two or three drivers required, because with the ready escape exit at hand the deer will seldom elect to stay around to play their circling and sneaking games.

The funnel drive, type 2. The second type of funnel drive is very similar to the one just discussed in that the animals are pushed through a narrow neck of cover, but there are two differences. First, this type of funnel drive is designed for draws, hollows, canyons, and similar types of lengthy bottomland terrain which is saturated with cover and has very steep walls or hillsides bordering its length. Second, the standers are positioned in a slightly different manner in order to intercept deer attempting to widely circle the drive line.

Seven hunters are usually sufficient. Four take stands while three act as drivers. Two of the standers locate themselves to watch the narrow neck or gap through which the deer may attempt exits. The drivemaster places the other two standers on high promontories or outcroppings, or simply high on the hillsides, but in any event located about one-third of the way down the length of the hollow to be driven.

The drivers space themselves relatively close together so that it is absolutely impossible for deer to sneak back through the middle, and all of the drivers very slowly and quietly still-hunt the length of the canyon. In most cases, the deer will travel the entire length of the cover and then through the neck in order to gain access to the

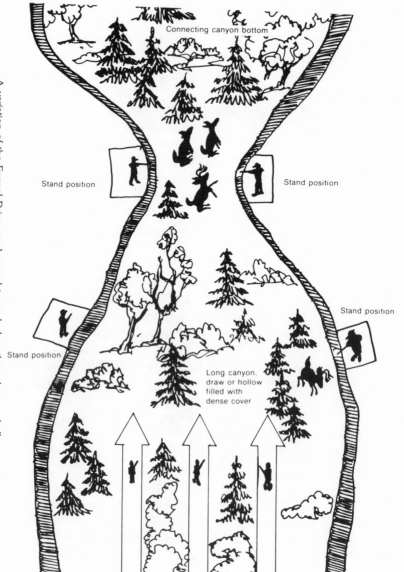

Connecting canyon bottom

Stand position

Stand position

Stand position

Stand position

Long canyon,
draw or hollow
filled with
dense cover

A variation of the Funnel Drive can be used to push deer through steep hollows, ravines, or canyons.

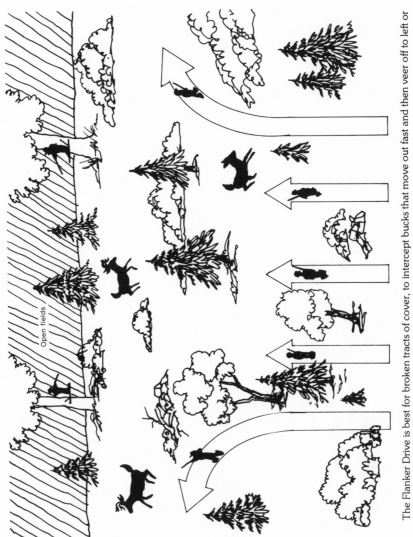

Open fields

The Flanker Drive is best for broken tracts of cover, to intercept bucks that move out fast and then veer off to left or right to circle widely.

presumed safety of a connecting hollow, swamp, river-bottom area, or whatever. Again, the standers overlooking the narrow gap should have easy shots at unsuspecting, loping animals.

Now and then, however, bucks jumped from their beds may travel straightaway for only a short distance, then move perpendicular to the drive line, and next try to sneak around the end drivers to get behind the drive line. If this is attempted, those standers situated high on the hillsides of the hollow or draw will see them and have setup shots at very slowly sneaking deer.

Drive with flankers. If you watch much pro football on TV you know what flankers are and how they move. In driving deer, flankers carry out similar maneuvers. This drive is perfect when the drive party is confronted with a larger than usual tract of mixed cover where there are interspersed open clearings separating swatches of multiflora rose, cactus, immature pines, scrub oak, cedars, felled trees, and so on.

Eight hunters are sufficient. Three are designated as stand hunters, three as drivers, and two as flankers. The drivemaster posts the stand hunters an equal distance apart along the far border of the cover and in such a way that they can easily view open clearings along that edge. The five other hunters line up along the opposite edge of the cover with the flankers perhaps just a bit more widely spaced from the three middle-line drivers.

In driving this type of cover situation, any bucks that are rousted from their beds may proceed all the way through the cover to present themselves as easy targets to the standers. But they may also attempt to angle away from the drive line in an oblique direction, since it is common for whitetails, after they have traveled straightaway for a distance, to then fade off to either left or right.

The flankers are the first to begin very quietly still-hunting in a straightaway direction, and then just as they are about 75 yards ahead of the drive line the left flanker begins flaring off to the left and the right flanker to the right. Simultaneously, the three middle-line drivers commence slowly moving through the cover, all of them sounding off with normal voice conversation.

The flankers have better chances of shooting than the standers, because they will be in position to intercept those bucks which are angling off to the left or right instead of heading straightaway in the direction of the stands. And they will also be in prime locations for spotting bucks attempting to circle widely in their efforts to get behind the drive line.

The line drive. Your hunting party consists of only a few individuals and you're spending the early morning and late afternoon on stand, but you'd like to stage drives during the midday hours when deer are customarily bedded. There aren't really enough people present to have hunters waiting on stand and drivers as well to push deer to them, so the best bet is the line drive.

The line drive is most effective when three or four hunters are available and when they are hunting heavy cover saturating an approximately rectangular piece of terrain that is surrounded by wide-open areas. The three or four drivers approach one of the longer sides of the cover, spacing themselves a considerable distance apart so that each hunter can just barely see an occasional flash of orange as his partners to either side very slowly still-hunt through the cover. Not a smidgen of noise is made; each of the hunters assumes the role of still-hunter on his own behalf but simultaneously a driver for the others.

When a buck is jumped from his bed, rather than move out in a straightaway direction and very soon be at the far side of the cover where openness begins, he'll move out only a very short distance and then cut sharply to the left or right to sneak the long length of the cover, and this will see him moving perpendicular to the direction of the drive.

Any particular hunter may or may not have a shot at a buck he jumps himself, depending upon how far out the deer is when it moves from its bed. But he will almost certainly have a shot when a buck is jumped by a hunter to either his left or right, and in most cases it will be a broadside opportunity at a slow-moving deer.

Technically speaking, the line drive can probably be said to be nothing more than a variation of still-hunting, since there are no hunters waiting somewhere on stand. But no matter. Call it whatever you want as long as you call it highly effective! (I'm prejudiced because the line drive was how I tagged the biggest buck of my career—a ten-point, 240-pound monster.)

The one-man drive. The one-man drive may be the perfect technique when all members of the hunting party desire to wait on stand and yet one member who has already filled his tag wants to help his partners get their bucks.

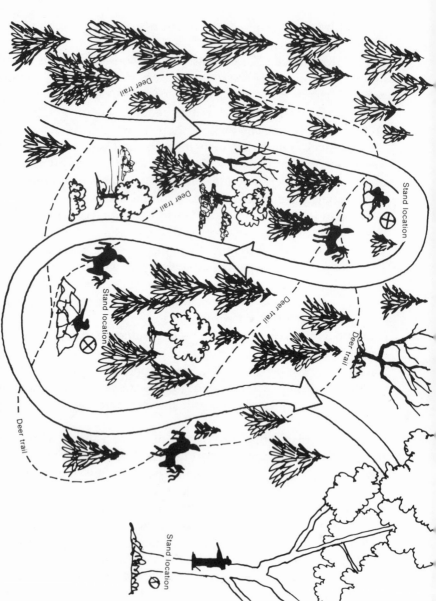

The One-Man Drive sometimes works when partners would rather use stands. Stands should overlook trails, and a single hunter walks to keep deer moving on routes that are familiar to them.

Deer trail

Stand location

Stand location

Deer trail

Deer trail

Deer trail

Stand location

The Line Drive is best when you have only three or four hunters. This is a quiet drive, and deer move perpendicular to the drive line to sneak around the end.

There is one very important element to the one-man drive if it is to be successful. The cover may be very heavy, only moderately dense, or there may be cover formations separated by open clearings, but the members of the party must know *exactly* where all the primary deer trails in the vicinity are located. Stands should then be installed (or they can be built in advance) in those places where two or more trails either cross or come together to form a major runway. However, the stands should not be so widely spaced from one another that the lone driver is faced with seemingly endless miles of walking; if there are to be five stands, for example, I would want them to be situated within a maximum distance of 750 yards of each other.

Standers take their positions, and the lone driver begins hiking a methodical pattern back and forth across the terrain, paying special attention to the types of heavy cover deer like to bed in or near. He doesn't make a lot of noise, but neither is he entirely silent (I often whistle softly to myself as though on a routine summer hike). And for safety reasons he should be dressed in blaze orange.

Since deer frequently see farm hands, forestry personnel, and others on regular assignments in their domain, the whistling and hiking activity of a lone person doesn't alarm them. It is readily identified for what it is; the "working" man has never posed a major threat in the past, and so the animals simply get up and quietly move out of his way, sneaking along those trails that are familiar to them as everyday travel routes.

One man coursing back and forth through the cover can sometimes keep the deer circulating all day long, as they will never entirely move out of their home ranges. But the all-day hiking is seldom necessary, because with partners stationed over the animals' primary travel routes, it usually isn't too long before shots begin ringing out in the distance.

These, then, are what I consider to be the very best methods for driving whitetails. They are not all my inventions but in part have been gleaned from some of the country's most proficient deer hunters.

It's important to keep in mind, however, that they are only drive *concepts* that may necessarily have to be revised, altered, or specially tailored as cover and terrain situations dictate. For example, if the drive with flankers doesn't produce results, and the members of the drive party are confident the cover contains deer, the animals are probably sneaking back through the drive line. Therefore, it might be wise to drive the cover a second time, still using the flankers but with one or two of the middle-line drivers executing buttonhook movements as well. Or, in the case of the one-man drive, if the cover is very dense the animals may simply remain bedded until the lone driver passes. Therefore, perhaps two drivers hiking through the cover, spaced about 50 or 75 yards from each other, may better succeed in rousting the deer.

But in any of this, the seed to be planted is that driving whitetails is no longer a raucous, disorganized hodgepodge of numerous hunters ramming through the woodlands. That kind of stuff is as ineffectual as loading up with rubber bullets.

9

Choosing
the Right
Deer Rifle

Nowadays, it's difficult for any hunting writer to approach the subject of rifles and calibers suitable for deer hunting, because for no other game species is so much in the way of acceptable armaments available. Compounding the problem, so much diverse opinion has already been penned that for many the issue seems hopelessly clouded.

Everything from the .222 Remington all the way up to, believe it or not, the .375 H&H Magnum, with perhaps as many as seventy-five intermediate calibers married with various bullet weights, has at one time or another been either used or promoted for whitetails. Using the .222 and other similar smallbores, of course, is little more than deplorable stunt-shooting because of the high ratio of animals only crippled, and at the other extreme the .375 is a classic instance of overkill.

Something else that aggravates the problem, when it comes to published advice regarding deer rifles, is that many of my gun-writing cohorts in the business—and I say this affectionately—are

The subject of deer rifles, calibers, handloads, and all the rest has become unnecessarily complicated. More important, once practical considerations are out of the way, is a hunter's familiarity with his rifle so he can use it quickly and cooly when big bucks like this are suddenly in the sights. (Photo by Bill Byrne)

overindulgent romantics, technical freaks, and constant fiddlers. They frequently go overboard debating the efficacy of highly specialized trigger assemblies that must be imported from some place like the Tortugas (with a three-year waiting list and at a price that would gag an Arab sheik), or inventing bizarre wildcat calibers. They ponder whether an additional 4.26 grains of this powder or that to achieve 50 extra feet per second of muzzle velocity is fully justified in view of the slightly shortened caselife sure to be in the offing. No wonder so many of their readers finally throw their hands up in despair!

This is certainly not to imply that there's anything wrong with poring over ballistic coefficient tables into the wee hours of the night, experimenting with sundry powder-bullet-primer handloads, or investing more than one can really afford in what often amounts to little more than purely cosmetic rifle surgery. But in a decade of Sundays none of this is likely to have any more influence upon the end success of the whitetail hunter than will a giraffe-hide golf bag upon the prowess of some white-ball tournament contender.

Of far greater concern should be the ever-unpredictable human element in the shooting/hunting equation. And the reason is that it's a fact of life that any rifle taken off the shelf and into the field, and fed with standard factory loads, will shoot better than 95 percent of all hunters can hold. I'm not talking now about bench-rest firing with sandbags and earphones and spotting scopes and measured distances to paper targets under good lighting conditions and with all the time you need in the world to squeeze the trigger. I'm talking about actual hunting encounters in the field, with live game in the sights, the need to shoot offhand or sitting or standing, with intervening cover under poor light conditions, and with your heart hammering even harder each time you look at the size of those horns.

In other words, the lifetime success percentage any hunter is likely to enjoy in his favorite deer cover is indeed at least partly determined by his selection of a practical caliber, bullet weight, weapon design, and sighting apparatus. But other factors are even more crucial: the intimate familiarity he has established with his chosen rifle; the efficiency and coolness with which he can put his rifle into use; and most important of all, his deep knowledge and understanding of whitetail behavior so that he may more consistently over the years find himself in the right place at the right time when Old Bushy Head comes prancing into view.

So read no further if you're looking for Holy Writ on whitetail armamants and sophisticated ballistic claptrap beyond that which is fundamentally necessary for the hunter. I hereby assign all of that make-problem ballyhoo to the guys with the slide rules and micrometers, most of whom never go hunting anyway.

WHAT CALIBER IS BEST?

In the case of any hunter, selecting the deer rifle that is right for him will be partly determined by whatever firearm restrictions or regulations may exist in his state or in those locales where he plans to do most of his hunting.

This taken into account, however, too many hunters make the great mistake of deciding first upon a particular action (such as an autoloader or pumpgun) or brand name, and then almost as an afterthought accept almost any caliber the clerk happens to have on hand in the certain firearm he fancies. This is entirely backwards! The caliber should be selected first, then the rifle model and design to handle it.

In looking at specific calibers, as good a place as any to begin is with the seemingly forever-eulogized .30/30. I won't unequivocally say the .30/30 is absolutely worthless (for generations, sagging camp meatpoles have offered contrary testimony). It is just that there are many, many other calibers that are far superior for the myriad tasks any deer hunter may be called upon to perform at any given time. And this is based upon the solid premise, subscribed to by most of the country's leading gun experts, that to be an adequate caliber for deer any given cartridge should deliver a bare-bones minimum of 2000 foot-pounds of energy at the muzzle. The .30/30 does not.

Ballistically, a 150-grain slug leaves the muzzle of a .30/30 at 2410 feet per second and with 1930 foot-pounds of energy, and at 100 yards the slug has slowed down to 1960 fps and has retained only 1280 foot-pounds of smack. At 200 yards a 150-grain slug has only 875 foot-pounds of energy. With 170-grain slugs, the .30/30 yields 2220 fps of muzzle velocity and 1860 foot-pounds of energy; at 100 yards, the 170-grain is down to 1890 fps and offers only 1350 foot-pounds of energy.

Inherent in the problem of the .30/30's rapidly diminishing velocity characteristic is that slugs of any weight, beyond 100 yards, begin taking on a very prominent rainbow-type loop in their trajectories. And aside from the pitiful energy beyond 100 yards, this can and does making aiming calculations a dubious affair. So the .30/30 is what we might hesitatingly call an "acceptable" deer caliber, but only if the hunter is realistic in appraising the caliber's capabilities and then accepting its limitations. In short, it is my contention he shouldn't be using the .30/30 in the first place. But if he insists, he should probably be willing to pass up shooting opportunities when the range is more than 125 yards—shooting

One of the auithor's favorite hunting companions is Mike Wolter, who displays here the four favorite calibers for whitetails. From left to right, the .243 Winchester, .270 Winchester, .30/06 Springfield, and .308 Winchester.

opportunities that would be a piece of cake for almost any other firearm manufactured to handle fodder possessing more ooomph—because of the distinct probability of the bullet's only wounding the deer.

That brings to front stage those centerfire rifle calibers I consider the very finest for any variety of whitetail campaign. They are the .243 Winchester, the .270 Winchester, the ever-popular .30/06 Springfield, and the .308 Winchester. All are excellent for close-in work, and yet because of their sizzling bullet speeds and consequently very flat trajectories will reach way out while still retaining plenty of punch. Further, midrange trajectories for all (at 200 yards, using the recommended bullet weights for deer) are in the vicinity of only 2 inches or so. Therefore, initial sighting-in procedures and subsequent sight pictures at various ranges during most in-field hunting operations require almost nothing in the way of furled brows.

Categorically, a 100-grain slug thrown from a .243 verily smokes along with a muzzle velocity of 3070 fps and 2090 foot-pounds of energy. By the way, never use the 80-grain slug available for .243 caliber; this is a varmint load. At 200 yards the 100-grain is still pushing over 2500 fps and has retained over 1400 foot-pounds of wallop. Midrange trajectory is only 2.2 inches at 200 yards, making it one of the "flattest" calibers available.

The .270 Winchester is a streaker as well, with basic factory loads available in 100-, 130-, and 150-grain bullet weights. The 130-grain leaves the muzzle at 3140 fps and at 200 yards is still chugging along at over 2600 fps. Energy at the muzzle is 2850 foot-pounds and at 200 yards is still a very healthy 2000 foot-pounds. The 100-grain slug trips along a little faster, but connects with less wallop, and the 150-grain, by comparison, is a mite on the languid side but in return offers 2800 foot-pounds of energy at the muzzle. Midrange trajectories for all, at 200 yards, average out to only slightly more than 2 inches.

As to the .270's clean-kill capabilities, I have the utmost in confidence. Doubtless, as I'll detail later, *shot placement is in truth the deciding factor as to any caliber's effectiveness.* But on most occasions, when executing long shots (over 150 yards) at bucks with my pet Ithaca bolt-action, the deer had no idea what hit them and it might as well have been lightning. And a good percentage of other whitetails that have been taken at closer ranges (less than 100 yards) went down so quickly it was as if they had fallen through a trapdoor. So I'm indeed very biased (and wish I had a nickel for every other hunter who is convinced the .270 is one fantastic caliber).

The .30/06 has been a celebrated caliber for many decades, partly because of its adoption by the armed forces and then its wide availability to sportsmen, but also because when chambered with various loads it serves well as an all-purpose piece for the "one-gun" man. Like the .308, which will be discussed shortly, the .30/06 is a proficient caliber for both whitetails and mule deer, pronghorn antelope, moose, elk, caribou, black bear—in fact, for virtually any sort of game that might suit your fancy.

.30/06 slugs may be had in 110-, 125-, 150-, 180-, and 220-grain weights; the lighter slugs, of course, are faster but have fewer foot-pounds of energy, and the heavier bullets are by most standards quite slow but do have considerable clout. The 125-grain slug leaves the muzzle at 3200 fps and with 2840 foot-pounds of energy. The 150-grain comes out at 2970 fps and with 2930 foot-pounds of energy. Yet they have a midrange trajectory at 200 yards of only 2.2 and 2.4 inches, respectively. By comparison, the 220-grain slug (not recommended for whitetails) has a midrange trajectory of almost 4 inches at 200 yards, and almost 10 inches at 300 yards!

Al and Mike Wolter are fans of the .308 Winchester (this is the 7.62mm NATO cartridge, which has been available to hunters since the mid-1950s). The Wolters originally hail from Minnesota but pursue deer in many other states on a regular basis. And between the two of them, their young hunting careers have already seen them hang up over fifty whitetails. Certainly they are both outstanding hunters, but with a diversified background of success like that it is easy to see the .308 is an excellent prescription for big bucks living anywhere.

The .308 may also be fed with five different bullet weights— 110, 125, 150, 180, and 200 grains. With either the 125- or 150-grain bullets, midrange trajectory at 200 yards is only slightly more than 2 inches. The 125-grain .308 slug moves out at 3100 fps at the muzzle and with 2670 foot-pounds of energy; the 150-grain comes away from the gate at 2860 fps and with 2730 foot-pounds of energy.

But wait! Arms experts and experienced hunters may contend, and they are entirely right, that there are many other calibers that are comparable to those described above with respect to both long-range and short-range performance capabilities. Examples that readily come to mind include the 6mm Remington, .25/06 Remington, .257 Roberts, .264 Winchester Magnum, .280 Remington, 7mm Mauser (7×57), .300 Savage, 8mm Mauser, and perhaps still many others as well.

But poll any cross-section of veteran deer hunters. You'll probably discover that while not everyone uses a .243, .270, .30/06, or .308, invariably these particular calibers are nevertheless the ideal types or "standards" by which most others are judged, and that is reason enough for singling these four calibers out for special mention here.

USE LIGHTWEIGHT BULLETS

An important consideration for any deer hunter is the bullet weight he plans to shoot, and as we have just seen there may be several options in the various popular calibers.

But inherent in all of this is a myth that has been perpetuated for much too long, and we need to dispel such notions right now.

The fable is that gunners residing in the East require slow-moving, heavy bullets because they hunt in tangled jungles of vegetation, branches, brush, and other cover they must plow through with their ill intentions if they are to experience minimal bullet deflection and succeed in hitting their marks. And that Midwestern and Western deer hunters, on the other hand, require lightweight, fast bullets because they have to reach out long distances over terrain that is typically wide open and cover-free. Further, that Eastern deer hunters require weapons that are short, light, and preferably equipped with open sights, while those on the other side of the Mississippi are better off with something long and equipped with a high-power scope.

All of these assertions, dear reader, are unfounded blanket generalizations. Or in more abrupt terms, pure bunk.

We'll look at weapon actions and scopes later, so for the moment let's deal here with the lightweight/heavyweight bullet controversy.

It is indeed true that lighter, faster bullets are more easily deflected by cover than heavier, slower slugs. But I have seen hunting situations in Pennsylvania, upstate New York, Vermont, and even throughout the Southern and Southeastern "swamp" states where, taking a solid "rest" position, entirely feasible shooting opportunities out to 300 yards or so have frequently presented themselves.

Conversely, in the plains states of Nebraska and South Dakota, throughout the arid Southwest, and even to the westernmost reaches of the whitetail's range, I've more than frequently been in such heavy cover that deer approached to within 20 yards of my stand before I even suspected their presence!

Therefore, in my opinion, it is entirely unnecessary for the hunter to use heavyweight bullets, if for no other reason than that heavy slugs, at any time or in any locale, place the hunter at a distinct disadvantage by making him less able to handle longer shooting opportunities as they periodically arise.

But there is much more to it than that. Knowing that a particular bullet weight is less susceptible to deflection, in my mind, may even precipitate careless or dangerous shooting. The hunter, hoping his heavyweights will cut a swath through the impenetrable cover and eventually find buckskin, perhaps more often takes impulsive shots he might not attempt with a lighter, faster slug. Too often, because even the heaviest of slugs will be somewhat deflected when hitting branches and vines, the unfortunate end result is an only superficially wounded deer. The animals deserve better, and the ethics of the sport demand it if those who would have hunting outlawed, claiming sportsmen are inhumane barbarians, are not to have still another lever for influencing public emotion.

Looking at it another way, lightweight bullets may encourage conscientious behavior on the part of the guy behind the trigger. He comes to accept the fact that his slugs are easily deflected, and so he learns to select his shots with greater care. He becomes, by sheer necessity, a highly competent marksman. A sniper. And so he becomes less willing to blast away through a dense screen of cover at some fleeting glimpse of what he "thinks" is deerhide. Call the whole thing unrealistic idealism, if you must. But it would indeed make it a far safer proposition for other hunters in the field, while similarly helping to reduce the tragic number of deer each year that are only crippled by the brushbusters, and that is a goal worth striving for.

Following this line of reasoning, 100-grain slugs would undoubtedly be the best bet for the .243; for the .270 I exclusively use 130-grain bullets; and for the .30/06 and .308 I recommend either 125 or 150 grains of lead. To be sure, we may be compromising a bit in several departments, since it is impossible to have the best of everything in one package. But with them, close-in work is a cinch. And yet because of their high velocities and flat trajectories, which allow for easier-to-calculate sight pictures, any buck out to 300 yards or so is in very serious trouble.

The main point to be made is that the whitetail hunter does not require specific calibers or bullet weights for different regions of the country or certain variations of cover. From Maine to Colorado, and from Washington to Florida, and everywhere in between, the accomplished hunter who demands versatility from his weaponry can use the same high-velocity, flat-shooting calibers and light-weight bullets.

The type of bullet also deserves mention. What is desired is that the slug penetrate well, at both long and short ranges, and then expand or mushroom within the animal with great shocking power and tissue destruction, killing the deer as quickly as possible but without turning it into deerburger in the process.

Whitetails are relatively thin-skinned and possess a rather fragile bone structure, compared to many other species of four-footed big game, so slug penetration is seldom a major concern when the popular deer calibers we have been discussing are employed. Proper bullet expansion, however (which is so vital to a clean, humane kill), may sometimes not be achieved if the hunter has unknowingly selected the wrong type of slugs.

I recommend jacketed bullets in which most of the lead, except for the tip, is covered with a tough alloyed metal, or where the tip has a thin coat of metal but is notched to facilitate expansion. In either case the jacket gives the bullet good accuracy, performance, and penetration, allowing the slug to hold together upon impact but then begin peeling back from the tip and flattening as it opens a large path. Just two examples of such bullets are the Winchester Pointed Soft-Point and the Remington Core-Lokt.

Full-jacketed bullets or solids, on the other hand, invariably pass entirely through the deer, leaving only a very small hole and sometimes not inflicting shock or tissue damage necessary to prove immediately fatal. Subsequently, a very long tracking job is often in store if the animal is to be recovered at all.

WHAT RIFLE ACTION?

Various regions of the country are known for the types of rifle actions that deer hunters residing there prefer most. Throughout the Northern border states, and into the East and Northeast, the most popular seems to be a toss-up between the lever-action and the autoloader. In the Plains, Western, and Southwestern states, nine out of ten are seen toting either a bolt-action or a lever-action. And in the Midwest, South, and Southeast, you'll see mostly autoloaders, with someone in the crowd occasionally carrying a pumpgun.

There is no advantage in being a conformist, however. Choose what *you* want, based upon whichever type of action you've used most in the past, perhaps in other types of hunting, and therefore feel most comfortable and adept with.

Those who, throughout the year, engage in considerable target shooting with various calibers, or enjoy occasional groundhog forays, are almost certain to be strongly in favor of bolt-action rifles when they enter their favorite whitetail haunts. The bolt-action is the most accurate of all the actions (thus the reason it is unanimously chosen by match shooters and varminters, who typically require precision accuracy and sometimes plunk their targets from extremely long ranges). It is also the most rugged and trouble-free and the easiest to keep clean.

Barrel length in the bolt-action need be no more than 24 inches, and in my estimation even better are the shorter tubes of only 22 inches. An average bolt-action rifle will weigh around 7 or 8 pounds. Add to this the weight of the scope (with its base and rings) and now the rifle suddenly weighs 9 pounds. Then there's the weight of the sling and fully loaded magazine. And believe me, each additional few ounces here and there will feel like pounds when climbing a mountain or trudging across some blistering hot saguaro flat, especially at the end of a long day. If the total weight of the rifle, scope, sling, and cartridges can be kept close to 10 pounds you've done a good job.

In looking at other firearm actions, however, there is the distinct possibility that the Kentucky rabbit or coon hunter will feel most at ease with a pumpgun (slide-action) when he later in the season ventures afield for deer. The pupmgun is not as accurate as the bolt-action but is faster to use, since chambering additional rounds can be easily accomplished without taking the gun from either the cheek or shoulder and thereby destroying the sight picture. Barrel lengths for slide-actions average 22 inches. And stripped down, such rifles come in around 7 pounds or so, which means that fully outfitted the hunter can again count upon an eventual 9- or 10-pound rifle afield.

The lever-action is as familiar a sight in the scabbards of Western horsemen as are grits on the breakfast platters of Southerners, and that's one reason why it is their logical choice when the deer season rolls around. But the lever-action has drawn an even greater calling among Minnesota, Wisconsin, Michigan, Pennsylvania, New York, and New England whitetail scouts who more commonly prefer to engage in still-hunting and driving deer than occupying stands for endless hours; with them, continually on the move as they are, a rifle that still feels light at the end of the day is just the ticket. Barrel lengths average from 18 to 20 inches, and stripped down most lever-actions weigh somewhere in the range of 5½ to 6¾ pounds.

The lever-action as well allows fast use, because it is not necessary to remove the rifle from your cheek to engage consecutive rounds. But as in the case of the pumpgun, the lever-action is not as strong as the bolt-action, nor as accurate.

The autoloader (or semi-automatic) is not impressively accurate. And it is not overly rugged; feeding and extraction malfunctions or "jams" are common when the firearm is not immaculately clean, whenever the weather is unusually cold, and sometimes when the user is working with handloads. Barrels average 18 to 22 inches in length. Stripped-down autoloaders weigh in the vicinity of 7½ pounds, and stripped-down autoloading carbines average 5½ to 7 pounds.

Some hunters feel the autoloader's deficiencies (susceptibility to malfunctioning and lesser accuracy potential) are compensated for by the fact that this particular action is by far the fastest. But still others, myself included, feel even this is a distinct drawback. The reason is that I firmly believe that in the great majority of hunting circumstances it's the hunter's first shot that should and indeed probably will count. He may not get another, but if he luckily does, how *fast* he can put that additional lead into the air is absolutely meaningless, and perhaps can even be said to fall into the category of irresponsible shooting.

Don't get me wrong. There's nothing immoral about taking consecutive shots at a buck, or sending your greetings to one that is running flat out. But in my mind, each shot should be taken with deliberate care and to the very best of the hunter's aiming ability so that the chances of only wounding deer are minimal.

Yet the autoloader seems to encourage a hunter to send too much lead flying too quickly. I've even found myself falling victim to this unconscious reaction when using autoloading shotguns for bird and small-game hunting as well as in hunting deer. And that is why I nowadays use bolt-actions almost exclusively for whitetails instead of slide-actions, lever-actions, or autoloaders. By their very mechanical nature, bolt-actions force me to slow down, and when I'm shooting slowly and purposefully my accuracy skyrockets.

I don't care what the cover may be like, or consequently how quickly a buck may be capable of vanishing from sight. You can make book that the hunter who uses a pump, lever, or auto solely because he can get off a lot of shots in a hurry is one of the poorest and most inept marksmen in the woods.

YOU NEED A SCOPE

Since who knows when, iron sights and aperture-type peep sights have enabled hundreds of thousands of hunters to place millions of pounds of venison in their freezer lockers. And there is no question open sights will be with us for many, many open seasons to come. On the plus side, they are extremely rugged, almost entirely fail-safe, fairly inexpensive, and will usually do a creditable job of reducing a buck on the hoof to so many steaks and roasts, provided the deer is standing within 125 yards when the shot is taken.

But telescopic sights, or scopes, have it all over iron sights and peep sights. In fact, they are so superior that the hunter who still insists upon some type of open sight, if I may be allowed the observation, is as behind the times as the guy who is still not yet willing to trade in his 1941 Nash and has block ice delivered for his refrigerator.

Some hunters still think scopes are fragile, easily knocked out of alignment, and not as fast to use. This is not true. Scopes have been much improved during the last fifteen years or so. They are now precision-made, extremely durable, and very fast to use when the right scope has been selected, and of course they allow a hunter to take advantage of shooting opportunities far beyond the range capabilities of open sights.

One difficulty not the fault of the scope but of the hunter—and this can indeed cause one to blow a chance at some big buck—is that of using a glass of greater magnification than the shooting situation warrants. With any scope, the higher the power the more limited or restricted the field of view at the closer ranges, and many times this prevents the hunter from quickly finding his target and centering the reticle upon it. This is especially the case when a deer is on the move and there is intervening cover. Likewise, since the higher magnifications tend to reflect the slightest of normal body tremors, holding steady on a faraway target sometimes becomes a precarious venture at best.

I am strongly in favor of the variable-power wide-angle scopes now on the market, instead of the standard-field, fixed-power scopes that predominated for years, because they are so versatile.

My favorite is the Bausch and Lomb 2.5 − 8×, which I use on a variety of weapons. I mount it on various shotguns when hunting in states where only smoothbores are legal for deer, on rifles for both whitetails and mulies elsewhere, for long-distance shooting at antelope and woodchucks, and for very close work on moose and bear. In other words, the hunter who goes after more than just whitetails during the course of the year could easily, if he employed only standard-field-of-view scopes with fixed magnifications, find justifiable use for maybe as many as five or six different scopes, each intended for a specialized task. But with only the one described above, I can do it all.

When still-hunting or waiting on stand for whitetails in very heavy cover or when participating in drives, all of which are likely to see very close shots regardless of the type of weapon used, I keep my scope turned down to its lowest setting (2.5×). Yet if a buck is ever sighted a good distance away there is usually more than ample time to crank the Bausch & Lomb up to a slightly higher power (from 3× to 5×). About the only time the still-higher magnifications are used are when I have a very long shot across rather open terrain, as in antelope, mule deer, or varmint hunting, and there is enough time to assume a prone position and make use of a very stable rest.

The above scope, though, is certainly not the only choice the deer hunter has available for his inspection, for there are many others of high quality, too. For example, when I travel far from home and am not restricted to the amount of gear I can take along,

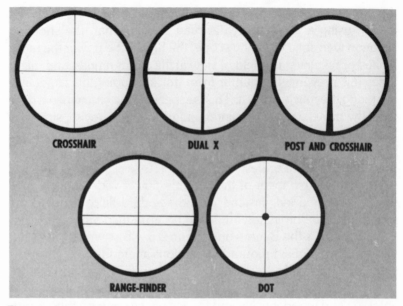

CROSSHAIR   DUAL X   POST AND CROSSHAIR

RANGE-FINDER   DOT

These are the most popular telescopic sight reticles, with the dual X being the most favored among deer hunters.

I pack a "backup" rifle upon which is mounted a variable-power wide-angle Weaver scope in 2.5 — 7× (the rifle is usually another bolt-action in .270 caliber, but sometimes a .243 or .308). Al Wolter is partial to Redfield's Widefield model in 1¾ — 5×, and hunting crony Barry White likes Leupold's 2 — 7× Vari-× II. Still other quality scopes are made by Bushnell, Browning, Lyman, and Nickel.

So I advise the hunter to visit his local gun shop and make his choice, keeping in mind that the variable-power wide-angle scopes will see him through a broader range of hunting situations. He should also remember that while hunting it is best to keep the scope turned down to its lowest magnification (usually somewhere between 1.5× and 2.5×) until there is a clear need for a higher power; this should see him perfectly ready for any close-in shot that may suddenly present itself, even in the most densely saturated regenerative or tropical growth.

I am personally an advocate of the cross-hair reticle rather than the post, dot, and other types, which I feel obscure too much of the target at the longer ranges. Cross-hair reticles are available in fine, medium-fine, medium, and coarse thicknesses, and also in what are known as "4-Plex" or "Dual-X" designs in which the thick outer extremities of the cross-hairs gradually taper down to fine at the center. All are excellent, with any particular choice being governed by personal preference more than anything else. There are also various types of "rangefinder" scopes now on the market that, through the use of a type of scale as seen through the glass or calibrated dial on the side of the scope, enable the hunter to judge long distances more accurately in order that aiming calculations can be more precise. These are of excellent workmanship, too, but the hunter will have to determine for himself whether the few times they might be called into use for whitetail hunting warrant the added outlay of cash.

A few other things can also be mentioned in favor of scopes, to further convince you of their merit if that is still required. I noted earlier that in heavy cover a hunter using almost any caliber rifle but throwing lightweight bullets must take greater care in selecting his shots. Scopes allow this very thing! The hunter using a telescopic sight is better able to find openings or shooting alleys through branches and vines, which is seldom possible using open sights at ranges beyond 60 yards or so.

Additionally, scopes offer what is sometimes referred to as "light-gathering" help. This means that target resolution, or its degree of "brightness," is far greater through a scope than what the human eye can ordinarily discern by itself under poor light conditions. This can be an important safety as well as trophy consideration during dawn and dusk periods when the distance is appreciable, since low light levels (when hunters are most likely to see action) characteristically diminish the human eye's depth-of-field capabilities (how far one can see). Consequently, a hunter can more accurately study his game if he is strictly after a trophy. But even if he's willing to settle for something less, a scope can aid in determining which deer are legal and which are not (as in the case, for example, in certain states that allow only those bucks to be harvested that have certain minimal antler configurations, such as forked horns). But whatever the case, when using a scope there is little likelihood of a hunter ever making the unforgivable mistake of shooting at anything but his intended quarry.

Finally, still another advantage of telescopic sights is that nearly all of them nowadays have a rear eyepiece that can be focused during sighting-in procedures to accommodate any hunter's particular visual deficiencies. This can be and usually is beneficial for those who have seen many deer seasons and whose eyesight may not be as keen as it was in earlier years.

Many rifles, off the shelf, will not accept scope rings (which contain the scope tube itself) unless first the receiver is "tapped" and an appropriate scope base or mount installed. Since this can be tricky work, and since it is imperative that scopes be mounted rigidly, it's not a good idea for the hunter to attempt this himself. Nor is it wise to wait until a week before opening day to confer with his gunsmith on the matter, because no doubt he'll be up to his knickers with other rush orders at this time. Further, throughout the hunting season it's always a good practice to check the various screws holding the scope in place; sometimes they have a tendency to work loose after a while.

Once a scope has been installed, the next thing is to check for proper eye relief, or the distance from the eye that will be looking through the scope to the ocular or rearmost portion of the tube. A scope that is mounted too far forward in its rings does not allow a complete sight picture. Loosen the scope rings a bit and slide the tube to the rear until a clear and complete sight picture is gained. And a scope that is too far to the rear may, when the rifle recoils, clout the shooter in the eyebrow region. It hurts! For most hunters, proper eye relief is somewhere between 2½ and 4 inches.

SIGHTING IN THE DEER RIFLE

All firearms manufacturers and makers of scopes include with their products various pamphlets that detail the easiest ways to achieve proper sighting in with that particular line of equipment, and the deer hunter should thoroughly read these instructions before heading for the target range. However, for the sake of completeness, we should nevertheless cover the fundamentals.

Using any of the four popular calibers discussed earlier in this chapter, along with the most appropriate bullet weights, most hunters will want to have their weapons sighted in so that on the target range the slugs consistently group as closely together as possible, printing 3 inches high of point of aim at 100 yards.

Sighting in the deer rifle is easy and takes only a few minutes. It's best to first "bore-sight" the rifle to get slugs on paper. Then fine-tune the scope by adjusting elevation and windage knobs one click at a time.

Since the lung region will be the most desired aiming point during encounters with deer (I talk about this in detail later), this allows the hunter to hold almost dead-on at any range from pointblank out to 300 yards or so with the assurance that he will connect with a sure hit in the chest cavity. (In wanting to be as precisely accurate as possible, however, in most cases he will probably hold slightly low when targets present themselves at ranges closer than 150 yards, and just a tad high at anything beyond 275 yards.)

A short cut to sighting in with a scope is to "bore-sight" the rifle. Most gunsmiths will do the job when the weapon is left with them to be outfitted with a scope base, rings, and scope, by using a gadget called an optical collimator. But anyone can just as easily bore-sight a weapon himself.

If the rifle is a bolt-action, completely remove the bolt and cradle the weapon securely in V-notches cut out of two opposite sides of a cardboard box. Then, looking through the barrel, adjust the position of the weapon so the bull's-eye, 100 yards away and as seen through the bore, is as perfectly centered as possible. Now, being careful not to move the rifle, turn the scope's windage and elevation knobs until the cross-hairs are likewise centered on the bull.

A spotting scope makes sighting in easier, and earphones are highly recommended. Sandbags cradling the rifle ensure extraneous movement does not influence placement of shots.

If the rifle is a pumpgun, lever-action, or autoloader, bore-sighting can also be accomplished, although in each of these cases the target is placed only 25 yards away. Open the weapon's action, cradle the rifle in a box as before, and then insert into the open breech a small bore-sighting prism manufactured for the purpose. Or, as Al Wolter suggests, use a small fragment of broken mirror. Continue to adjust the position of the rifle until the bull's-eye, as seen in the mirror or prism, aligns perfectly with the bore, and then again adjust the scope's cross-hairs.

The purpose of bore-sighting is simply to get the hunter's slugs "on paper" as quickly as possible (otherwise, there is no telling how many shots it might take in pure guesswork fashion). This done, he is then able to proceed on to the matter of making fine-tuning adjustments with his scope.

Fine-tuning a scope is easy. To make the rifle shoot higher or lower, the elevation knob is adjusted; adjustments to the right or left are made by turning the windage knob. Most such knobs have arrows on them, indicating the direction the dials should be turned if point of impact is to be raised, lowered, or sent to the right or left. Both knobs are also, in most cases (check your scope's instruction booklet or inside the dial caps), graduated in click stops with each click representing an angle of .25 minute (at 100 yards, 1 minute of angle is 1 inch). Therefore, for example, if slugs are consistently printing 1 inch high at 100 yards (which is 2 inches below the desired point of impact) and 4 inches to the left of point of aim, the shooter would turn the elevation knob "up" by eight clicks and then he would turn the windage knob to the "right" sixteen clicks.

Good advice when making these fine-tuning adjustments is to shoot from a bench-rest position with the weapon cradled securely in sandbags to ensure that it is perfectly steady at all times. You can make such sandbags yourself in little time; all you need are a few scraps of discarded canvas or denim and a quick trip to your local beach. Also, since the slightest amount of extraneous movement may drastically influence the point of impact of any particular shot, most hunters fire three-shot groups for each aiming adjustment. Of course, the closer to each other those three shots print, 3 inches high of point of aim at 100 yards, the better.

You'll read of shooters regularly making ½-inch and ¼-inch groups. But I have my suspicions that most of these are shot with typewriters rather than by whitetail hunters with their deer rifles. If through practice and patience you can consistently achieve 1½-inch groups at 100 yards, with occasional 1-inch and ¾-inch groups now and then to further bolster your confidence, have no worry. You'll eat venison this winter!

Finally, every deer-hunting rifle should be outfitted with a leather sling. There are many types, but I like those with extra-wide straps because they stay on the shoulder better and do not cut into the skin (which can be important in warmer climes where heavy hunting jackets are not usually worn).

There are two distinct advantages to a rifle equipped with a sling. The weapon can be shouldered, which allows free use of the hands when navigating steep terrain, carrying into the field a portable tree stand, or dragging out a deer. And the hunter can use the sling to help steady the weapon when making shots from the offhand, kneeling, or sitting positions. Place the elbow of your gun-holding arm between the sling and the rifle. By swinging the elbow out against the sling you'll tighten it against the back of the upper arm, affording much more weapon stability.

10

Shotgunning for Whitetails

Shotguns are playing an increasingly prominent role in whitetail hunting, especially throughout the East, South, and Midwest. The main reason is that increasing population density, suburban sprawl, and a renewed trend toward rural living have prompted many states to rewrite their hunting laws in favor of supposedly safer shotguns, which do not have the effective distance of high-powered rifles; the maximum range of a 12-gauge slug fired at a 30-degree angle of elevation is only 2400 feet. As this is being written, nine Eastern and five Midwestern states strictly forbid the use of high-powered rifles for deer hunting.

Deer hunters who are by law required to use smoothbores should know, however, that just any old rabbit plunker, upland bird piece, or waterfowl gun may be totally inadequate for deer. Okay then, what kind of shotgun *is* best for deer hunting? Well, that is a many-faceted question which can best be answered by systematically eliminating a number of variables, so let's look at everything pertaining to shotguns in a categorical sense.

USE THE BIGBORES

I noted in the chapter on deer rifles that the first order of business should be selecting a suitable caliber. The same consideration should be given shotguns with regards to their various gauges.

In shotgunning, it is the slug's energy we count upon to drop a deer. And contrary to popular belief, the .410, which is the smallest gauge manufactured, will indeed kill a whitetail. But on the other hand, so will a few well-placed swats with a ball-peen hammer if you can get in close enough. With a .410 the hunter must be within extremely close range—not more than 25 yards—and he must be able to place his round precisely. That is a feat not many are able to execute when some snorting patriarch of the bush jumps unexpectedly from his bed and makes a zigzag escape flight through jumbled undergrowth with rockets on his heels.

The .410 rifled slug weighs only $^1/_5$ ounce, and at 75 yards it is pushing along ("lumbering" is probably a better word) with only 250 foot-pounds of energy. I have a pal who tongue-in-cheek claims that at 100 yards he can "shag" a .410 slug with a catcher's mitt! This is an exaggeration, of course, but because the .410 is so grossly deficient it is an illegal load in most states; even if there are no such restrictions in your locale, please don't attempt to use this peashooter for whitetails.

The 28-gauge is the next size larger in which rifled slugs are available (you'll have to search long and hard), but like the .410 it too will only result in many crippled deer left in the woods. Use the 28 with appropriate shotshell loads for woodcock, quail, snipe, and other diminutive quarry, not for game that may easily tip the balance at 175 pounds or better.

It is very wrong, but a large number of misguided hunters will this year also use 20-gauge shotguns for deer hunting. Some of them may luck out and kill deer with close-in shots, but the 20 is incapable of throwing a slug a reasonable distance while still retaining the punch needed to mortally wound a whitetail. It is true that with a ⅝-ounce slug and 2¾-inch shell (the standard loading) the 20-gauge has the same velocity as the 12-gauge (with standard load consisting of ⅞-ounce slug and 2¾-inch shell). *But at 100 yards the 20-gauge has retained only slightly more than half the foot-pounds of energy as the 12-gauge.* Most arms experts agree

Not all shotguns are necessarily good deer guns, although the particular model you have may well be. Try it and see. Twelve gauge is best and if you can hit the target at 50 yards the gun is probably okay. The next step is to add better sights and experiment with different brands of slugs. This is Ed Linscott, checking how well his grouse gun performs with slugs.

that any shot over 50 yards is a very long one for a 20-gauge shotgun.

Shaking out on top, then, as the most effective bores for shotgun deer hunting are the 16-gauge and 12-gauge. The 16-gauge (the standard load consists of ¾-ounce slug and 2¾-inch shell) offers 2175 foot-pounds of energy at the muzzle (more than the .30/30 caliber rifle!), and the 12-gauge commands a walloping 2485 foot-pounds. Both, although they come from the muzzle at only 1600 feet per second, are capable of extending a hunter's larcenous intentions out to slightly more than 100 yards, though barely so. Inside this range, however, they possess more than enough clout to cleanly kill any deer; by comparison, at 50 yards a 12-gauge slug packs nearly as much energy as a 150-grain .30/06 bullet.

Some hunters, likely those who are also gun collectors, may even wish to hunt whitetails with 10-gauge shotguns. These are entirely suitable, because of the substantial foot-pounds of energy they offer, but a major problem is that rifled slugs are difficult to obtain. The hunter usually has to "roll his own," or order them special, and so for this reason alone 10-gauges are not among the recommended shotguns.

In summary, there is little doubt that the 16-gauge and 12-gauge are far and away the very best choices for shotgun deer hunting. And the one you have, or are contemplating buying, may prove to be the most lethal medicine ever unleashed against whitetails in your area. On the other hand, it may be a real turkey. So read on.

CONSIDER SHOTGUN ACTIONS

The first scattergun I attempted to use for deer, although more years ago than seems possible, is not difficult to remember. It was a break-open single-shot with no significant value other than countless invested memories afield. But things like nostalgia count for little when face to face with whitetails.

Sure, with the break-open single I was able to "drive tacks" from 50 paces on the firing range, and had a mentally retarded buck stepped before my paper targets it would have been his last mistake. In the field, however, shooting conditions are seldom the same as those on the range, and the single-shot had three drawbacks which serve as worthy enough rationalizations as to why the two of us never brought home venison.

For one, the hammer had to be cocked by hand, and it always fell into its ready position with a highly audible metallic click that was sure to spook any whitetail mincing along the trail to my stand. The barrel, characteristic of most singles, was also much too long, and swinging its 32-inch length in the juniper and scrub-oak tangles where I often jumped deer was a near impossibility. And of course I had only one shot. That first and only round expended and resulting in a clean miss allowed any deer yet within range to give me a good snorting raspberry and still have time to disappear through the cover before I was able to extract the spent hull, chamber a fresh load, cock the hammer again, and aim.

Fortunately, I realized all of these deficiencies at a malleable age and soon gave up all hopes of any break-open single ever being a suitable deer shotgun. Yet even to this year I still see many of the same types of weapons hanging on gun racks in deer camps, their owners clinging tenaciously to the less than probable hope that Old Betsy will do the job on a trophy buck. Some of these hunters will take home deer meat, but they're the few lucky ones that also win all the poker money. Otherwise, the odds are surely not in their favor. Then too, there are the legions of proud fathers who anxiously await the eventful day when their sons or daughters kill their first deer. Unknowingly, many of them greatly reduce the possibility beforehand by handing them a single-shot. Or worse yet, a .410 or 20-gauge, which cripple more deer than they ever cleanly kill.

I also tried using a double-barrel as a deer shotgun. I'd start the hunting season in hot pursuit of upland gamebirds and small game, for which purpose the side-by-side was ideally suited. And I savored the anticipation of opening day of the deer season because now I had a relatively short-barreled weapon and *two rounds* available if the buck of my dreams materialized before my stand. But I'd made a poor choice again.

It is a basic nature of slugs fired from doubles to "cross over" during their trajectories, partly because of the canted way in which the barrels are married to the receiver and partly because the twin tubes nearly always possess different chokes.

In my particular side-by-side, for example, which I guess is fairly representative of most that are around these days, the right barrel, bored "modified," sent slugs as much as 8 inches to the left of point of aim. From the left tube, bored "full choke," slugs printed as much as 11 inches to the right of point of aim! Now I suppose a mind quicker than mine could make rapid calculations and then compensate for these shooting vagaries. But I am of the notion that deer hunting is tough enough without penalizing yourself with a gun that doesn't shoot where you aim. In fact, the idea is so hairy that I wouldn't want to even be in the vicinity of someone using a double.

I did see one season of success with the side-by-side, though, in the South, where buckshot, not slugs, has been used for nearly seventy-five years. Typically, buckshot loads with their garden-hose spraying effect are devastatingly lethal out to about 40 yards but highly inaccurate when used beyond this range.

To some extent, it may be argued, buckshot loads have been improved in recent years. Regarding efficiency, hunters now know that magnum fodder tremendously outperforms standard loadings. Also, there seems to be a definite trend away from the historically favored 00 buckshot to No. 1 pellets. When the shot is buried in a type of polyethylene powder called "grex," as most manufacturers are now doing to lessen flattening of the shot during its passage down the tube, accuracy and effectiveness have been extended to about 50 yards. Despite published opinion, however, full-choke barrels do not always yield the best patterns, as in many cases the tubes are actually overchoked for the big balls; nearly always, a modified choke is better.

But despite these changes for the better, using buckshot or any other similar shot-pellet loading for deer must still be classified as a very short-range proposition, and a dangerous one at that when other hunters are in the immediate vicinity. Resultantly, the use of shot loadings for deer is gradually being outlawed in most regions of the country, even in the South where years of heritage have seen hunters waiting on stand, listening to the singing sounds of hounds trailing whitetails through jungles of palmetto and swampland hardwood. Presently, there are *no* states where hunters are required by law to use buckshot. Fourteen other states, where shot loadings are still permitted, nevertheless "recommend" the use of single projectiles instead. And twenty-three states (where only shotguns are legal) absolutely forbid the use of shot.

Another variation of the double-barrel shotgun, the over/ under, presents similar crossover problems with regard to throwing slugs. I have tested only a few of these weapons but in all have noted that slugs emanating from the lower barrel seem to print consistently high and those from the upper barrel seem to print consisently low.

Bolt-action shotguns are a step in the right direction, but unless the hunter already owns a bolt-action, I can't advise going this route either. It is a rocky road, because arms manufacturers, in my opinion, have not devoted their engineering expertise to bolt-action shotguns as they have to their line of bolt-action centerfire rifles. There may be many reasons for this, but it's probably because of the very low demand for bolt-actions for any kind of smoothbore hunting.

Then there were the autoloaders I tried during the course of several seasons in my continuing search for the ideal deer shotgun. The lessons I learned were equally pleasant and disastrous. Of the favorable qualities, autoloader barrels can be had in relatively short lengths (20 to 26 inches), and this means such shotguns are

Every shotgun has a personality all its own and will throw various brands of slugs with wide degrees of accuracy, so experiment to find out which your shotgun likes best. Shown here are the most popular. From left to right are the Winchester Western Super-X; Smith and Wesson sabot-riding slug; Remington Express; Brenneke; and finally, a 12-gauge loading of buckshot which the author feels should be made illegal because of its gardenhose spraying effect.

easy to maneuver in heavy cover and tight quarters. And up to five rounds are available, all of them pushing through the same choke and thereby printing as consistently as can be expected of a shotgun. Most, stripped down, come in around 8 pounds, so when the firearm is fully outfitted the hunter has not too heavy a piece to carry afield.

But overnight, in one deer camp I was privileged to share, the mercury dipped to minus 10 degrees and the gun's inner workings slowed to a molasses-like crawl. Eventually the damn thing froze up altogether. At another camp, with another autoloader, I slipped one day on slushy snow and fell face-down upon forest duff. From then on the auto never functioned properly until after I had entirely disassembled and cleaned every moving part (that deal cost me one fine buck). So it is not likely that I will ever again wait twelve long months for the opening of the deer season, spend the time, energy, and money to travel to some distant hunting locale, and then depend solely upon an autoloader to see me through hard use and frigid weather. A few others who hunt in milder climes and under less abusive conditions, however, tell me they have few problems with their autoloaders.

It should not be difficult to guess that my search for the elusive best-suited deer shotgun next led me to the pumpgun category. The one I purchased was a real peach. It was short and light, offered a five-round capacity, and was quite accurate at the longer ranges. And the manual slide mechanism was unfailing, even under adverse weather conditions and in the presence of quantities of debris which usually manage to find their way into the internal components of any firearm during long hunts. Not surprisingly, those companies that make special deer shotguns (which are discussed later) do so in greater quantity in pumpgun design. Second in popularity are the autoloaders.

We are narrowing the field. Of the collection of shotguns any avid hunter may have in his gun rack, only those of 16 gauge or 12 gauge, and only those of autoloader or pumpgun design, are worth still further consideration. And in my opinion, the 12-gauge pumpgun heads the list. But let's look at a few other things that will also have their critically important influences.

WHAT TYPE SLUG AND CHOKE?

Unlike a high-powered rifle that has spiraled lands and grooves on the inner surface of its barrel, which impart spin to the smooth-surfaced bullet and so are responsible for bullet stability during its trajectory, a shotgun barrel, and the slug that emanates from it, works on a slightly different principle.

In order to achieve shotgun-slug stability, since the inner barrel surface of a shotgun is smooth, manufacturers have had to specially design the slug itself. In most cases, this means that the spin-imparting lands and grooves (or what are sometimes, in the case of shotgun slugs, called "fins") have been molded into the soft lead slug itself. But also, most shotgun slugs these days, such as those made by Winchester and Remington, take on the appearance of a weighty round-nose design with a hollow base, a configuration which (in cooperation with the "fins") is said to prevent the slug from tumbling during its flight.

However, there are other shotgun slug designs, too, which afford comparable stability, such as the German-made Brenneke slug, which is more squared-off at the nose, is cylindrical in length, and has a fiber "stabilizing wad" attached to its base. A slug recently discontinued but still in good supply on many dealers' shelves is the Smith & Wesson sabot-riding shotgun slug, which looks like an hourglass-shaped rocket housed between two protective plastic sleeves inside the hull, that fall away the same as a shot-pellet cup when the slug leaves the barrel.

The performance of any shotgun slug is largely regulated by the amount of choke in the barrel, but also to a certain degree by the peculiarities of the shotgun itself. Allow me to explain.

Of all the chokes available in shotgun barrels, cylinder or improved cylinder is the best. It should be mentioned that a hunter can shoot slugs from any choke without worrying about damaging his firearm, because like a load of shot pellets a shotgun slug constricts as it passes through the muzzle. But the greater the choke the more the slug's soft lead stabilizing fins must compress as the slug negotiates the narrowed fore section of the tube and consequently the less accurate the slug is likely to be. With minimal choke constriction, however, the flight of the slug is less impeded and accuracy invariably better.

Regarding specific brand names of slugs and their characteristic designs, my extensive tests have revealed that all are excellent, but that the particular slug you should use is a decision you should allow your shotgun to make. It sounds terribly unscientific, but from my experience every smoothbore has a personality all its own and will therefore throw certain brands of slugs better than others.

For example, my friend Russ Thomas owns a Winchester pumpgun and with Brenneke slugs he can't hit a washtub at 50 yards. But the instant he switches to Remington slugs he's able to clip wings off gnats at substantially beyond that distance. His brother Ron chases after whitetails with a Savage autoloader, and he swears that Brenneke slugs are the best thing to come down the pike since beer, girls, and pizza (not necessarily in that order). I own two Ithaca shotguns, one in pumpgun design and the other an autoloader, yet the pump is most accurate with Super-X slugs and the autoloader insists upon Remingtons.

So it's always a good practice to invest in several boxes of slugs by different manufacturers and then spend an afternoon on the target range. It shouldn't be too long before it becomes readily apparent that your shotgun shoots one brand far more accurately than the others.

The hunter who has a 16-gauge or 12-gauge autoloader or pumpgun, with a bore that is as wide open as possible, plus several boxes of slugs by different manufacturers, can at this stage, on the target range, make a final determination as to whether his shotgun is suitable for deer hunting.

Here is what to look for. With a standard shotgun bead sight you should expect 6-inch groups at 50 yards, 10-inch groups at 75 yards, and 18-inch groups at 100 yards. If your shotgun is capable of this, or nearly so, using only a front bead sight, you can be fairly confident that later adding a rifle-type sight or scope (which I'll discuss shortly) will enable you to get far better groups at the same yardages. Remember, of course, to shoot from a bench-rest position during this test period so that extraneous movement doesn't influence your firearm's performance.

But let's say you've tried a variety of slugs by different companies and your shotgun just doesn't want to consistently send them anywhere near where you aim; you're getting "flyers" on almost every other shot. If that is the case, which is very common and probably due to too much choke in your muzzle, there are three alternatives.

Those on a very tight budget may elect to have a gunsmith simply cut down the muzzle of the barrel by several inches (or you can do the work yourself). It's a hacksaw job to be sure, but a little sanding with emery paper and then a touch-up on the bluing will patch it up. Cutting down the length of the barrel removes the choke, leaving an open (but permanently altered) tube. According to Al Wolter, who recently performed such surgery on his Remington autoloader (which was previously bored modified), slug accuracy immediately jumped from "disgraceful" to "amazing."

SPECIAL DEER SHOTGUNS

The second alternative might be the purchase of an interchangeable slug barrel for your present shotgun. This will allow you to retain the weapon's dual-purpose function (for example,

The serious whitetail hunter will probably want to eventually own a specialized deer shotgun. These are made especially for deer hunting and render far better performance than makeshift rabbit guns that have undergone a facelift. Here, Al Wolter displays the author's deer shotgun. It's a 12-gauge Ithaca Deerslayer, in pump-action, with Bausch and Lomb 2–8× variable power scope. Additional features include leather sling, recoil pad, receiver-dovetail for mounting scope, and special rifle-type sights for those who prefer not to use the scope.

the capability of throwing slugs through an open bore when deer hunting but then at any other time switching back to, perhaps, your full-choke tube for goose hunting).

Interchangeable slug barrels are available for most of the popular makes of pumpguns and autoloaders, such as those made by Winchester, Remington, Mossberg, Browning, and so on (for other makes of firearms, contact the manufacturer or your local gun dealer to find out if slug barrels are available—they probably are). In most cases, slug barrels cost about 40 percent of the total cost of the shotgun, and they can be installed yourself in a few minutes with no special tools.

Upon first inspection you'll quickly notice that a slug barrel is different in appearance from a conventional scattergun tube. One thing is that it is very likely to be somewhat shorter; most slug barrels average 20 to 24 inches in length, which does not appreciably affect long-distance accuracy but does make the gun lighter and quicker. Another noticeable difference is that instead of a small bead sight near the muzzle and nothing toward the receiver you'll get special rifle-type sights. These usually consist of a front elevated sight on a ramp and some variation of adjustable notched rear sight—a combination, like the open sights on high-powered rifles, that allows for at least passable accuracy to 75 yards or so. One thing you won't be able to notice, but it's there, is that the inside of the barrel's length is of a special open boring which perfectly accommodates rifled slugs, and it is this feature that is most responsible for its accuracy.

The third alternative is the purchase of a special deer shotgun. These are made for the express purpose of deer hunting, nothing else, and thereby eliminate the need for annually performing a facelift on some cherished fowling piece. The weapons are light (between 7 and 8 pounds) and equipped with slug barrels ranging in length from 20 to 26 inches. They have rifle-type sights and often boast other extras as well, such as sling swivels, recoil pads, and receiver or rear-barrel-mounted dovetails for those who wish to install scopes on their weapons for even better accuracy at the longer ranges.

The Deerslayer, made by Ithaca and available in both pumpgun and autoloading actions (in 12 gauge), is one of the most popular makes, as Ithaca was the first to pioneer the field of deer shotguns. According to an independent testing laboratory the Deerslayer, at bench rest, is able to produce slug groups measuring 7 inches by 5 inches at 100 yards! I have conducted further tests with both Deerslayer models and a variety of telescopic sights. Using a 4× glass and shooting from the bench, I have been able to group slugs in a 10-inch bull at 130 yards. With a 7× scope, at the bench, I've been able to achieve 13-inch groups at 150 yards.

A word of caution, however! Keep in mind that this is only "circus shooting." Regardless of whatever accuracy you may be able to achieve on the target range, it counts for little in the field, because a shotgun slug, energy-wise, diminishes very rapidly. Shooting at a deer 100 yards away is a long poke for any shotgun. And even if the firearm is one of the special deer shotguns equipped with a scope, it's my belief you should personally set an absolute maximum shooting distance of no more than 125 yards. Whitetails are a highly renewable resource but they are nevertheless much too valuable to waste. And this is exactly what happens when hunters bust caps at ranges beyond their shotgun's clean-kill capabilities.

Other deer shotguns which have only more recently found their way onto the market include the Remington Model 870 Brushmaster, the Browning Buck Special, the Marlin 55, the Savage Model 30, and the H&R Topper Buck. All of these as well are superb (by shotgun standards) in regards to accuracy and handling; their most significant differences lie only in aesthetic features, and therefore price.

SIGHTS AND SIGHTING IN

Once a hunter has selected a shotgun for deer hunting, he should next give serious thought to the type of sight that is likely to prove best under those conditions he usually hunts. The open rifle-type sights that come on slug barrels and special deer shotgun barrels are certainly much better than conventional shotgun bead sights. But even better are any of the many peep-sight variations available, such as those by the Williams Gun Sight Company or the Redding Gun Sight Company. Or you may want to investigate the Quik-Point shotgun sight made by the Weaver Company, or the Single-Point shotgun sight by the Normark Corporation. Both of these look somewhat like elevated scopes, they readily attach to any gun's receiver, and they project a fluorescent orange dot into infinity; this dot subtends 8 inches at 50 yards and is extremely fast to center on the target under low-light conditions and when the cover is heavy.

But I am one of those apparently few hunters who insist that some type of telescopic sight be mounted on my shotgun's receiver, regardless of whether I'm using an improved-cylinder "rabbit gun," a smoothbore that has been graced with an interchangeable slug barrel, or one of the special deer shotguns. As in the case of high-powered rifles, scopes offer several advantages over all other sights, one of which is far better accuracy at ranges of 75 to 125 yards, and another of which is the ability to find shooting alleys through the cover to lessen the chance of a slug being deflected. Also, as I noted in the previous chapter, scopes afford light-gathering help, which is invaluable when the cover is dense or light is poor.

Since smoothbores are short-range firearms, a scope used for shotgun deer hunting should have a wide field of view, and this is most easily accomplished by using either a very low-power scope or one of the wide-angle varieties. Many hunters like the 1.5× scopes which only very slightly magnify the image but do offer light-gathering help and better accuracy at the longer ranges; this, however, is a fixed-magnification scope. But I again lean toward the variable-power wide-angle scopes (an excellent example is 1.5–3×), because when a shot presents itself at the longest ranges of which a shotgun is capable, and when I'm able to assume a steady rest position, I like to use something in the range of 2½× to 3×. Yet this is nothing more than personal preference.

An adequate deer shotgun and sight combination decided upon, the final and most important effort should involve becoming exactingly familiar with the combination.

I know former high-powered rifle hunters, for example, who upon moving to some state (or taking out-of-state hunting trips) where shotguns are required initially find difficulty converting to smoothbores because of the substantial "loop" of shotgun slugs along their trajectory. At 100 yards, a ⅞-ounce slug from a 12-gauge shotgun will drop slightly more than 10 inches, and a ¾-ounce slug from a 16-gauge will drop almost 15 inches.

This makes a good case in favor of plenty of practice on the firing range before opening day. Look at it this way. Deer hunting always requires an investment of not only time but a good chunk of change. There are clothing and equipment purchases every hunter must make, of course, and the cost of the license. Then there are long days spent in the field scouting for concentrations of deer sign and then building a stand. Yet all of these preparatory arrangements may be for naught if the hunter is unable to use his firearm quickly and accurately. It's as simple as that.

I won't hesitate to say that of all my hunting-related expenditures, the money paid out for at least fifty or a hundred practice slugs at the outset of each new season represents one of my most important investments.

With any shotgun variation in which rifle-type sights or peep sights are to be used, practice at 25, 50, and 80 yards. If you're using a slug barrel, or one of the special deer shotguns, and either is equipped with a scope, you'll also want to know how your shotgun performs at 100 and 125 yards.

My Deerslayers are sighted in to hit 5 inches high at 75 yards (using scopes). They are about 3 inches low at 100 yards, and about 7 inches low at 125 yards. But these are only personal preferences; with your chosen shotgun and sight combination, some other formula might be more to your liking.

There are many gun enthusiasts who stalwartly proclaim that shotguns are worthless for deer hunting, and there is no argument from me that such guns are far from ideal. But each year hundreds of thousands of hunters do indeed take fine bucks with smoothbores, and if the present trend of population expansion continues we can probably expect still more states to outlaw the use of high-powered rifles. With no choice in the matter, all it takes from there is a realistic appraisal of what shotguns can and cannot do, an understanding of which types of shotguns yield the best performance, a good sight, and plenty of practice with the right kind of slugs.

Practiced Hunters Get Their Bucks

The location was Winconsin's Chequamegon National Forest, and I cannot recall more miserable weather.

Twelve inches of new-fallen snow, with drifts to 5 feet, are more than enough to test the mettle of the most enthusiastic of hunters, and they likewise have the effect of greatly restricting all wildlife activity. That meant trail-watching had become an exercise in futility.

"My feet are five-toed blocks of ice," I moaned to my partner, Ted Williams (not the former baseball player), when we rendezvoused at a designated location for a noontime break. "And in this wind my wool jacket feels like a sieve. I hereby cast my vote in favor of going back to camp and spending the rest of the day poking the fire and nursing a few glasses of Old Scalplifter."

"We have to get a buck before any of that," Ted answered encouragingly, reaching into his daypack for a thermos and lunch

When a handsome buck like this busts out of the cover, any hunter could get lucky and score a good shot. But a hunter who has practiced stands a far better chance.

bag. ''And since the deer aren't moving around on their own, I suggest a cooperative still-hunt. Not far away there is a low, swampy area where cedars and brush are protected from the wind by surrounding hillsides and thick stands of balsams. The hike over there will warm us up, and I'm sure one of us will get some shooting.''

Next, Ted scratched out a map in the snow, explaining to me the logistics of the proposed maneuver. With our strategy agreed upon we then loaded up and began tramping off in the direction of the morass. It was not long before I was once again feeling the warm glow and fast pulse of typical deer-hunting excitement. Sensitivity was returning to my feet. The wind's whistling assault was now, somehow, more tolerable. The sandwiches and steaming hot coffee had been good revitalizing agents. Yet neither of us had the slightest notion that for Ted the hunt would be over only twenty minutes later, and that I, moreover, would be filling my own deer tag shortly after that.

We had just stepped inside the leading edge of the expansive marsh, spaced only 75 yards apart because of the upside-down

cover, when unexpectedly, just in front of and between us, powdered snow in the middle of a blowdown exploded as if someone
had lobbed in a hand grenade. I reflexively jumped backward out
of startled surprise, failing even to flip off my rifle's safety.

It was a buck! A fat six-pointer, and he came straight up through
the felled tree's twisted branches like a Polaris missile, his after-
burner wide open and his gray matter pumping explicit orders to
go anyplace else, but do it fast! The deer touched down on the
other side of the blowdown and in less time than it takes to tell was
airborne again, this time in an attempt to clear a hedge of waist-
high huckleberry bushes.

Even if I had been alert, the acute quartering-away angle of the
deer's departure would have meant a very chancy shot. But Ted
was in good position and I heard his rifle crack. The shot took the
deer high in the ribs and it literally collapsed in flight, as a grouse
folds when a pattern of shot pellets has found its mark.

I remember us next plowing through the snow full steam ahead,
Ted shattering the cold air with the familiar warwhoop he always
bawls when a good buck is down for keeps, and me pounding him
on the back with congratulatory slaps that almost brought him to
his knees. When we reached the deer, only 40 paces away, it was
stone dead.

A very lucky shot? Well, there is probably a certain element of
luck in every successful kill, especially when shots are taken at
animals that are really hauling the mail. But Ted's shot was acceptable to him because it was at very close range, the deer was
perfectly broadside to him, and he was ready. All of those
qualifications therefore made the attempt a far less risky one than if
I had started blasting away. But maybe having an even greater
influence, Ted regularly engages in several specific types of preseason practice for shots identical to this one or others he most
frequently is given.

With the two of us at work, field-dressing the animal took only
five minutes. Then we propped open its chest cavity with sticks and
washed our hands in the snow. Since the cold temperature offered
a tailor-made deep freeze to cool and preserve the meat, we
decided to simply leave the buck where it lay. Ted said the swamp
was sure to contain other deer because it offered the only source of
concentrated food and major security cover anywhere in the area,

and under the present weather conditions that would serve as a natural drawing card for every whitetail in the vicinity.

"Let's continue to sneak-hunt," he advised. "We'll work the thickets and blowdowns with you always on the high side to be in position for the shot if any deer bust out. At the end of the day the shortest route back to camp will mean retracing our footsteps and we can retrieve my deer on the way."

I would not have believed it possible, but only 200 yards from where Ted killed his buck six more deer bounded from a small depression as if they had been hurled by catapults. Five were does, and running with them was a buck with one of the highest racks I have ever seen.

I desperately tried to find that deer in my scope, but the trophy was dodging left and right around small cedars while at the same time going up and down through the deep snow as if he was strapped to a coil spring. I do not know how that buck managed it, but there was always at least one bouncing doe between the two of us, protecting his hide from my line of sight.

Finally when all of the deer vanished over a small rise I lowered my rifle and before or since cannot recall feeling more depressed. Reflecting back, however, a round fired would have definitely been an Annie Oakley shot at best; banging away might have enabled me to collect that buck but there was the probability of only crippling him or hitting one of the illegal she-deer.

I like to think my decision not to shoot was rewarded with a consolation prize, because not long after that episode I spotted a perfectly respectable forkhorn buck pacing slowly along the edge of a white pine plantation.

"Mister, you have problems you can't even begin to imagine," I silently said to the buck, raising my bolt-action, centering the cross-hairs on his lungs, and remembering the dozens of times I had made this exact kind of shot during preseason shooting exercises. The 6mm Remington barked with the sharpness of breaking glass and the young buck could not have dropped more quickly if he had fallen off the edge of the world. The distance was 75 yards, and at the very instant the deer fell I heard Ted's victory yelp the second time that day.

Both of those bucks were killed by shots that hunters enjoy recounting for years to come, preferably around a fireside with an attentive audience present. Yet seldom, as evidenced by this

Taking a stable "rest" position offers pinpoint sight pictures, and a rest should be taken whenever possible. But since most encounters with deer are unexpected, learn to shoot offhand. The sights will wobble at first but that is what practice is all about.

particular Chequamegon Forest adventure, is the distance involved an important or emphasized point of the storytelling, at least as far as an increasing number of whitetail scouts are concerned. You'll hear them just as often tell of shots they made at 50 yards as at 250, and with considerable pride, provided that they resulted in quick, clean kills. But you won't hear much bragging from the man who gut-shot his deer, even if it was a fine buck he eventually recovered. Nor will too many dwell upon the deer that should never have been shot at in the first place and were only wounded and got away, or ones that were so mutilated by misplaced shots that their choicest cuts of venison were suitable for little other than sausage and stew meat.

There are probably as many reasons for missed shots at deer as there are embarrassed hunters every fall and winter, and perhaps just as many explanations for shots that tragically result only in maimed deer or too much prime meat needlessly wasted. But the most common are undoubtedly direct results of the hunter's failure to engage in the right kinds of sufficient shooting practice prior to the hunting season, his inability to judge distance when shooting at stationary deer, or his inability to calculate the proper lead when shooting at moving targets. And still other important reasons (covered in the next chapter) are his lack of knowledge of the deer's anatomy and therefore where to place his shot, or, indeed, *when not to shoot,* and nervousness or inaccurate aiming that are the products of "buck fever" or flinching.

In the field, one exercise that should continue through all forms of practice is learning to accurately estimate distances, which can be very deceptive in various types of cover, across irregular terrain, and under various lighting conditions.

You may well be equipped to bring down a whitetail at 300 yards with your chosen centerfire rifle, but how far *is* 300 yards? And, more specifically, is that deer 300 yards away, or is the distance really closer to 450?

I noted in the chapter on shotguns that under no circumstances should shots be taken beyond 125 yards, even when using 12-gauge slugs and special deer shotguns equipped with scopes, because of the reduced velocity of slugs beyond that range and their beer-belly trajectories. So is the deer you're centering cross-hairs upon within the 125-yard shooting capability of your shotgun? Or is the distance closer to 160 yards? If it is the latter, and you attempt the shot, you'll probably either miss or cripple.

The best way to learn to estimate distances is by doing it. You'll hear some hunters claim they can estimate distances by the length of shadows cast by objects at certain times of day, or by learning to estimate 25 yards to the inch and then "guesstimating" farther ranges in 25-yard increments from one intervening object to another, and there are probably dozens of other techniques as well.

But I've found the best way is simply to pick out some object in the field, carefully judge the distance, and then actually pace it off. My stride is about a yard, but I'm long-legged; your stride may be somewhat less. So simply walk a short distance where your footprints are visible and then with a ruler figure the average distance between each step. Then in the field estimate and pace off yardages uphill and down, through dense cover, and especially spend

A valuable type of practice is shooting at paper deer targets. Make sure you have a safe backdrop. This allows for simulated shooting of the same type as you'll be doing when the season opens. Bowhunters shoot at deer targets religiously; gunners should do so as well if they want to better their chances of collecting venison.

some time estimating distances under low light levels such as at dawn or dusk when depth perception is usually impaired.

SHOOTING OFFHAND

The types of shooting positions I most diligently practice are those in which I'm either standing or sitting, and from both positions I shoot offhand. The case may be different for any other hunter, depending upon the types of whitetail hunting he enjoys most. But 80 percent of my hunting is accomplished by sitting in a tree stand (watching a trail or scrapes, or being a stander during a drive). The other 20 percent of the time I'm on the ground and moving (either as a driver, or during the course of still-hunting).

If another hunter predominantly works more open country in which deer are first glassed from long distances and then stalked, and then a shot is usually made from the prone position, then prone-position practice shooting might take precedence. On the other hand, if a hunter prefers to watch trails from a ground-level blind, he'll probably want to emphasize shooting practice from squatting, sitting, or kneeling positions.

But whatever the actual shooting position, I strongly urge the hunter to do the bulk of his practice firing offhand.

This is not to contradict the age-old and worthy advice, when actually hunting, of taking a "rest" position whenever possible, as this affords tremendous weapon stability and pinpoint sight pictures when aiming. Using a rest might mean bracing your shoulder against a tree trunk, grabbing onto a sapling with the hand and then laying the forearm of the stock over the wrist region, supporting the rifle-holding hand and backarm on a rock, log, or stump, or perhaps even cradling the stock of the firearm on a rolled-up coat or across a light backpack.

But whatever the situation, it is never wise to sacrifice the "quality" of the shot for whatever increased firearm stability might be gained by using a rest.

Let's say, for instance, that you are still-hunting and suddenly spot a buck 100 yards away. The cover is rather open, affording you almost no concealment. At the moment the deer is totally unaware of your presence. You have a choice. You can very slowly raise your rifle to your shoulder and shoot offhand at a stationary, unsuspecting animal; or you can attempt to move slowly a few yards to one side or the other to where you can drop to a prone position so you can lay your rifle across a log for a very stable rest, but in so doing likely be faced with a shot at an animal now almost certainly alerted to your presence and bounding away through the woods. Obviously, taking the offhand shot at the stationary deer is a better bet.

So regarding rest positions, the best rule to follow is to by all means make use of a rest, *if* you can assume the particular rest position quickly, quietly, and with a minimum of movement so as not to alert or spook your quarry. But since this will not be possible or practical most of the time, encounters with deer usually being of an unexpected nature, devote most of your practice to offhand shooting. The cross-hairs in your scope will wobble at first and acquiring steadiness will take time. But that is what practice is all about, and the reason for it.

Offhand accuracy will come more quickly if you learn to concentrate upon what you are doing and control your breathing. For me, the best method is to think very seriously about the estimated

Hitting deer on the run involves learning how to lead a moving target. At 100 yards, a deer running flat out at 30 mph would require about 8 or 9 feet of lead.

yardage and simultaneously the sight picture that range requires, and to check with the side of my index finger to ensure that I've taken the rifle's safety off. Then I inhale (but not too deeply), allow half of my breath to escape, hold my breath from that point on, and very slowly s-q-u-e-e-z-e the trigger. But whatever the *modus operandi*—and it may vary among individuals—there is simply no substitute for practice shooting under simulated hunting conditions, shooting a little bit more, and then shooting some more after that.

Exactly how much shooting is necessary depends upon the experience and expertise of each hunter. But always, any kind of practice yields more beneficial results when taken in small doses over a period of time. In other words, much better than shooting for eight hours one day just before the opening of the season would be to shoot for half an hour a day for sixteen days before the season.

SIMULATED SHOOTING

Several times I've mentioned "simulated shooting," and now is a good time to clarify exactly what this means. It means shooting under those terrain and cover conditions you expect to encounter when hunting deer and at targets that in some way further resemble what you'll later be shooting at for real.

I like to obtain life-size paper deer targets, which are available in most sporting goods stores (don't get the kind with bull's-eyes on the front of them). A curious thing about life-size or silhouette deer targets is that bowhunters use them religiously but gun hunters almost not at all; the reader can draw his own implications as to why this is so, but I sincerely believe the "average" bowhunter is a better deer hunter than the "average" gunner, because he is much better practiced and spends far more time afield engaging in simulated shooting with his chosen equipment.

With a small stapler I attach my paper deer targets to upright stakes, brush, between saplings, and so on. Then I practice shooting at the targets with the rifle or shotgun I'll be using during the upcoming deer season and from as many different angles and positions as I can conceive. I shoot at them from uphill and downhill positions, across hollows and small canyons, across large and small clearings, through dense cover (this gives me practice in picking out holes or shooting lanes), and from quartering-away, broadside, and quartering-forward angles. While most of the practice is either from a standing or sitting position, some is also from my portable tree stand about 12 feet above the ground, with deer targets at various distances around me, and all of the shots, of course, are taken offhand.

HITTING THEM ON THE RUN

I've been talking about shooting practice and what I have said so far has dealt primarily with stationary targets. Now and then, however, there may be opportunities for shots at deer on the move, and I very heartily recommend rolling-tire shoots as one of the best ways to practice for hitting deer on the run.

Very simply, two hunters gather half a dozen discarded tire casings (you can get them for free at the city dump or county landfill). Cardboard inserts can easily be fashioned for the tires to register the placement of shots. Then one of the hunters rolls the tires, one at a time, down any steep or gently sloping hillside where safe shooting is afforded at them by the partner stationed below. Preferably, the terrain should have occasional intervening cover and irregular ground features. And the shooter should be positioned so that as the tires roll by he has first quartering-forward shots, then broadside, and then quartering-away shots.

The tires hit rocks, mounds of dirt, clumps of weeds, and so on, alternately slowing down, speeding up, and bouncing along just as a running deer might do. Sometimes the downhill shooter has as many as three or four shots or more at each tire, but regardless of the number, each should be taken with deliberate care and to the best of the shooter's aiming ability. After the tires have been fired upon and are lying at the bottom of the slope, they can be examined to find out where the slugs hit and then the bullet holes covered with pieces of masking tape and the practice renewed.

The main advantage of rolling-tire shooting exercises, of course, is that a hunter learns to calculate "lead," which is an essential ingredient in hitting running whitetails. At first, he'll probably discover he is shooting far behind the moving targets, and the reason for this is the tendency to aim at where the tire (deer) presently is rather than where it will be when the rifle bullet or shotgun slug arrives. Correcting this entails swinging the rifle or shotgun much in the same way as an upland hunter learns to follow through on a flying gamebird; the deer hunter must likewise keep his rifle or shotgun moving, gradually overtake the target, and then continue the swing as proper lead is mentally calculated and the trigger depressed.

There are many complex formulas for figuring out how much to lead a running deer, because there are solid facts about the distance a deer can move while the bullet is enroute to its target. But the practical deer hunter can assign such sliderule busy-work to the guys in the white coats if he'll just keep a few basics in mind.

Deer walk briskly at about 4 miles per hour, trot at 10 miles per hour, and are capable of running at 30. At 30 miles per hour, a deer running broadside to you is covering 44 feet per second. Therefore, if he is 100 yards away, a high-velocity rifle bullet will take about .1 second to get there, and most hunters require an equal amount of time to squeeze off a shot once they have mentally committed themselves. In that $1/5$th second the deer has traveled 8 to 9 feet, which gives a rough idea as to how much lead may be required for a proper sight picture if the round is to strike the animal's chest cavity.

Of course, if the deer is running at an angle, lead can be slightly reduced. Keep in mind, too, that even spooked deer seldom run flat out at 30 miles per hour. And any cover present will make the animal's speed erratic as the deer bounds slightly to the left and right in negotiating its escape; thus the reason for shooting at rolling tires, which can be intentionally rolled at various speeds and angles, or will many times do so because of the irregular terrain they are bouncing over. In time the hunter will get a feel for how much lead is necessary when shooting at targets moving at various speeds and angles, and this learning experience can then be tempered with good judgment and adapted to one's personal gun handling when actually hunting deer. This may not sound very scientific, and the "instinctive" shooting experience gained will probably be something very difficult for the hunter to explain to someone else, but it works! Liken it, if you will, to the quail or pheasant hunter who achieves a degree of lead practice by off-season shooting at clay pigeons.

LIVE GAME PRACTICE

Another type of practice I find invaluable is to actually go hunting, but this is not a suggestion to jump the gun and illegally shoot at deer before the season opens. In many states there are no closed seasons or bag limits on woodchucks, groundhogs, coyotes, cottontail rabbits, or jackrabbits; in fact, most landowners are glad to have these animal populations reduced. Use your deer rifle or shotgun and the same type of slugs you plan to chamber for the deer season; this may be taken as blasphemous by dedicated small-game hunters and varmint shooters, but what we're concerned with is refining your familiarity with your firearm and your knowledge of estimating distances and other aspects of shooting.

Groundhogs, especially, are extremely wary creatures, and they also present themselves as very small targets. Both factors allow considerable practice and development of shooting skills which later in the season may make shooting at a 175-pound whitetail seem easy.

12

Shooting Your Deer

Contrary to the beliefs of modern sportsmen, deer hunters, and conservationists, the market hunter of sixty to a hundred years ago was not entirely a scoundrel and reprobate. It is true that early market hunters played a major role in the devastation of this country's existing deer herds (and other wild game species) around the turn of the century. But it must be remembered that that was an era in which fish and game agencies (on both the state and federal levels) were in their infancy, sophisticated game management programs were almost entirely nonexistent because no one ever considered we might actually run out of game someday, and the harvesting of enormous quantities of venison for sale was perfectly legal.

Well, we've long since learned that without viable laws and management techniques numerous species could find themselves in trouble. But the point to be made is that while market hunters, in a conservation sense, are typically looked back (and down) upon as irresponsible exploiters and plunderers, they had their better qualities as well. In fact, I might even crawl as far out on the proverbial limb as to say they were the most expert deer hunters this country has ever known. And in certain regards, the modern deer hunter should emulate the same attitudes and philosophies such hunt-for-cash men lived by.

You see, the early market hunter was a one-shot artist who lived by the code of clean, quick kills. With ammo being comparatively expensive, sending off a fusillade of bullets at any given deer greatly cut into the expected profits he might hope to realize. Also, a barrage of rounds sent after a fleeing whitetail, it was known, because such hurried attempts are nearly always inaccurate, often resulted in wounded deer that escaped. And those crippled animals which *were* recovered often had the "money meat" damaged. So the market hunter was, in terms of "overhead" and other business costs, very sensible. Expend as little ammo as necessary to get the job done; recover every deer shot at and as quickly as possible; and ruin absolutely none of the various cuts of prime venison destined for sale. In short, the market hunter was a meat hunter. And those who were the most successful (and well paid) were those who had learned to pick their shots. They learned as well that those shots that were the surest and deadliest were also the ones that left all the steaks, roasts, and better portions of venison undamaged.

Should the modern deer sportsman be a meat hunter? You bet! But clear evidence that this is often *not* the case can be seen during a brief visit to almost any meat-processing plant that butchers deer and other big game for hunters. Go there about two or three days after the local deer season has opened, when most of the carcasses are being brought in, and I guarantee you'll be in for a very unsavory surprise. To be sure, you'll see carcasses in prime condition, with single bullet holes through the chest cavities or other vital regions, made by expert hunters. But far outnumbering these will be does, spike bucks, forkhorns, and big bucks too that have been shot (many times, riddled) through the front quarters, through the hindquarters, and high along the backbone—the hams, tenderloins, and chops in many cases all but reduced to bloodshot deerburger.

One major reason for wounded deer, or damaged venison, is that hunters place their shots in the wrong location. Or more to the point, too many hunters aim for the entire deer, not realizing that a whitetail possesses only a few body regions where a bullet will be almost instantly fatal and result in little or no wasted meat.

None of this is meant to imply that any hunter should feel guilty or receive reprimands from his partners for shooting a spike buck or forkhorn, or even a big doe, provided that the animal is legal and that the particular deer is one the hunter is willing to settle for. Nor is there anything at all immoral (though many other writers say it is) in attempting a shot at a running deer, provided the hunter has quickly evaluated all conditions (distance of the animal, speed at which it is moving, angle at which it is traveling, degree of intensity of intervening cover, and so on) and feels reasonably confident he can score a good hit in a vital region because he has many times, in one manner or another, practiced such shots.

STANDARDS FOR SHOOTING

In picking his shot, the sportsman belies the "slob" image too often given the hunter. He becomes very choosy and selective. The deer he shoots at must be one that fulfills whatever expectations he has established for the hunt, and the shot, if there is the slightest possibility, must be set up just the way he wants it. If the deer he spots is not what he is really after, he unhesitatingly passes it up in the hope that something better will come along. If the deer *is* one that he wants, but the shooting circumstances are not, he pauses in the hope that the position of the animal or its relation to cover will change. In short, it is he and he alone who controls the shooting atmosphere, not the deer, and certainly not other hunters back at camp who have "status" because they've already filled their tags!

The deer a hunter should be willing to settle for, however, is a very individual and personal choice, and absolutely no one should berate his decision. The gourmet chef may be pleased to bag a yearling doe (where legal) or forkhorn because of the palatability and tenderness of the meat. The young son or daughter who is just starting out, under the tutelage of a parent or some other instructor, has every right to feel extremely proud of his or her first deer, even if it is only a spike. The veteran hunter who has bagged dozens of deer during his lifetime may derive the greatest personal satisfaction from trying to outwit some particular mossyhorn he has seen from time to time that no one else has been able to collect. And in attempting such a task he may be perfectly willing to pass up shots at six- and eight-pointers, even though those back in camp may call him foolish. Yet the strict trophy hunter may elect to let even heavy ten- and twelve-pointers go about their business, hoping for a rack of such massive and perfect symmetry that he will be awarded the distinction of having his name etched in the record book.

So the deer that any hunter should settle for is the one that fulfills his expectations and thereby completes a successful outing he can happily remember.

But there is more to it than that. Even if any particular deer fully meets any hunter's standards, there will often be shots that should not be settled for. One is the shot through extremely heavy cover with no holes or shooting alleys. Because of bullet deflection, which is bound to occur to at least some degree in such situations, this will probably only result in a wounded deer. It may even result in an illegal kill, as happened to a North Carolina hunter a number of years ago.

He had been waiting on stand, scanning the cover, when he happened to look to his left and see a good six-point buck standing on the far side of very thick blueberry bushes. All that could be seen was the buck's head, and so the hunter "guessed" at where the animal's lung region would be and touched off a round. The buck bounded from the cover and disappeared in short order, completely unscathed. The hunter walked over to where the buck had been standing and on the other side of the hedgerow found a dead doe with a bullet hole in the neck.

Apparently she had been standing in front of the buck, with her head lowered to feed, and the hunter never even suspected her presence in his haste to get on with the matter of shooting. Since the hunter knew that reporting the incident would mean a $100 fine, that his hunting license would be suspended for two years, and that the illegal doe would be confiscated by the authorities, he simply left the deer where it lay and beat a hurried retreat. It was a tragic waste of not only a game animal but about 80 pounds of prime meat, and it was all needless because this hunter did not exercise care and good judgment in waiting for just the right shooting opportunity.

Another shot every hunter should pass up is the one in which numerous animals are running together and it is impossible to see anything but occasional flashes of polished antlers as the buck keeps a shield of doeskin between the two of you. And there are countless other ways in which certain types of shots may present themselves that are not to be desired or attempted. But these fall into that gray area in which every hunter, and he alone, will have to make the decision, and often he will have to do so within scant seconds. Upon occasion he may miscalculate lead or something else, and there may be times when deer will make sudden and unexpected moves. But these constitute that margin of error and unpredictability over which no one ever has any control. We can only hope to keep the margin of error as low as possible by acquiring the necessary shooting skills, taking only those shots that we are fully confident we can make, and in all other regards demonstrating personal responsibility. No one can ask more of any hunter.

WHEN TO SHOOT

The moment to shoot at a deer is when it is as close as it is believed it will ever be, when it is presenting itself in a broadside manner, when it is standing still or moving very slowly, and when there is little or no cover between the line of fire and that particular vital area the hunter is aiming for. An ideal, you say, that seldom exists in true hunting situations? Well, maybe to a degree, since there is never one shooting situation that is exactly like another. But if we know what perfect shooting conditions are, and strive to set them up, then we are better able to make more responsible judgments when less-than-ideal shots are offered.

I do not mean to dwell again on the ethical or moral conduct of deer hunters in various shooting situations, because we have been over that ground before, but rather to stress that if a hunter learns to anticipate what the deer he encounters are likely to do he'll stand a far better chance of scoring. And regardless of whether he is waiting on stand, still-hunting, participating in drives, or pursuing deer in some other manner, there are a few basic guidelines that can be applied.

For one, when a deer is spotted that fulfills a hunter's wishes and that he desires to take, it is wise for the hunter never to take his eyes entirely off the animal; because of their coloration and evasiveness, it is simply too easy for them to melt into the cover. Yet at the same time a hunter should learn to see not only the deer he is watching but with peripheral vision keep on the lookout for other deer that may also be nearby while simultaneously trying to second-guess the directional movement of the deer. This is important, because while the buck you are concentrating upon may be totally unaware of your presence, perhaps a fawn or bossy old doe you did not see is giving you the once-over and is about to blow the whistle on the whole situation the instant you make one more move to raise your rifle. Or perhaps an unaware feeding buck is moving slowly through heavy cover, stopping here and there to rip up green shoots. If finding a good shooting lane through the cover is difficult, maybe it would be better to wait until the deer has progressed another 40 yards and is more in the open. There have been several times when I have agonizingly waited as much as five minutes (that is pretty long, if you time it) for a slowpoke buck to step from behind a screen of saplings so that my line of fire would be unobstructed.

Though many hunters do not know it, the whitetail often gives clues or advance notices of its intended actions. And one of the most important signs the hunter should be able to read is the manner in which the animal holds or moves its tail. If the tail is down and perhaps occasionally swishing from side to side, the buck has not yet sensed danger, although you can bet he is always monitoring every aspect of his environment for some alien sound, sight, or scent. When so alerted, his next move will likely be no move at all! He'll freeze in position, hoping to identify whatever it is that has triggered his sensory apparatus. The hunter should freeze as well, even if in an awkward position, because there are many things (songbirds, rustling squirrels, falling hickory nuts and dead branches, and such) that precipitate such behavior on the part of deer, and usually they eventually conclude nothing of danger is around and lower their heads to resume feeding.

If a whitetail erects his tail so that it is sticking straight out, he has decided that his continued presence in the area is not healthy. The same applies if he loudly exhales or snorts. In either case the hunter has only a precious few seconds to react, because the deer's next move will be to throw his flag all the way up and then he will be off for parts unknown. One exception to this manner of holding the tail aloft pertains to does. If the flag is not all the way up as she comes trotting along, but instead is being held straight back and perhaps to the side a bit, don't even blink. She's in heat and waiting to be bred by a buck following close behind!

Another visual clue whitetails give that indicates their present state of mind has to do with their ears. If they seem "cupped," held high, and pointed in some direction or another, the deer is curious, alerted, or otherwise trying to classify something it has heard or hopes to hear again. If the animal lays its ears back, however, the hunter should be prepared to shoot quickly or not have a shot at all, as the animal is only a fraction of a second from bolting. Whitetails pull their ears back in such a manner so they will not be "stung" as they weave their escape flights through the thorns and buckbrush.

It has been written many times that the best time to take a shot at a deer is when the animal has its head lowered to feed because the deer must first raise its head before it is able to bolt. This is true, but few hunters realize how quickly a whitetail can execute this maneuver. Moreover, in addition to waiting for a buck to lower his head before beginning to very slowly raise my rifle, I also like whenever possible to wait until his head is turned away or slightly behind a tree or other screening cover so that his range of vision is obscured.

When to shoot at deer on the move is an altogether different question, because in most instances the hunter is faced with the prospect of making quick judgments and then either reacting or not reacting at all. But it is again possible for him to hurriedly anticipate future shooting conditions.

For example, a deer that is moving in your direction (as when the deer has been pushed out by drivers) should be allowed to come as close as possible before the shot is attempted. The closer the deer is, the less lead must be calculated, and the easier it will be to pick out shooting alleys through the cover. When a deer is rapidly moving away from the hunter's position (as when a deer scents or sees a hunter on stand and bolts), usually it is best for the hunter to shoot as quickly as careful aiming will allow, because of the reduced lead factor and the better chance of finding shooting holes through the cover when the deer is in close. But sometimes, if the cover is extremely heavy and the hunter has an elevated vantage point, it might be wiser to hold off shooting until the animal is a bit farther away but more in the open, even though lead will have to be increased slightly.

WHERE TO AIM

Whitetail deer possess several vital regions where shots, if they are properly placed, will kill them very quickly if not instantly. But some of these locations, at least in this author's opinion, are far less desirable than others, so let's look at them categorically.

A shot anywhere in the brain or skull region of the head will drop the deer in his tracks. But the head of a whitetail is a very small target. Consequently, a shot that is off by only a very slight margin may either miss entirely or inflict a wound—one that eventually results in death, when the animal is far away—by shattering the jaw, superficially grazing the windpipe, or penetrating a fleshy part of the neck. Since the head shot is so chancy, I don't recommend it. Another thing is that even successful head shots will invariably ruin the head for mounting purposes.

Expert hunters occasionally attempt neck shots, as a bullet placed at the base of the neck where it joins the body severs the vertebral column and results in instant death. But making this shot requires a precise knowledge of a deer's anatomy; missing by a few inches one way or another can result only in a wounded deer capable of traveling many miles before it eventually expires. Even when it is properly placed, however, the neck shot may ruin several nice roasts, and for sure the cape (neck skin) will be damaged and therefore present problems if the animal is to make a trip to a taxidermist.

A heart shot will also either drop the animal on the spot or see it dashing only 50 or 75 yards before piling up. But again, the heart is a very small target to aim for (about the size of a grapefruit) and it lies very low in the chest cavity. A shot that is off by only a couple of inches may result in a deer with one or two broken front legs, a gut-shot animal, or one with a superficial wound in the forward part of the brisket.

A spine (or backbone) shot will drop the deer instantly, either killing it immediately or paralyzing it so that a finishing round can be placed. But this as well requires a good knowledge of exactly

The best possible shot is the lung shot. It is the largest vital area, ensures a quick, merciful kill, and results in no lost meat. Cross-hair placement here shows aiming location, just behind the front shoulder. (Photo by U.S. Forest Service)

where the spine is located, and the best meat of all, the tenderloins, will be damaged.

Some hunters, when a deer is directly facing them, shoot for the white throat patch. If the shot is true, the deer goes down as if it had stepped into an abandoned well, but it is a small target to aim for and ruins the cape. Other hunters, when a deer is directly facing away from them, shoot for the back of the neck, which is yet another small target. Or they shoot for the animal's rump, hoping either to drive the slug forward between the hams and into the chest region, or to hit the root of the tail (the very end of the spine), which paralyzes the animal, or to break the rear hip, which brings the deer down but requires a finishing shot. The rump of a deer is admittedly a very big target, and one way or another the animal eventually dies. But just ask an old-time market hunter for his opinion of such shots, and the condition in which they leave the hindquarter roasts!

To penetrate the chest cavity and hit the lung region, cross-hairs will have to be adjusted to the position of the deer. For deer that is facing on, this sight picture is best. (Photo by U.S. Forest Service)

That brings us to the shot I consider best: the lung shot. The lung region of a whitetail is about the size of a basketball, and with a deer standing broadside it is located directly behind and slightly to the rear of the front shoulder. The reason I recommend the lung shot is that it is the largest vital area a deer possesses (and therefore the easiest to hit, regardless of the stance of the animal), it is either immediately or almost immediately fatal, deer that travel short distances afterward are easily tracked and recovered because of the quantity of blood usually left behind, and no meat is damaged. Also, since the lung region is surrounded by still other (though smaller) vital areas, a shot can often be off by as much as 6 or 8 inches one way or another and still cause a quick and merciful death. If the shot is a bit too low, either the heart or major blood vessels to and from that organ will be hit. If the shot is just a bit too high, the spine will be severed. If the shot is just a tad too far to the rear, you've got him in the liver, which is quickly fatal. And if the shot is too far forward, you've got him at the base of the neck, in the windpipe/esophagus area, or perhaps in major blood vessels feeding the brain.

Without a doubt, because an increasing number of noted marksmen and gun specialists are writing stories about big-game hunting each year, we can expect the controversial "where to aim" issue to be brought up again and again as each writer expounds his own theories. But when the smoke has blown away and we've returned to pragmatic considerations, it is still every respectable hunter's desire to score a hit in a vital area which kills the animal quickly and with little damage to the venison. Hit the lung region and you've got your deer, and your meat!

In placing a round in the chest cavity, however, the hunter must always keep in mind the stance of the animal. If the deer is standing perfectly broadside, no problem. But if the animal is facing directly to the front, the slug should be placed on the animal's centerline where the neck joins the body. If the deer is quartering away, the slug will have to sometimes be placed very far to the rear of the short ribs (depending upon the angle) so that in driving forward it will eventually penetrate the chest cavity. If the animal is quartering toward you, the slug may have to be placed well forward, sometimes as far forward as to go between the neck and front shoulder, to angle backward into the chest cavity.

If the deer is quartering away, shot placement will have to be farther back, behind the short ribs, to angle forward into the chest region. This depends upon the speed of the animal, however, as "lead" may also have to be calculated.

In summary, no hunter should be so eager to kill a deer and fill his tag that he willingly accepts poor shooting conditions—conditions in which the proper placement of his round is very unlikely. There is immense pride and satisfaction in shooting ethics of this sort, once a hunter has achieved it.

BUCK FEVER

Buck fever is an unpredictable, cursed malady that every year causes countless hunters to blow easy shots at deer. Sometimes it is an unconscious thing. A buck appears before a hunter, his gun is properly sighted in and he knows how to use it, but for no apparent reason the deer is cleanly missed. Other times a hunter is well aware of his buck fever because all composure is obviously lost. He chokes up—freezes—and is unable to raise his firearm, aim, or pull the trigger. Or in the process of aiming he is shaking so violently that the sights wobble all over.

There are many explanations for buck fever, and it would take a psychologist to evaluate any particular hunter's mental makeup to determine how and why the fever afflicts some but not others or why it affects various hunters in different ways. But generally I feel buck fever, whatever its manifestation or frequency, is most likely to have its effect when a deer, without warning, suddenly appears at very close range before an inexperienced hunter.

This is definitely *not* to imply that buck fever is something to be ashamed of. Even the most expert hunters, if they are candid, will admit to at least a little queasiness, unsteadiness, tremor, or elevated blood pressure when a buck steps into a clearing before them. I experience buck fever in varying degrees all the time. But with me it presents itself in a slightly different form. After years of hunting I am able to concentrate, maintain cool control of myself, and execute good shots. Then, *after* the kill, I sometimes go all to pieces.

A couple of years ago, for example, I killed a huge mule deer in Colorado. In fact, it was the biggest mulie of my life. Cool, calm, and collected, I centered the cross-hairs of my scope on the deer and at the shot he tumbled over as though he had been poleaxed.

I hiked over to the deer, admired him for brief moments, and then since it seemed very warm (I later learned the temperature that day never once rose above 25 degrees!) I decided I'd better immediately get on with the business of field dressing. But after repeated attempts I realized I was having trouble unfastening the leather thong on the sheath of my belt knife. I looked down at my hand and it was shaking as if I were doing some new kind of teenage dance!

Finally I sat down, leaned against a quaking aspen (which was appropriate to the circumstances), and smoked a cigar. It was fifteen minutes before I felt competent and composed enough to handle a sharp blade.

There are several ways to guard against buck fever. The best, of course, is experience. The veteran who has collected venison every season for twenty years is not as likely to experience the fever, or at least not likely to the same degree, as the tyro who is just about to kill his very first deer. But this is not something that can be controlled. You simply pay your yearly dues to the deer-hunting fraternity and gradually, in time, buck fever, if it continues to occur at all, will be of a lesser degree—until that one special big buck of a lifetime comes along!

More practical, in reducing the possible influence of buck fever, is for the hunter to spend as much time as he can around deer, observing them. Visit a zoo on a regular basis, or a game ranch, or preserve, or some other place open to the public where live, penned deer can be watched from relatively close distances. It won't be too long before you feel very comfortable and at ease in the presence of whitetails. Even if you've never killed a deer before, such preseason close-contact encounters will afford a type of confidence and self-assurance that will greatly lessen the possibility of feeling your heart in your throat when a deer is suddenly spotted from your stand or while sneak-hunting.

Another method, one that I use frequently as I'm a full-time outdoor writer, is off-season photography of animals in their natural habitat. This is also good practice for actual hunting, because shooting color slides rather than bullets requires getting much closer to the quarry than is otherwise necessary. Therefore, the hobbyist who has been successfully photographing deer for several months before opening day is not likely to go bananas when a buck or doe eases down the trail toward his stand.

WHAT TO DO ABOUT FLINCHING

Flinching is altogether different from buck fever. This is the unconscious physical reaction of muffing shots as the trigger is being depressed. Perhaps the shooter squints, winces, or closes his eyes just before pulling the trigger. Or he may turn his head from the stock or jerk the firearm. But whatever the nature of the flinch it is almost always because the shooter anticipates and fears the noise (muzzle blast) of his rifle or the recoil when the stock pounds his shoulder.

The irony here is that flinching is born during target shooting, because the hunter is more acutely concentrating upon his firearm and muzzle blast and recoil are therefore more noticeable. Yet in the field, during the course of hunting excitement, with live game in the sights, nearly all hunters claim their quarry so occupies their attention that they seldom hear a loud noise when the gun discharges and rarely feel any kick; the encounter—the moment of truth—is that entrancing and captivating.

Since flinching can be very difficult to cure, every measure should be taken to prevent it in the first place. One way this can be accomplished is by using rifles of either low or moderate recoil and muzzle blast. The four calibers recommended earlier (.243, .270, .30/06, and .308) fall nicely into this category, at least compared to the shoulder- and ear-torturing cannons many hunters unnecessarily carry into the field for deer hunting.

Also, add a recoil pad to your firearm if necessary. Wear a hunting coat or shooting vest with a padded shoulder pocket. And when target shooting, place a sandbag between your shoulder and the butt of the rifle.

Speaking of practice, it's always wise to spend as much time as possible shooting your firearm year-round. The shooter who fires his .30/06 only once a year, just before the deer season, is likely to be far more sensitive to recoil than the hunter who makes a trip to the practice range several times a month throughout the year.

With regards to muzzle blast when the firearm is being practiced with, wear ear plugs or some type of protective headphone set; this is recommended by doctors, anyway, to prevent a partial loss of hearing by those who do a lot of shooting.

Sometimes a hunter will find he is suddenly having great difficulty hitting the targets (or deer) he's aiming for. He may vehemently proclaim he is not flinching, and may even sincerely believe this to be the case, because recoil usually covers up a flinch. Here is the way to find out for sure. Head for your local target range with your partner, and give him instructions to hand your rifle to you, sometimes loaded with live ammo and sometimes with only a spent case in the chamber. With your rifle in hand, now take a bead on a target downrange and squeeze the trigger. If you've contracted flinching it should be readily apparent to both you and your partner on those occasions when you pull the trigger and the firing pin falls on an empty round.

If flinching is evident, there are a couple of possible ways to cure it, although none is guaranteed. First, try switching to a smaller-caliber weapon (say, from a .308 to a .270) that racks the shoulder less on recoil and is not as loud in report.

If your flinch doesn't gradually go away, next try what the psychologists refer to as systematic desensitization. This means shooting with numerous firearms, starting with very small calibers and gradually working back up to the bigger bores as each new step feels more comfortable. You may have to borrow six rifles from various friends, starting out shooting fifty rounds every other day of .22 Shorts. After a week, move up to .22 Long Rifle shells. Then shoot for a week with a varmint rifle such as one of the hot .22 calibers (.22 Hornet or .222 Remington). Next try the .243 or 6mm Remington, gradually progressing up the line until you're once again able to handle your .30/06 or other big caliber.

During actual hunting, with regards to either buck fever or flinching, mental control is another deterrent to double-trouble. Train yourself not to think of recoil, muzzle blast, or the visual "shock" of that big buck that has just materialized before you. This can easily be done by learning to concentrate instead upon the specific part of the anatomy you wish to aim for, the proper sight picture you must have in accordance with the distance away the deer is, remembering to flip off the safety, and anticipating the movement of the deer through the cover so you can plan ahead for the right time to take your best shot.

Training yourself—forcing yourself—to think of such things allows no opportunity for your mind to mull over muzzle blast and recoil. Take your time. Take a breath. Very likely your buck is moving only a few steps at a time and then stopping to nibble browse. He doesn't see you. He has no idea you're even around, so you can play it cool.

Whenever his head is partially screened by cover so that his line of sight in your direction is blocked, or when he's turned slightly away and looking in the other direction, or when he has his head lowered to feed again, very slowly and quietly raise your gun to your shoulder. Take your time. Don't risk the chance of a quick shot when he's not standing just the way you want him. You are in control of this deal. Quickly scan the cover to make sure there are no branches or saplings in your intended line of fire. Easy now. Settle your sights on his lung region. Take another breath. Let half of it escape. Steady. Slowly squeeze the trigger.

13

Following Up the Shot

A couple of years ago, in the heart of Maryland's farm country, my pal Bob Pelletier came very close to losing a whitetail buck of any hunter's dreams. Exactly what happened is worth relating here, because any deer hunter could sooner or later find himself in a similar situation.

The buck was sneaking along the far edge of a lowland clearing, and Pelletier watched anxiously as the animal next bounded across an open stretch and began working his way up a hillside. The deer was still 200 yards away, but headed straight in the direction of Pelletier's stand! The deer gradually came closer and closer.

Then something happened which Pelletier had not counted upon. The buck suddenly changed direction, angling off to his left for a distance of about 25 yards to where it then stepped into a dense tangle of tall grass and two-year-old pines. The range was 75 yards. It was not the best shot Pelletier had been hoping for, but then again, with the animal almost stationary as it milled around, neither was it a very risky shot. But Bob knew he would have to act fast; the buck was apparently going to bed there and once he dropped down he would be entirely out of sight.

In slow motion Pelletier raised his shotgun and a moment or two later pulled the trigger. Immediately, and with no indication whatever that he'd been hit, the buck made a few leaps on nimble legs and was gone. Whether or not Pelletier had made a good shot was entirely uncertain, and that is why the next thirty minutes of waiting on stand were probably the longest of his life.

"During the course of many years of deer hunting with my older brothers," he later explained, "I had been tutored to wait on stand after each shot for as long as possible. The theory was that a deer, regardless of where it was shot, would travel only a short distance before lying down and stiffening up."

By the time Bob Pelletier finally climbed down from his tree stand, with tottering legs as he later admitted, he had pretty well convinced himself that he had scored a clean kill and that the buck would probably be lying not more than 50 yards away. And he was almost ecstatic when he saw scattered droplets of crimson on the pine boughs where the buck had been standing. But closer examination of the area next revealed splashes of blood on the ground which contained bits of green and yellowish matter—a positive indication the buck had been gut-shot—and that is when his happy thoughts began turning gloomy.

The only thing to do, he figured, was to take to the trail ever so slowly, following single specks of red at a time and on hands and knees if necessary. It caused him to remember just the previous season and how his older brother George had lost a dandy buck when the blood trail eventually gave out, and he said a few silent words in the hopes that the same thing would not happen to him. However, that is precisely what happened after only ten minutes on the trail. The amount of blood sign grew fainter by the minute until it finally quit altogether. The ground was hard and bone-dry, so following tracks was out of the question.

Only by sheer luck did Bob Pelletier eventually find his trophy. He had hung his blaze-orange cap on a bush where the last sign of blood had been spotted. And from there he began fanning out, making progressively larger circular passes ahead in the hope of coming upon additional specks of scarlet. Some 300 yards far to the left of where the last blood had been seen, and just as he was about to give up the search (after almost two hours), he suddenly noticed a very small splash of sunlight upon a single antler tine in dense brush cover. The deer was dead.

Bob considered himself very fortunate in many ways, because subsequent searching of the surrounding area gave no hint that the deer had headed in that direction. Had it been an overcast day, or perhaps only late in the afternoon, the buck would probably never have been recovered.

There is still more to Pelletier's experience. Having almost lost a superb trophy, and still a bit shaky about the entire episode, Bob very slowly and carefully field-dressed the deer. Evidently the shot had been a "flyer," as he had indeed hit the buck far back and high in the paunch, just barely creasing the liver but otherwise nowhere near anything that could have proved immediately fatal. He also discovered why the blood trail had given out. Not being pressured, the deer had apparently slowed to a walk to conserve energy, and this allowed the blood, which had only been dribbling to begin with, to coagulate. Soon both the entrance and exit holes made by the slug were plugged with tallow, soft flesh, and clotted blood. Examining these, and shuddering at the thought of such a deer almost escaping him, Bob Pelletier began seriously questioning whether he had made the right decision in waiting on stand so long after taking his shot.

Therefore, savvy tactics in following up shots taken at whitetails constitute a very important part of every successful hunt, and this may entail many considerations. The hunter, whether using a slug-loaded shotgun or high-powered rifle, should first understand how deer are likely to react when hit in various body parts. Sometimes this may be difficult, because deer often display no signs at all of being hit as they line out for distance or cover, and this may often cause any hunter, at first thought, to believe he missed completely. After any shot, and regardless of whether an obvious hit has been scored or whether there is some doubt, the hunter must next decide either to sit tight for a while or take off after the animal immediately. Being able to recognize and interpret various types of blood sign, tracks, and other clues, and understanding the behavior of wounded deer, are also critical requirements in recovering animals which have been hit but do not immediately fall.

DEER REACTIONS AT THE SHOT

To my knowledge, no data has ever been compiled on the subject, but without a doubt only a minority of deer hit with fatal shots drop right at the spot of impact. A hunter can usually expect this to happen only when devastating damage has been done to the animal's central nervous system. This means a shot somewhere in the brain region of the head, in the cervical column (vertebrae sections of the neck), or somewhere along the spinal column. Those animals struck in the area of the backbone far to the rear of the body will usually fall due to instant paralysis of the hindquarters, but a second shot will be required to finish them off.

The great majority of deer are hit in some location other than those listed above, and they can usually be counted upon to travel at least a certain distance before dropping. The farther the hit is from vital organs, major blood vessels, or nervous-system components, the farther the animal is capable of going, though a shot anywhere in the main body trunk is certain to result eventually in the animal's death.

This is a good case for always making the first shot count. And as indicated in the previous chapter, there can be no dispute that the lung region offers the largest and surest target. But deer hunting is as unpredictable as it is exciting, with trophy evaluations and shots often having to be made within fleeting seconds if they are to be made at all. Even under the most favorable conditions the best of marksmen are not always "right on," and this is especially true when a shot is taken at an animal on the move or when the range is considerable.

Many times, but not always, deer react in telling ways upon being hit, and this may give the hunter an idea as to what follow-up tactics he should next put into play. An animal hit in the paunch, for example, will frequently hump up his back before taking flight, and a long tracking job is probably in store. A lung-shot animal will often kick his rear legs like a bucking horse. Yet still another lung-shot deer, and many times even those drilled squarely through the heart, may show absolutely no initial reaction or break in stride, although they are certain to pile up within 100 yards. A liver-shot animal may react still differently. I have seen them travel as much as several hundred yards at full speed (even outdistancing other deer they were running with) until they gradually fell behind and then suddenly dropped.

Therefore, it's always important to watch a deer carefully after a shot has been taken. Whitetails are one of the most graceful of all four-footed big game, and any noticeable break in stride or labored movements usually means a solid hit in a vital area. In other cases, though, a deer may only momentarily droop his head or ripple his skin and muscles in the vicinity of where he has been hit.

The major problem encountered in following up shots taken at deer is that the species are nearly always in or around heavy cover. Normal patterns of movement seldom find them in wide-open areas. Because of this basic nature of whitetails—their inherent instinct to expose as little of themselves as possible and only for very brief periods—they will most often be out of sight only seconds after the shot. Then, almost any hunter's first decision will be whether to take to the trail immediately or stay put for a while.

RUNNING DOWN WOUNDED DEER

There is no question in most hunters' minds that under conditions of steadily falling rain or snow the quarry should be pursued as quickly as possible. Significant amounts of precipitation will quickly wipe out blood sign or obliterate tracks, and an animal hit in the lungs, heart, liver, or with major blood vessels severed isn't going far anyway. But aside from existing weather conditions, and regardless of where the deer may in fact be hit, an increasing number of hunters are adopting the philosophy of pursuing their game immediately after the shot. Since this is contrary to the schooling of many previous generations of hunters, a few words of explanation are in order.

A wounded deer is afraid—aware that something is wrong—and most often its first inclination is to place distance between itself and that which it fears. That distance achieved (which may be only 100 yards if the cover is heavy), he'll then slow to a walk, searching for a place to lie down where he can rest and hide. The act of resting causes his body functions and responses to slow back down. And therefore, if the animal is capable of moving from his bed sometime later, in order to elude a hunter who has played the waiting game after his shot and is now slowly following the trail, the deer may not leave much blood sign, if any at all.

On numerous occasions I have found pools of coagulated blood where hard-hit whitetails have lain down to rest, but no blood trail at all leading from the location when forced to their feet again sometime later by a slowly tracking hunter.

The idea of promptly taking after a deer, then, rather than

Following a blood trail is an art because the hunter must learn how to identify blood sign of different color or quantity. Here, Bill Weiss puts a hat on a bush to mark the last location of sign when following a trail.

waiting on stand, and pressuring him into staying on the move, makes good sense. If the animal is never permitted to lie down but is forced to remain on his feet and always one jump ahead of an eager hunter, his heart will continue to frantically beat. A rapidly pumping heart maintains a high level of blood pressure, and consequently the wound never has a chance to close or become obstructed or plugged with a mixture of tallow and clotted blood. Further, the deer is never given the opportunity to rest and regain lost strength. If the weakened animal does fall, he probably won't be able to get up again. But even if he is able to stay on his feet he'll gradually slow to a stumbling walk, allowing the hunter to catch up and place a finishing round.

TRAILING AND TRACKING

Exactly how hard any deer is hit, and where, can very often be diagnosed by the amount and type of sign present when the hunter immediately takes to the trail.

Large amounts of blood usually mean that major arteries or organs in the chest cavity have seen damage. In this region blood pressure is always highest, because of the arterial blood vessels and organs close to the heart, but also because the region contains greater quantities of blood than outlying body areas. As a result, blood will often be sprayed several feet to one side or the other of the animal's tracks. This is most notably the case if the slug has passed entirely through the body and therefore pushed a quantity of blood ahead of it and out the exit hole like an atomizer.

Small amounts of blood mean lesser vessels have been damaged or the animal is bleeding internally. When major veins are struck, blood released is on its return route to the heart and therefore not under great pressure and will be found next to or between the animal's tracks.

Regardless of blood quantity, bright blood is always oxygen-laden, meaning a hit in a major artery within the chest cavity or perhaps even through the heart itself.

Bright blood which takes on a frothy or bubbly appearance practically always means a good hit in the lungs or the major arteries from that organ.

Dark, rich-colored, nonbubbly blood in large quantities most often means a hit in the liver.

Of course, blood containing digestive or fecal matter means a paunch hit or one far back in the intestinal tract.

Chips of bone in bright, frothy blood are usually from the ribs, indicating the slug penetrated the chest cavity. But chips of bone in small quantities of very dark blood mean a hit in either the front quarters or hindquarters, and most likely in the lower-leg regions.

Very frequently a shotgun slug or rifle bullet will also shear a large tuft of hair from the animal's hide, and this sign may be scattered about the impact site. A general but not infallible rule is that light-colored hair means a shot low in the body; darker-colored hair means a hit higher up.

The toughest of all follow-up situations is when no blood trail is evident. This is frequently the case when a slug enters through a fleshy, tallowy area, does not exit through the opposite side of the body, and the entrance hole self-plugs as blood trying to flow outward pushes matter into the opening. When this happens the deer bleeds internally and leaves behind little or no sign. The deer may be dead on his feet, but you'll have to follow other clues, often far distances, if you are to have any hopes of eventually stringing him on the camp meatpole.

When no blood is present, tracks are the first type of sign that come to mind. Tracks can be relatively easy to follow if the ground

Following tracks across dry ground is tough, but much easier if there is snow. If your wounded deer's tracks become lost in a jumble of other tracks, one trick is to stay on the trail of those tracks which are continually splayed. An injured deer is wobbly and unsteady, and for better balance he'll spread his hooves even when walking slowly.

is soft or muddy, and very easy if snow is present. An animal hard hit in a vital area is usually weak and will leave tracks in an erratic, wandering, and stumbling manner. But an animal hit high in either the front quarters or hindquarters will often leave tracks with one of the imprints taking on "dragging" characteristics, because the flank or forequarter muscles are damaged and the deer is incapable of lifting the limb from the ground. When a deer has been shot in the lower portion of any leg, close examination of all of the tracks will reveal one of them to be missing; the animal is hobbling along on only three legs, holding the injured one above the ground.

If there are complete sets of tracks on the ground, meaning four imprints, and all appear of equal indentation, then the deer is known to be capable of placing an equal amount of weight upon all legs. You've hit him someplace else.

Very difficult tracking conditions are seen when the ground is hard, dry, or rocky. In southern Ohio, where I live and hunt whitetails every year, we often see very mild winters with significant amounts of snow not usually coming until well after the season closes. But it is still possible to follow tracks and related sign, and these tactics often prove equally effective for me when hunting in arid Southern states where snow almost never appears.

I have learned, for example, to pay close attention to the leaves on the ground. On a rather dry day the tops of the fallen leaves will be dry, yet their underneath sides will nearly always be a little moist and darker-colored. When these are scuffled or turned upside down by a running, stumbling deer the trail is clear. Just the opposite applies during rainy periods which occur after long dry spells. The tops of the fallen leaves will be shiny wet, but their underneath sides, in many places, will often have dry places exposed when they are turned over. Sometimes dry ground will be exposed. On very cold but otherwise dry days, especially during the morning hours, the tops of the leaves will be thoroughly sprinkled with frost particles; when scuffled by a running deer, the leaves' dry or wet frost-free undersides will show, leaving an easily discernible trail.

On parched, rocky terrain, where there is no blood sign present, it is often necessary to get down on all fours and closely examine any ground debris laying about. This happened once when Joe Burns and I and two others were hunting whitetails in western Oklahoma. Our group took four nice bucks during a week-long campout on a mile-long sagebrush flat that was bordered on two sides by brushy gullies, but one of those deer required serious tracking efforts. Many times the trail would have been lost had it not been for the discovery of single overturned pebbles, bits of shale, and sticks. They were sun-bleached on top, but quite dark underneath; the exposed darker sides indicated that a staggering animal had kicked them over with his hooves.

Game animals, and particularly whitetails, since they are creatures of deep-rooted custom, feel most comfortable and safe using the same general travel routes day after day. They also use the same escape routes. And in regions where deer populations are high it is a frequent and frustrating experience to lose the animal being trailed in a jumble of other hoofprints about the area. One trick, when in doubt, is to stay on those tracks which are continually splayed. A hard-hit animal invariably weaves and wobbles. And he'll spread his hooves with every step, for added balance, regardless of whether he's running or walking.

Another trick is to meticulously examine each of the deer's four tracks when the chase is initially undertaken. Many times it is possible to find some clue that may further aid in their proper identification when they sometime later become lost in a scattering of other hoofprints. I'm thinking here, perhaps, of one toe that is slightly larger than the other, maybe a telltale split in the rim of one of the hooves, or an actual chunk out of part of the hoof. All of these, and more, are as uniquely characteristic to individual deer as are variances in fingerprints among humans.

One situation in which tracking a wounded deer must be undertaken very slowly and tediously occurs when the trail has to be taken up again after being temporarily abandoned. This is commonly the case when the shot is taken at dusk. If an immediately fatal hit is not scored, many hunters elect to defer their tracking until the following morning when ample light allows them to again follow the trail. By then the deer may be a good distance away. In such instances, one effective tactic is for several hunters to return to the last sighted blood or other sign. One hunter follows the sign very slowly and methodically while his partners work much faster and farther ahead, in large circular patterns, trying to find shortcuts.

But my partner, Al Wolter, refuses to wait until the following morning. His reasoning is that unexpected rain, snow, or wind during the night hours may entirely wipe out blood sign and erase tracks, and therefore I recommend his follow-up strategy as the best of all.

When it becomes too dark to follow sign, Al hotfoots it back to camp, where he enlists the help of others. Several hunters then light gasoline lanterns which are capable of throwing wide, strong illumination and they return to the last sighted sign, which Al has marked by hanging his white T-shirt in a branch at that location. Usually tired after a long day of hunting, they nevertheless stay on the trail, sometimes far into the night. Al believes (and I agree and many times have participated in such searches with him) that no effort should be spared in the prompt recovery of any deer.

WHEN YOUR DEER IS LOST

It is not unusual for a hunter to immediately take to the trail in pursuit of his trophy after scoring a good hit, and as diligent and careful as his tracking efforts may be, still have the blood sign and other indications of the animal's direction quickly dwindle to nothing. But that doesn't mean the game should be considered lost and the search abandoned. By the type and amount of blood, tracks, and other sign at the impact site it probably will not be too difficult to make a judgment as to where the animal was hit. With this knowledge at hand, the hunter can often second-guess what the deer is likely to do, or more specifically, where it is likely to go.

If all indications point to the animal being hit in the front quarters, for example, the deer will in all likelihood head for higher ground. Locomotion, under these circumstances, is provided in bulk by the hindquarters, with the deer not wanting to place heavy body weight upon the injured front leg (which is required to a greater degree when traveling on the level or downhill). Conversely, an animal struck in the hindquarters will more than likely stay on the level or head downhill, because damaged muscle tissue in the hindquarters makes it very difficult for him to push the weight of his body up steep inclines. Therefore, when a hunter knows his shot has been "off," he usually has a pretty good idea as to whether he led the animal too much and hit only the front quarters, or did not lead the animal enough and struck the rear quarters; searching of either higher or lower elevations in the area may subsequently turn up additional sign, or perhaps even the animal itself.

A frequent subject around hunting camps, and one that often reaches heated argument proportions, is whether a wounded deer, hit in a vital body region, will head for the heaviest cover in the vicinity or whether he will avoid heavy cover. One school claims that heavy cover is much too difficult for an injured animal to navigate and he will thus take the easiest escape route available to him, often covering open ground if necessary. Opponents claim a seriously wounded deer will always seek the safety of heavy cover where he can rest and hide.

I am inclined to take the latter viewpoint, if for no other reason than personal experience. Many times when the trail has seemingly evaporated, a search of isolated patches of very heavy cover nearby has revealed the downed animal or a pool of blood where it has stopped to rest (keep on the alert, in heavy cover, for traces of wet or dry blood located a couple of feet off the ground where the

When your deer is lost, check higher or lower ground, depending upon where the deer was hit. Also inspect heavy cover and known sources of water. When you finally see your buck, approach with caution. Prod his hindquarters with a stick and check to see that his eyes are open and glassy. Of course if the deer is still alive, mercifully kill him then and there.

deer has brushed against vegetation and other cover while pushing through it). Even in the case of farm-country bucks, which are often shot at in semi-open places such as the edges of orchards, meadows, and croplands, the animals will predictably line out in the direction of woodlands, tall grassy swales, brushy hollows, or toward other difficult or rugged terrain features in the distance that may offer concealment.

I have also seen times when seriously injured whitetails have headed directly for water. Perhaps a severe wound causes thirst. Or there may be some internal mechanism, probably a carryover from previous generations, in which pursued animals instinctively took to the water to evade predators hot on their scent. These conjectures would be difficult to prove, but known sources of water in the area are always good places to check if the trail has grown thin and all other attempts to recover the deer have proved unsuccessful.

APPROACHING YOUR DOWNED DEER

We should say a few things about the recommended procedure for approaching a deer that is down, whether it is an animal dropped on the spot or one that has required trailing for a considerable distance.

If the deer is obviously still alive there is only one thing to do, and that is to mercifully end his life as quickly as possible. Approach to within 25 or 30 yards, but no closer, so that you can make the killing shot count. The deer will in all likelihood be stuporous, dazed, in shock, and not aware of your presence. Most hunters prefer to take very careful aim and place a shot in the neck, to break the cervical column. The deer should drop on the spot and be instantly dead.

Let's say, however, that your deer is down but you are not certain whether or not it is dead. Be careful, because the animal may still have some life left and greet you with a swinging rack or slashing hooves.

Approach to within about 25 yards so that you can see his eyes. If they are open and either glassy-looking or glazed over, the animal is almost certain to be dead. But just to be sure, quietly approach from his backside and give his hindquarters a prod with a long stick. If the eyes are closed, there is a good chance the animal is still alive, so play it safe and place a finishing round in the neck.

14

Field Care
of
Your Trophy

I am not exactly sure why it is so, but a tremendous amount of what has been written, professed, or taught about the field care of deer is pure garbage. It seems that sometime every season I sooner or later reach the point of astonishment and total disbelief.

So if you ever hear a hunter or dinner guest speak of his or her dislike for venison because it is tough or it's too gamy or some other reason, you can bet cold cash there was some person involved in either the field dressing, the butchering, the storage, or the actual meal preparation who had absolutely no idea what he was doing and therefore resorted to guesswork or fable.

The purpose of this chapter, then, is to set the record straight. A lot of things you'll read may contradict what you've read elsewhere or what you may have been lead to believe by some hunting pal, and this may create a bit of animosity, but it's high time the truth was leaked.

Too many hunters believe in superstition and old wives' tales when it comes to dressing their deer. There's no need whatever to cut off the scent glands or plunge your knife blade into the throat. Simply remove the deer's insides to cool the meat as quickly as possible. The text gives detailed instructions about this.

GUTTING, THE RIGHT WAY

To begin with, it's never necessary for a hunter, when his deer is down, to go fooling around with the musk glands. These appear as dark tufts of hair located midway on each rear hock. When a deer dies, the glands become inactive, so if you leave them entirely alone there is no way for them to adversely affect the meat. The few times in which I have seen musk glands present a problem have been when an exuberant, ignorant hunter began needlessly cutting at them, did a horrendously sloppy job, and then without washing his hands or the knife he was using began handling the meat, allowing some of the glands' oil to be transferred. Good advice is simply to exercise a bit of caution to *not* touch or otherwise disturb the glands and if you do that, you'll have no trouble whatever with them.

Nor is there any need to slice open the deer's throat to bleed the animal. If the hunter has scored a good shot in a vital region, using either a shotgun or a high-powered rifle, the deer will have automatically bled itself and 98 percent of its blood will have drained into the chest-cavity region; you'll notice this for sure when you open the deer up and the stuff pours out.

It *is* imperative that the deer be field dressed as soon as possible, to quickly reduce the temperature of all those steaks and roasts, and this is done by removing the animal's internal organs and viscera, and draining the chest region of all that warm blood. From the time the animal dies until the time the venison is eventually reduced to packages for the freezer, keeping the meat cool is the number-one concern.

Start the gutting procedure by rolling your deer over on his back, with his belly up, and position the animal so his head, neck, and chest region is slightly uphill. This will permit the blood and entrails to roll out more easily and flow downhill and away when you open him up.

The best way to begin the field dressing is by straddling your deer, facing the chest region. The job is a lot easier if a partner is available to hold either the front or rear legs upright. If this isn't possible, the deer may tend to roll or flop over on its side; some hunters like to straddle their deer in a kneeling position, holding the deer carcass upright and in place by exerting pressure with the insides of their knees.

Grab the deer's belly skin firmly between the thumb and forefinger, lift the skin up, and very carefully, with the tip of your knife blade, slice a 1½-inch-long hole in the skin. The reason for lifting the skin up is so the knife blade, if it happens to go just a tad too deep, has no chance of cutting into the intestines lying directly underneath.

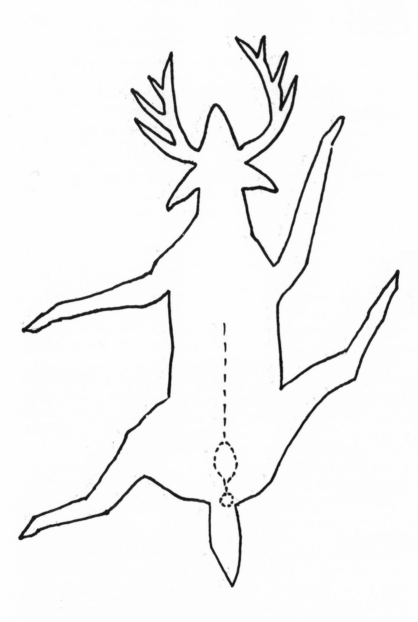

No need to chop open the rib cage. Here are the only knife cuts you need to make. Exercise care not to allow your knife to cut open any of the internal organs. Take your time. Then clean out the body cavity with dry grass or leaves.

Now slip two fingers (the index and middle fingers, palm up) into the hole you've just created, spread the fingers slightly and lift up, then carefully place the tip of your knife between your fingers with the blade edge facing up, and while continually lifting up the abdominal skin guide the blade from the reproductive organs to the base of the rib cage. The intestines and paunch will now bulge up and begin to spill out. Be careful not to touch them with your blade or you'll soon have messy digestive matter all over the place.

Now, using mostly your hands, begin gently pulling the remainder of the paunch and viscera out of the abdominal cavity. It should come away rather freely, but here and there you'll have to slice the various peritoneum tissue that formerly held the intestines and stomach to the inside walls of the body cavity.

With the offal lying on the ground beside the deer yet still connected to the reproductive area, next attend to the removal of the heart, liver, and respiratory organs. In doing this, there is no need to go borrow a double-bit lumberjack axe and begin chopping away at the rib cage, as I have actually seen some hunters do. Simply roll up your sleeves, kneel, and with your knife in one hand extend both arms as far as you can reach up through the chest cavity and into the neck region and grab onto the esophagus and windpipe. These will feel, in your hands, like two tubes lying one on top of the other: a small ¾-inch-diameter soft one, and a 1½-inch-diameter ribbed tube.

Completely sever this twin-tube assembly as high up as you can reach and then withdraw the hand holding the knife. With the other hand get a firm hold on the esophagus/windpipe and begin pulling backward, and the heart, liver, lungs, and other higher-up organs will come back and out just like peeling a banana. Any additional cuts that have to be made will be in the area of the diaphragm, and this will be only to sever small ligaments of restraining skin. With the chest-cavity organs entirely removed, set them aside and we'll further tend to them in a moment.

The next order of business is completing the removal of the intestines and reproductive and excretory organs. Again, don't go fetch a hatchet and start chopping away at the pelvis or aitch-bone or anything else, as it is totally unnecessary; so many hunters do this that it is unbelievable, and nine times in ten they succeed in puncturing the bladder, rupturing the colon so that fecal matter spills out, or in some other manner damaging one side or the other's hindquarter meat sections.

Initially we made a cut into the abdomen and worked upward toward the chest region. Now we want to reverse our line of travel and work backward to remove the reproductive/excretory organs. So turn around and face the hindquarters, still straddling the deer. If the abdominal slice has not gone all the way to the base of the penis, lengthen that cut at this time.

Next grab onto the penis itself and lift it gently while carefully cutting around both sides; since it lies on top of the skin, the cut does not have to go deep. Still holding onto the penis, extend the cuts straight back along both sides to pass the testicles. As you are doing this the organ should easily begin lifting away, but to repeat, make sure your slices do not go too deeply and damage the hindquarter meat lying immediately underneath.

As the two cuts pass on either side of the testicles and approach the region of the anus they will come slightly closer together but then will necessarily have to be expanded to go all around the anal opening. Once this circular cut has been made, the anal opening will appear as though it has sort of a small edge or flap of skin all the way around the orifice. Grab onto this skin and with the very tip of your knife blade begin gently cutting and separating the anal tube from the inside of the pelvic canal. Here is where a partner really comes in handy, because he can grab the two hind legs and lift up, better exposing the anal region for you to work on. If no partner is available, one trick is to stand facing away from the deer but backed up against it with the hind legs *behind* your thighs; as you back up just a step more, then, the anal region is raised and exposed.

In "reaming out the bunghole," as it is commonly referred to, the circular cut is made to a depth of about 3½ inches, and the deeper you go, entering through the pelvic canal, the more care must be exercised to not slice into the bladder deep inside. Once a sufficient depth has been reached it's better to stop working from this direction and begin coming in from the other end (the abdominal side).

Grab onto the lower intestine region, pull it back slightly, and begin executing the same circular cutting motion down through the pelvis. Soon, cuts made from this direction will meet those from the other side and you'll be able to pull out the entire reproductive and excretory tract intact and undamaged.

All of this may sound terribly complicated, but with a little experience it becomes the easiest and most efficient way to gut a deer. After doing it only two or three times it will even begin seeming incredible that anyone should want to try doing it any other way. And when you become truly expert, the job should take, from beginning to end, no more than eight to ten minutes.

The deer's insides should now be entirely cleaned out. I like to roll the carcass back over on its belly, with its legs spread wide, so that the body cavity may further drain for a few minutes. During this time I work on the chest-cavity organs, carefully separating the heart and liver from the rest by making judicious cuts here and there. They, in turn, are next laid upon a clean rock, log, or clump of ferns to drain. Just before I'm ready to head out, I secure them in a plastic bag; an old bread wrapper is ideal.

With the deer carcass now fully drained, roll the animal over on its back again and use several handfuls of clean leaves, moss, snow, or dry grass to further wipe out the inside of the body cavity of any debris yet remaining. It's not necessary to spend a great deal of time in this because you'll be doing a more thorough cleanup job back at camp.

DRAGGING HIM OUT

Improperly removing a deer from the field is another way in which I have seen too many hunters make far more work for themselves than is necessary.

For example, you've seen magazine pictures of two guys carrying out a deer that is trussed upside down to a long pole they are supporting over their shoulders. The scene is exciting, outdoorsy, and makes the models look like macho woodsmen and all that stuff, but just try it! You'll continually stumble and fall off balance, because of the bouncing, shifting carcass, which is dead weight with a high center of gravity. And by the time you get the animal out of the woods your neck will throb with pain and your entire shoulder will be rubbed raw.

Simply grabbing onto the antlers and heaving is just about as impractical. Since the dead-weight center of gravity is now very low to the ground, and so too the head region, you'll have to bend over to grab the horns and drag while continually hunched over. By the time you arrive back at your parked vehicle it will feel almost impossible to stand straight up again. Also, using this method, if you ever slip and stumble those sharp antler tines will go right into your calf muscles. Ouch!

Perhaps the height of stupidity—and believe it or not, pictures of this method have even been allowed to appear in several national sportsmen's magazines as well as a few other deer-hunting books—is to use the fireman's carry, whereby the deer is transported on top of the shoulders, around the neck, with the hunter holding onto the legs. Should the hunter stumble and fall, that enormous weight coming down on top of him could be fatal; it could break the hunter's back or snap his neck, or one of the deer's antler tines could go into him like a spear. Just as important, traipsing through the woods with antlers, a deer head, buckskin, and a flopping white tail hung about your neck is a dandy invitation to have some dolt take a shot at you. It has happened!

There is only one right way to drag out a deer, and amazingly it also involves the least amount of effort. First, extend the buck's front legs, lift up the hooves, and place them behind the animal's antlers; this gets the legs up and out of the way, to eliminate the resistance they would otherwise cause if allowed to drag on the ground. Now loop your drag rope around the base of the antlers, perhaps taking a few additional turns around the hooves as well to prevent them from working loose, and tie a secure knot. Then look for a drag stick lying around somewhere. It should be sturdy, about 2 inches in diameter, and about 25 inches long.

The other end of the drag rope should now be tied to the middle of the drag stick and then wrapped around as many more times as is necessary so the stick is eventually brought up to within about 2½ feet of the deer's head. With your hands behind your back, grabbing onto the stick, you can now begin relatively easily dragging your deer home. Further, you can stand at normal height while dragging to lessen fatigue or strained muscles. With a partner, of course, each hunter grabbing onto one side of the stick, the job is even easier. In any case, gloves make pulling on the stick a lot more comfortable.

If it's an average-size buck, you'll have to stop to rest every so often. I suggest stopping every 50 yards, and here's why. In the past I've found that after my deer has been dragged out I've had to

The easiest way to drag one or two deer is this way. Note that the front legs are tied behind ears to minimize drag on the ground.

make a second trip back to the kill site to retrieve my portable stand and other gear. Therefore, I now eliminate this extra work by bringing my deer and hunting gear out in leap-frog fashion. This trick also eliminates toting the extra weight of my rifle while dragging my deer.

In other words, I drag my deer 50 yards, stop, go back 50 yards to pick up my stand, rifle, and perhaps other gear such as heavy coat and binoculars, carry them 50 yards further beyond my deer, and so on. This change of pace, I've found, makes dragging out a deer far less tiring. But also, as I'm carrying forward my equipment I have the opportunity to do a little scouting for the easiest drag route, to take advantage of slight changes in the elevation of the terrain, so I'm able, as much as possible, to drag across level ground or downhill. In checking out this forward 50 yards, I also take the time to move aside any logs, rocks, or other obstacles that may be blocking the intended drag route.

At a deer camp, deer are traditionally hung on a meatpole, for cooling purposes, to keep the meat free of insects, and certainly so the game can be admired a while longer. The best way is to hang the animal by the hind legs high enough so the head is about a foot off the ground. This allows body heat to more easily escape; when deer are hung by the antlers, body heat, which has a tendency to rise, is trapped in the chest and neck-cavity regions.

Use a game gambrel if you have one (the people that make Baker tree stands offer a great one for only $5), or a length of pipe, sturdy green sapling, or something of this nature. First make two small slices, one each at the hock through the thin skin that separates the leg joint from the Achilles tendon, insert the gambrel, spread the legs slightly, and hoist 'er aloft. A miniature block and tackle, which costs about $8, makes the job easy.

Since leaves, mud, and other debris are likely to have accumulated in the body cavity during the drag out, a more thorough cleaning of the carcass should now be undertaken. I begin by first trimming away fat globules, remnants of skin, dried blood crusts, and other matter that, if the temperature is warm, may encourage bacteria. After this, I may even use a garden hose (turned on low-stream) or a bucket of water hauled from a nearby stream to slosh out the body cavity and neck region of whatever blood residue may still remain. I believe this is especially important if the carcass is to hang and age for several days; the "dirty" water, when the deer is hanging by its hind legs, will drain all the way through, exiting from the nostrils. The only thing to remember in any use of water is that it not be allowed to directly contact bare meat—only the inside body walls of the carcass—and that the carcass be permitted to air-dry very quickly, as any prolonged moisture may cause spoilage.

You should now insert one or more sticks crosswise in the body cavity to spread the walls to speed cooling of the meat. If it's warm and there are flies and other insects about, wrap the meat with cheesecloth or pull a cloth game bag (made for the purpose and available through many sporting-goods stores and mail-order catalogs) over the deer. In consistently hot states such as Texas and elsewhere, hunters often build in advance small buildings in which to hang their deer; they resemble outhouses in size but are made of lightweight frames with entirely screened walls to facilitate the circulation of air. In other cases, when it is hot, many hunters believe, and they are right, that it is extremely important to get the hide off as soon as possible because of the insulating properties of the hollow hair; this is why nature has given the whitetail his heavy coat—to keep him warm—and so if rapid cooling is to be achieved, off it must come. When the carcass is free of its hide and exposed to the air, it will by itself "case" or "glaze"; this is the formation of a thin, protective, skinlike crust (it usually takes about eight hours). Then the carcass should be wrapped in cheesecloth.

When it's time to hit the road for home, whether immediately after the kill or after several more days in camp, remember that continual cooling of your deer carcass is critical. If the only place to put the deer is in the trunk of your car, be sure the sticks remain in place to keep the chest and abdominal cavities well spread, and leave the trunk lid ajar at least 12 or 14 inches or so, to allow breezes to pass through and carry out any warm air that may accumulate. But an even better idea, if you have a conventional automobile, is to lay the carcass on top of the trunk deck, near the rear window and lashed down on both sides. Or lay the carcass on some type of roof rack on the top of your car, station wagon, truck, or camper (this is preferred to laying the deer directly on the roof, which prevents circulation of air underneath the animal) and again ensure the body cavity remains open.

In other cases a hunter may wish to quarter his animal near where it was killed and then secure the meat in double-walled cardboard boxes, camp coolers, or gamebags that can be iced down in some manner. All of this, however, is assuming the weather is warm and that it's a long way home; if it's cold, nature provides the refrigeration.

HOW TO DO YOUR OWN BUTCHERING

With your deer now at home, the first thing is to decide whether or not to allow the meat to age. Aging has the effect of tenderizing the meat (all beef and most other domestic animals are aged for varying periods of time). If your deer was killed only that day, or very recently, you may wish to see it age for a few more days. If it was hanging in your deer camp for several days after it was killed, however, and then you had a long drive home, it has already undergone a good deal of aging and should require no more.

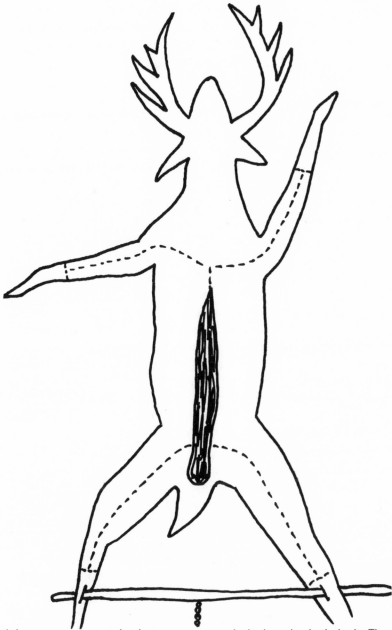

At home, or camp, prior to butchering, use game gambrel to hang deer by the hocks. Then cut on dotted lines as indicated to remove the hide. Be careful you don't cut too deeply and injure prime meat lying just beneath the hide.

If aging is to be done, the deer should hang upside down during the interim and in a place that is cool (ideally, somewhere that is consistently between 38 to 42 degrees), this might be in your garage or toolshed, in a barn, perhaps in your basement, or a similar place.

Whether or not the hide should be left on during the aging process is a matter of individual decision. Unless the temperature has been on the warm side and you've already peeled it off, I don't think it makes much difference. But for certain, the hide comes away more easily when it is removed as soon as possible after the deer has been killed.

With the deer hanging by its hind legs, I begin the hide-stripping process by first using a hacksaw to cut off all four lower legs at the knee. There is so little meat in the lower or shinbone areas, and it's so laced with sinew, that it's just not worth bothering with.

Next I make cuts through the hide, beginning on the inside of each hind leg and running all the way to the pelvis. Then I carefully begin separating the hide from the carcass, working continually around the deer's diameter. I let the hide just hang loose as I continue to work progressively toward the head region. It is important, when any cutting is necessary, not to go too deeply or you'll have slices in the meat directly underneath. In fact, one mark of an expert is that the knife is used only minimally; the rest of the time the hide is pulled and pushed away from the carcass in a downward direction, using only the hands and knuckles.

When you near the chest region, make cuts through the hide at the forelegs where you cut them off and extend them to a midpoint at the ribcage. Another cut can now be made, beginning where the field-dressing cut ended at the base of the ribcage, all the way to the lower jaw of the animal, and the remainder of the hide slowly and carefully peeled away.

Butchering your own deer is by no means difficult, and no hunter should be afraid to tackle the job. In time he'll develop a system, and after about his third or fourth deer should be able to reduce a whole carcass to individual wrapped portions of meat for the freezer in only a few hours. Now is also the time to give some thought as to the types of meat cuts you want from your deer—steaks, roasts, and the like. All of the various scraps and trimmings go for stew meat, burger, sausage, and so on.

An excellent idea is to make a quick trip downtown to your department of natural resources or state fish and game agency (some agricultural extension offices also have them) and ask for their big-game butchering guide sheets. These show either pictures or line drawings of animal carcasses with superimposed dotted lines indicating where to make cuts for various types of steaks and roasts.

For the record, however, I will explain how I cut up my own deer, though there is no reason why anyone else's methods or preferences are not as good.

There is one thing I should mention, though. With the exception of sometimes wanting round steaks, which are simply inch-thick slices from the hindquarter, I do not very often care to cut steaks or chops. The reason is that such cuts of meat require that the carcass be split vertically for its entire length, through the middle of the backbone, and then horizontal cuts made at whatever thickness you prefer your steaks. Both of these operations require a good deal of bone cutting with a saw, and this is something I do not like. When bones are sawed, marrow dust and cuttings are liberally sprinkled throughout the meat where the cuts were made. In the cases of beef, pork, lamb, and other domestic carcasses there is no problem, but bone marrow from deer is not at all flavorful and is partly responsible for imparting the gamy taste that many people complain of.

So instead of steaks and chops, I prefer the long backstrap (tenderloin) sections to remain intact and the remainder of the larger portions of meat to be cut up into roasts, as this tack requires only the use of a knife and no bone cutting. Additionally, I bone out all of the various roasts, mainly because boneless meat will keep longer and does not take up valuable freezer space. I've found that a razor-sharp fish-fillet knife with an 8-inch, thin, narrow blade is ideal for boning out various cuts of meat.

I begin by laying the entire skinned deer carcass out flat on a level surface such as the top of a picnic table, workbench, or counter top. Then, before actually starting to cut the meat into serving portions, I cut away any bloodshot areas. Sometimes, if the bloodshot area is in a prime cut, soaking the meat in salt water for a while will rid it of the discoloration.

Next I begin removing the two long tenderloin strips, each of

The tenderloins are the best cuts of meat. Al Wolter admires a backstrap from a Minnesota buck, which will provide a winter's worth of good eating.

which is roughly 3 inches in diameter by about 2½ feet in length. They lie directly along either side of the backbone, beginning slightly behind where the back of the neck joins the body and going all the way back to where the hindquarters begin. I begin working in the neck region, carefully guiding my knife along the backbone all the way to the beginning of the hindquarter and lifting up the piece of tenderloin as I go along; actually, what I do is fillet the thing right out. Each tenderloin strip is then cut into thirds and wrapped for the freezer.

Many hunters do not know it, but there are two additional, but much smaller, tenderloin strips *inside* the chest cavity, along either side of the backbone. They're about 13 or 14 inches in length, 2 inches wide, and ¾ inch thick, and they just may be the most tender and flavorful cuts from any deer. Very gently fillet them out, and keep them under lock and key!

The next step is to remove each of the two hindquarters and the two front quarters, and set them momentarily aside. Removal is accomplished by continuing the cuts at the rear and front, where the tenderloin cuts ended, and carefully going all the way around each leg all the way down to the ball-and-socket assembly. You'll notice that unlike a human ball-and-socket joint, which is rigidly affixed, those of deer "float" with a connective piece of cartilage that is easily cut with a knife.

Now cut lengthwise down both sides of the back of the neck and continue all the way through, leaving two large slabs of neck meat. These are the neck roasts. Sometimes we prefer to quarter each one to create eight smaller roasts; other times, all of the neck meat is reserved for grinding into burger and sausage.

Most of the meat has now been removed from the skeleton, but I spend a little more time going over it more thoroughly, such as between the ribs and along the backbone, to trim away every bit of meat that I can find. Toss all of these bits and pieces, as they accumulate, into a large pan to later be ground, and then discard the remainder of the now-bare skeleton.

The two hindquarters and the two front quarters, if you look closely, are not solid pieces of meat. Rather, they consist of large, irregular-shaped muscles lying on top of and beside each other to form the whole. Each of these muscles can be very carefully separated out as different kinds of roasts, which is the way we prefer, or with each hindquarter lying on its side you can use a large butcher knife to make diagonal cuts of whatever thickness you prefer to obtain round steaks. However you do it, there will usually be left over a number of thin slabs of meat that can be rolled up and tied with cotton string to create cuts such as rolled rump roast. In the case of the forequarters, I cut up the shoulder roasts, and the miscellaneous pieces left over go for burger and sausage.

That is about it for the major aspects of butchering. Some

of the larger roasts may now have to be halved or quartered, depending upon the individual needs of your family. And with regards to all portions of meat, you'll want to take some time to trim away as much fat as possible; the fat of a deer, unlike that of a beef steer, does not taste good, nor does it freeze well.

Butchering, as I said, is not at all difficult, but at least at first it does take time. If it becomes necessary to interrupt the butchering operation, place the various portions of meat still to be worked upon in some type of large box or container, cover them with aluminum foil, and store them in the lower compartment of your refrigerator.

15

Tomorrow's Deer Hunting: A Bright Future

It has been said that 95 percent of the greatest scientists who have ever lived are still alive today; we are technologically advancing that rapidly. And with regards to animal biology one of the more notable things we have learned in recent decades is that most wildlife species, but especially whitetails, while indeed a precious natural resource, are as well a highly renewable and consequently very manageable resource.

Game management, then, as defined by the National Wildlife Federation, is a science that seeks to maintain the optimum numbers and varieties of wildlife that our country's range or habitat can support, consistent with the best interests of man.

The first task in managing game is to provide, protect, and maintain habitat—areas where animals can find food, water, and cover in which to raise their young—because without habitat there can be no wildlife. But also, the science of game manage-

The science of professional game management calls for the provision of habitat for animal species. But it also calls for the careful harvest of surplus animals every year. Otherwise, the deer can multiply so fast they can easily destroy their own range and jeopardize the entire herd. (Photo by E.P. Haddon)

ment calls for the complete protection of any species which is endangered or threatened with extinction. It additionally prescribes and encourages the culling, cropping, harvesting, or thinning out of those particular species which are too abundant or threatened with overpopulation to bring their numbers back down to the carrying capacity of their range.

Enter the hunter, who has been instrumental in the annual harvest of game surpluses. It should be emphasized, however, that no brand of deer hunting or other hunting these days consists simply of indiscriminate killing, as was the case, for example, in the massive slaughtering of buffalo and passenger pigeons at the turn of the century or the fully legal market-hunting practices that continued through the late 1920s. Rather, it is now based upon fully researched, scientific principles that are formulated by wildlife biologists and wildlife managers who determine population levels of various species and who recommend the rules and regulations for hunting specific species—the seasons, the hours, the bag limits, and the restrictions on weapons. Since wildlife is much like tomatoes, peaches, and other perishable fruits and vegetables in that it cannot be stockpiled or saved, such programs allow hunters to make wise and conscientious use of those particular species the managers say are in surplus while never actually endangering the breed stock required to sustain the species within its range.

Unfortunately, there are many who believe man should not enter the wildlife picture to exercise controls and instigate annual harvests (which is as ludicrous as not picking this year's crop of apples). They believe nature should be allowed to take her course.

But contrary to popular and predominantly urban opinion, Mother Nature is not as benevolent and concerned for the welfare of her children as Walt Disney would have had us believe. In fact, she is a cantankerous, whimsical, and violent old bitch who more frequently than not deals the cards of life from the bottom of the deck. And one of the more important things she has repeatedly taught us around the country is that the let-nature-take-its-course method of managing wildlife is always a "boom and bust" proposition. It produces a bumper crop of animals, at first. But as populations peak, the animals—especially those that browse and graze, such as whitetails—eventually exhaust their food supplies. And when undernourished, if they don't simply die a slow and gruesome death by starvation, they become extremely vulnerable to parasites that literally eat them alive, and diseases such as anthrax. Virulent anthrax can wipe out 90 percent of a deer herd within a matter of days.

As an example of the reproductive capabilities of whitetails, an amazing experiment was performed at Michigan's fenced-in 1200-acre George River Game Preserve. Two bucks and four does were released into the confinement (previously, there were no deer there) and within the short time span of only five years, due to a geometric progression factor, the six deer had increased their numbers to 160! Indeed, the whitetail may very well be his own worst enemy, because without man's thoughtful and well-planned interference he can easily destroy his own range by overpopulation. When that happens, there will be a massive die-off of animals, and the detriment done to the range can make it virtually uninhabitable for any manner of wildlife species for many years to come. This very thing happened in Arizona, on the Kaibab National Game Refuge, when hunters were not allowed to harvest surplus deer populations. Over a period of fifteen years, the initial deer population there increased from 2000 animals to over 100,000. In the two years to follow, over 90,000 deer died of starvation. The remainder of the herd was very weak, diseased, and emaciated, and this, along with the tens of thousands of rotting carcasses, precipitated a major public health hazard requiring the closure of the plateau even to hikers, campers, and other lovers of the outdoors. Because of the extensive overgrazing of the range, which eventually allowed the massive erosion of the layer of fertile topsoil that previously supported the lush ground-story vegetation, even to this day, fifty-five years later, the plateau's habitat has not entirely recovered. Yet all of this could have easily been averted by the continued allowance of regulated hunting.

Still another alternative from those who would have hunting banned has been the suggested live-trapping of deer in high-deer areas and then transplanting them to other areas of low deer populations. This has actually been attempted in many regions of the country. But the building of box traps, the cost of sedating the animals (which is required to prevent them from thrashing around and injuring themselves while confined in the cages), the hiring of drivers and trucks for transportation purposes, the statewide

DEER TRAP

SINCE 1940 THE TEXAS PARKS AND WILDLIFE
DEPARTMENT HAS LIVE-TRAPPED AND TRANS-
PLANTED OVER 13,100 WHITE-TAILED DEER
FROM THE REFUGE FOR USE IN RESTOCKING
DEPLETED DEER RANGE THROUGHOUT TEXAS.
ARANSAS DEER HAVE ALSO BEEN SHIPPED TO
FOUR OTHER STATES AND TO THE VIRGIN
ISLANDS. APPROXIMATELY 10,000 DEER NOW
USE THE REFUGE. JAVELINAS, RACCOONS,
AND WILD TURKEYS HAVE ALSO BEEN TRAPPED
FROM THE REFUGE AND SHIPPED TO OTHER
STATES IN RESTOCKING PROGRAMS.

Those who would have hunting outlawed have suggested many alternatives. One is live-trapping and relocating of deer, which has been very successful but gradually phased out in most areas because of the prohibitive cost. (Photo by Luther Goldman)

studies that must be conducted to determine the high-deer areas and then suitable low-deer regions to receive stocking, and the overall supervision of such programs by trained biologists have been prohibitively expensive. Compounding the problem is that such programs are never one-shot deals, but because of the reproductive capacity of the species must be continually ongoing programs. And then what do you do when eventually *all* areas have high deer populations?

For instance, in northern Ohio, at a particular high-security space-research installation which sprawls over thousands of acres but is entirely enclosed by high fences, and where the live-trapping of deer was for a period the only allowable method of herd reduction, it was estimated by the Department of the Interior that the trapping and relocation of *each* deer cost approximately $200. And further, that to maintain a herd size compatible with the available habitat there and the way the animals were reproducing,

This deer, outfitted with a radio transmitter collar, is being released by biologists under an intensive study program that will enable the state of Indiana to increase the size of its deer herd. The cost of such programs is extremely high, and hunters traditionally foot the entire bill. Anti-hunting organizations clamor the loudest about their concern for wildlife, but historically have contributed no financial support whatever for wildlife's betterment. (Photo by Indiana Dept. of Natural Resources)

each year it would be required to live-trap and transplant 600 animals! Go ahead and calculate the staggering cost to the public if similar programs, in lieu of hunting, were to be implemented on a nationwide scale! Obviously, the space-research installation could ill afford an annual expenditure of $120,000 just to solve the problem of numbers of deer on their top-secret acreage, and the result has been that now controlled public hunting by lottery takes place sometime every fall.

It's well worth repeating at this stage that it is a proved and accepted fact among highly educated and trained animal scientists that barring natural disasters most species produce a surplus every year—that is, more animals than their range can sustain. Therefore, there is never any biological question as to _whether_ surplus animals must be removed from the range every year . . . only _how_. With songbirds and other nongame species, nature takes the entire surplus, and her methods of doing so are seldom expedient or pleasant. With game species, however, hunting is recognized as the most viable, effective, efficient, and _merciful_ method of reducing surpluses—if we are not to witness still more Kaibab tragedies in the future.

Hunting is consequently the one method of wildlife surplus reduction that is fully condoned by the federal government, by all fifty state governments, by all of the nation's major conservation organizations (don't allow yourself to be misled here; many are only "preservation" organizations that believe in the "look but don't touch" and "let nature take its course" approach), and all of the nation's reputable wildlife biologists.

In substantiation of this, according to the U.S. Council of Environmental Quality, as stated in its Fifth Annual Report: "Under American law and custom, sport hunting that is properly regulated and based upon scientific principles is considered a legitimate management technique as well as a form of recreation. Since the development of modern wildlife management in the 1930s, _no_ American wildlife has been exterminated by sport hunting. On the contrary, wildlife management has restored many depleted or threatened species."

Now comes the kicker—the point to be made in tying up all of these loose ends. Hunters not only harvest each annual crop of surplus wildlife, in accordance with and under the supervision of biologists, but they and they alone foot the bill for the many various wildlife management programs necessary to ensure that we are able to maintain the optimum numbers and varieties of wildlife that our country's range or habitat can support.

It is through the purchase of hunting licenses and special hunting stamps and other permits, and also through a special tax (which hunters asked Congress to levy upon them in the purchase of firearms and ammunition), that the hunter is wildlife's benefactor.

This money presently amounts to an estimated $600,000,000 annually, and every penny of it goes for wildlife management, which, by the way, as in the case of buying, preserving, and maintaining habitat, benefits nongame as well as game species. It pays the salaries of game protectors, wardens, wildlife biologists, zoologists, and the agency administration and equipment costs of their many activities. It pays for the acquisition of more and more public lands (habitat) every year, which in addition to providing hunting opportunities are enjoyed as recreation sites by nonpaying nonhunters such as hikers, backpackers, picnickers, outdoor photographers, birdwatchers, rock hounds, cliff climbers, spelunkers, and many others. It pays for the planting of various types of forage favored by wildlife. And it pays for government educational programs such as clinics and seminars which are open to the public and designed to acquaint them with wildlife species native to their area and related conservation practices.

In short, the hunter's dollars pay for everything pertaining to wildlife (game and nongame), and that makes it easy to conclude that without wildlife management—without the hunter—we simply would not have forty times as many deer today as a century ago. Indeed, as contradictory as it may appear on the surface, the hunter is wildlife's greatest ally.

It is interesting to note that during the 1970s both Ohio and Colorado have initiated "wildlife stamp" programs. These have been for the purpose of allowing nonhunters the opportunity to help wildlife, too, through the purchase of $5 stamps. The money is channeled into wildlife (game and nongame) programs to benefit the species, the same as is hunters' money from hunting licenses and taxes on firearms and ammunition. What is startling is that in the case of both states, after a number of years, it was determined that hunters bought 90 percent of the stamps! Six percent of the total sales of stamps were bought by stamp collectors, and only 4 percent bought by nonhunters and anti-hunters, who, curiously, are the ones who seem to shout the loudest when it comes to defaming hunters and hunting; given the opportunity to contribute something themselves, their shouts have turned to whispers and they've faded into the shadows, while the hunter has still again come to the cause.

I go to great length to mention these things because hunters are presently coming under a great deal of fire from extremely active, large, and well-financed groups that are determined to have all forms of hunting outlawed. Composing these groups in most cases are well-meaning, honest, and respectable citizens who either possess little background knowledge of the intricacies of wildlife management and the important roles hunters play or have been presented with downright distorted views of hunters by their profiteering group leaders. The bottom line, if any of these groups were to succeed, would see an end to our whitetail deer hunting. But of far greater importance, it would be a tragic consequence for every manner of wildlife on this continent.

There are many other things as well that tomorrow's deer hunters will need to be concerned with.

A few, for example, are beginning to complain about the increasingly high costs of licenses and permits, and the growing complexity of state hunting regulations.

Both of these are something we are going to have to learn to live with and accept, however, because license costs are going to go higher and higher and still more pages of fine print are going to be added to the pamphlets of hunting regulations.

Although it is an inconvenience to the hunter, these are actually for the good, and every sportsman should enthusiastically support their purposes. The reason for both, of course, is the increasing costs and sophistication of modern wildlife management programs. If the quality of our deer hunting is to remain at its same high level, and even be improved upon, it will take money. Hunters have always footed the bill and will continue to do so. The great majority would have it no other way.

Pertaining to money, we can also expect more and more hunting on private lands to be in the form of "fee hunting," and this, too, within reasonable bounds, is born of necessity.

Let's say a rancher has 1000 acres of land, upon which he runs 500 head of beef steers. Deer there consume a tremendous quantity of the lush grasses and vegetation that otherwise would benefit the stock. If the entire deer population could hypothetically be eliminated, the rancher could well increase the size of his herd by perhaps as much as 25 percent; naturally, therefore, the deer are costing him a good deal of money, and so he is not likely to be amenable to hunters coming in and asking to hunt them for free.

In effect, many ranchers and landowners today, then, are keeping and managing two distinctly different types of animal life and by all rights should be financially compensated for both.

A major benefit of fee hunting has to do with the "quality" of the hunting atmosphere. Since it is his land, the rancher has control over who is allowed to hunt and who is not. He knows the names and addresses of those given trespass permission, and since he is on the scene he knows of violations or ethical encroachments and those individuals who are responsible for them. In time, only those who are honest and respectable sportsmen are permitted on his property, while the minority of scoundrels who give the rest a bad name must find somewhere else to hunt.

Here is another thing I should mention, because it seems to be given more and more press these days than fully warranted, and that has to do with what has come to be known as the "slob hunter." In fact, many anti-hunting organizations are quick to mention the "hunter personality," with the related mention of fences being cut or torn down, illegal animals and even livestock shot at, vehicles driven through croplands, incidents of vandalism and littering—the list goes on and on.

I'll readily admit that a few hunters do indeed behave like this, but they are definitely in the minority, and any mention of them as representative of all is a low blow. We don't petition to have automobile driving outlawed because of the 2 percent of drunks and drag racers on the highways. We don't petition to have boating outlawed because of the few "hot dogs" who recklessly speed around. There are no organizations founded to see the elimination of golf because of the few dimwits who don't replace their divots or who leave golf-cart tracks across the greens. So as hunters we should no longer tolerate front-page headlines pertaining to those few who are now and then apprehended for trespassing violations, who are guilty of vandalism, or who hunt without buying licenses.

Another thing of paramount importance is the curtailment of poaching, which has increased tremendously in the last decade. But it should be emphasized that poachers are *not* hunters. They are simply criminals whose theft happens to be deer meat.

According to a recent study by biologists associated with the New Mexico Department of Fish and Game, approximately 50 percent of all deer killed are taken by poachers! This is an astounding figure, and it is so high because a poacher, like any other crook, is primarily concerned with not being caught, so deer shot at that

Hunters can be proud that their efforts have restored many depleted wildlife species. The money and time they contribute is also beneficial to hundreds—perhaps thousands—of nongame species that share the whitetail's habitat. (Photo by U.S. Fish and Wildlife Service)

do not immediately fall (the great majority of them) are therefore never chased after and diligently tracked down as a respectable hunter would do. In a single night, using spotlights which blind the animals, any given poacher might take home (for later selling) as many as six or eight deer, but he might have put bullets into thirty or forty!

Another reason for the rampant increase in poaching is a combination of public apathy as well as the public's unwillingness to become involved in an observed crime. Confirming this, the New Mexico Game Department employed an "operative" to visibly and outwardly "fake" illegal kills to test public reactions in farm and rural areas. The operative left evidence of or allowed himself to be fully observed in the simulation of 144 different deer kills. Yet only once were the agent's activities reported to the proper authorities, and that was by a rancher too far away to actually see what was going on; he thought the operative was trying to rustle one of his beef steers.

It is not necessary for any citizen to try to detain anyone observed committing a crime and risk personal injury. But if every citizen was willing to simply write down a vehicle license number or description of the person involved, and then immediately call his local game protector or sheriff, the incidence of poaching would be drastically reduced.

All in all, however, despite minor setbacks and other problems hunters seem perennially to take in stride, whitetail hunting will continue to have a very bright future indeed. We have more deer than our fathers and grandfathers were able to enjoy, with the number still growing! And that's something every hunter can take great pride in, because he helped to bring it all about.

INDEX